GW01606253

# THE GHOST OF 29 MEGACYCLES

*By the same author*

THE GHOST OF FLIGHT 401
THE AIRMEN WHO WOULD NOT DIE
THE INTERRUPTED JOURNEY

# THE GHOST OF 29 MEGACYCLES

*A New Breakthrough in Life after Death?*

*by*

JOHN G. FULLER

SOUVENIR PRESS

First published 1985 by Souvenir Press Ltd,
43 Great Russell Street, London WC1B 3PA



ISBN 0 285 62691 4

Photoset in Great Britain by
Rowland Phototypesetting Ltd,
Bury St Edmunds, Suffolk
Printed in Great Britain by
Biddles Ltd, Guildford

# *AUTHOR'S NOTE*

This is a strange story. It is either true, or it is not. That determination has to be left up to the reader. If it is true, it is a major breakthrough in communication beyond this life, and into the next. It is also persuasive evidence that life continues after death.

If it is not true, it raises an enormous question mark as to why a group of reliable, reputable scientists, physicists, engineers, electronic technicians, doctors, professors, administrators, clergymen, successful business men and others have spent more than half a million dollars over the course of a decade to probe into electronic evidence of life after death, and to come to the conclusion that there is strong evidence of communication.

In either of the two views, there is sure to be controversy and question marks. I found the story to be a fascinating exploration, and my own opinion constantly shifted back and forth between the two polarities. One thing I can say with certainty is that I am convinced of the honesty, integrity and competence of those concerned, and that they have displayed a great deal of courage in facing the critics who are fond of attacking anyone who probes the paranormal with an open mind.

# CONTENTS

# *PART 1*

# CHAPTER 1

## *Outrageous – or Awesome?*

In mid-August of 1981, I received an unusual letter. It was from a gentleman named George W. Meek. From the letterhead, it appeared that he headed a foundation called Metascience in Franklin, North Carolina. I had vaguely heard about Metascience as an organization engaged in research into the paranormal.

In the letter, Meek said that a project he had been working on had developed beyond his expectations. He was convinced that it could become a basis for a book that would be of tremendous importance to people all over the world. He hoped that I would consider the possibility of writing it. The letter went on to say that he was going to be making several trips near the Connecticut area where I lived in the coming months. He would very much like to stop and talk at some convenient time.

There was something about the letter that made me curious. But I was also busy. I had just returned from several weeks in Indonesia and was preparing to write a travel book. My schedule was tight. I wrote and suggested that he might give me a ring if he were in the area, and went on to try to catch up on a pressing deadline.

On several occasions in the past, I had received proposals about book ideas. But whether they were good or bad, they seldom fitted in with current plans and schedules. I had found, however, that it was particularly important to keep an open mind when it came to considering stories that border on the strange and unusual. This sort of story rarely floats on the top of the surface. It is the kind that has to be gently scooped up to measure its possibilities. When doing so the word is caution. The stranger the story, the greater the need for documentation, and the need to move slowly. At one time, I had learned about an unlikely story of a ghost on a modern jet airliner from several airline pilots and flight attendants. But it took many more months of verification by other airline personnel before I decided to write a book about it. Once I had learned of a bizarre UFO encounter from a police chief in New Hampshire, but checked for weeks before deciding to take on the story. Whatever the subject, the need for careful investigative reporting is critical.

What George Meek had in mind, I did not know. When he wrote again asking if he could drop by on November 22, he included a bio sheet that had little to do with the paranormal. There was a brief description of what Metascience was attempting to accomplish. It was apparently an organized research program exploring the nature of man and his possible survival after death. But Meek's general background bore little relation to that. Prior to starting his foundation, Meek had apparently been an eminently successful engineer and business executive. He had been the chief designer of the Weathermaster air conditioning system for the Carrier Corporation, a system found in many of the largest buildings in the world. At one time he had been on the embassy staff of Ambassador Averell Harriman in London. He had designed, developed and manufactured air and thermal pollution devices and the heat and mass transfer surfaces for cooling towers and waste water treatment devices used all over the world. He held scores of industrial patents that enabled him to retire at 60, and turn his attention exclusively to the question of life after death.

This question was also of major interest to me. I had explored it to a degree in several books, but at arm's length. I did not want to get bogged down in the vagaries of the occult world; I wanted to look at the subject in a clinical and objective way. In the process, I found there were two schools of thought most damaging to intelligent exploration of the subject. One was the point of view of the obdurate skeptic who set about to destroy persuasive evidence with a sledge hammer. The other was the gullible enthusiast who accepted weak and inconclusive evidence uncritically, and made himself an easy target for irrational rationalists to shoot down.

Because the question is probably the most important man can face, I was interested in learning what Meek had discovered in his research. It seemed that he had personally invested over half a million dollars of his own money in exploring the subject, and was approaching it from the point of view of an engineer and scientist.

This seemed to be a refreshing slant. I looked forward to the visit. But if I had known what a complex labyrinth it would lead me into, I'm not sure I would have let myself get involved. It became a detective story that would lead me through England, Germany, Switzerland and elsewhere in an intricate tangle of theories, experiments, and personalities who were exploring the mystery of life after death in new and fascinating ways – not theologically, not in the nature of gloom and foreboding, but in the sense of adventure and excitement. But as the time for my meeting with Meek approached, I still had great reservations, and would be very reluctant to make any kind of commitment that would leave me without an escape hatch.

* * *

Late autumn in Connecticut can be cold and blustery. November 22, 1981, was no exception. My wife Elizabeth was putting some things together for tea while I built a fire to take the chill off the living room which could be drafty at times. Meek had called earlier to say he and his wife Jeannette would be arriving about four in the afternoon, after which they would go on to their son's house for dinner in a nearby village. It was the first time I had heard Meek's voice. He spoke with measured precision, I guess the way an engineer is supposed to speak. Elizabeth was as curious as I was about a man who would ditch a successful career and plunge half a million dollars of his own money into the wispy and insubstantial region of life after death.

'What did he sound like?' Elizabeth said.

'Very deadpan, but cordial,' I answered.

'Should I be on my best behavior?'

'You're always on your best behavior,' I told her, which was close enough to the truth most of the time. Elizabeth always liked to analyze things, situations, and people. 'I'm trying to picture,' she said, 'what a methodical, pragmatic mind is doing digging so deeply into this subject.'

'We'll find out soon enough,' I said. 'I'm as much in the dark as you are.'

Our own interest in the subject had sprung up almost by accident. Elizabeth had been a flight attendant for Northwest Orient, and had helped me research the book that turned out to be *The Ghost of Flight 401*. That story had started out as an inquiry into why and how the occurrence of an apparition could be reported in such a technical, sophisticated environment as a jet airliner, more or less a space age myth. Instead of a myth, the evidence was strong enough to create a very serious inquiry into the possibility, if not the probability, of life after death. Elizabeth had written her own sequel to the book after parapsychologists discovered during the research that she had very real psychic abilities she had never before suspected. Since then, our own skepticism had diminished, although we remained cautious about the whole subject. What Meek had to say to us would be listened to carefully, but I doubted if we would go any further than that with the story.

When Meek arrived with his wife, we hustled them into the living room to warm up by the fire while Elizabeth served them with steaming mugs of tea. My first impression was that Meek had just stepped out of the executive boardroom of General Motors, and was taking his wife to a top-level corporate seminar at Boca Raton. He was tall, slim, distinguished. A carefully-moulded dark wool suit framed a white shirt and a dark foulard tie. Beneath his gray and thinning hair sat steel-rimmed glasses and a close-cropped beard. His wife Jeannette was serious, affable and equally well-groomed, with a shock of attractive white hair. Both appeared to be in their late 60s or early 70s. Jeannette, we learned, worked full time with George on his projects. What was unusual about their entrance was that Meek brought a video cassette player and an audio tape deck with him.

Since they were planning to arrive at their son's house for a late dinner, Meek got right down to the subject matter without delay. In brief, he was bringing all his technical knowledge to bear on the one question of survival after death, and was unsparing with his efforts and funds to do so. 'I pulled the curtain down on what I had spent my life on,' he said, describing his sudden cut-off of a successful business career. 'I started to read and travel and subscribed to some 35 journals in a variety of fields because I concluded that no one science could possibly come up with the answers to what I was looking for.'

As I turned on my tape recorder with Meek's permission, he went on to say that he had taken material from many different sciences and the best of ancient philosophy and religions, and then coined the term 'metascience' with the meaning of 'over and above science itself.' Before long, he had found nearly 40 professional and technical people over the world who seemed to have similar leanings. They included physicists, nuclear chemists, biochemists, psychiatrists and other professionals. In one scientific group in Philadelphia, a strange thing happened.

In an experiment with a medium, an apparent contact came through in one of the sessions in which a deceased scientist identified himself through the medium. The purported entity claimed that he wanted to co-operate with some living engineers and technicians to develop an electro-magnetic communication system between those living on the earth level and those in the discarnate state where he now existed.

'This was exactly along the line that I was working,' Meek continued. 'I had been figuring that it would at least be theoretically possible to develop a non-mediumistic channel of communication with at least some of the levels of the world of spirit.'

One of the first things the Philadelphia group worked on was to try to confirm the prior existence of the deceased personality coming through the medium. The medium himself was a sober and serious advertising executive with N. W. Ayer, one of the largest advertising agencies in the country. The discarnate voice claimed to be that of one William Francis Gray Swann, who had been a professor of physics at Yale, the University of Chicago, and Swarthmore. After checking out a long series of purported facts about Professor Swann, the group became reasonably convinced that the information they were receiving was valid. Most interesting to Meek was that Swann began to provide accurate technical electronic information on how communication might be accomplished through that sort of channel, without a medium. From this session on, Meek became determined to make that breakthrough.

'This wasn't at all easy,' Meek continued as Elizabeth poured him another mug of tea. 'It involved elaborate circuitry and equipment with no assurance we would get anywhere. Anybody would think we were crazy, designing and building equipment from instructions coming from someone who was no longer on this world. We had to remind ourselves that both Edison and Marconi had tried seriously to bridge the gap between the living and dead by electro-magnetic means. While they didn't succeed, neither of them had access to the sophisticated electronic technology available to us.'

As Meek spoke, I was trying to listen, to reflect on and evaluate what he was saying. I looked over to Elizabeth to see how she was taking all this, but she gave no sign in either direction what she was thinking. I was attempting mentally to join up Meek's executive suite appearance with his offhand and incongruous references to mediums, seances, and elaborate messages from the dead. There seemed little question that he was honest, intelligent and in firm contact with the pragmatic world of reality at the same time that he was reaching out into these rarefied zones. I had a lot of questions forming in my mind, but I decided to hold off until I got more information.

Meek told us that the equipment needed to be designed and built, had required large funding – up to $70,000 for this particular project alone. 'I was lucky enough to get Jim McDonnell, chairman of the board of McDonnell-Douglas, interested in the project,' Meek said. 'Jim had been interested in psychic research for a long time. In fact, he has left half a million dollars to Washington University in St Louis to set up a psychic research laboratory. I worked out a deal with him whereby he would let me go ahead and design and build the equipment. He would pay for it, and then lease it back to me for a dollar a year. This included the elaborate video equipment. It was a lucky break.'

Meek pointed out that all this was leading up to what he considered the first breakthrough. It didn't happen until several years later, in 1975. He had encountered a rough-hewn, intuitively brilliant medium in western Pennsylvania named Bill O'Neil. He was an eighth grade drop-out, but something of an electronic genius, developed from his days in the services at Pearl Harbor during World War Two. O'Neil lived with his wife on a remote farm in western Pennsylvania. He was apparently totally absorbed with his electronics. He was something of a recluse. He was also, according to Meek, rather irascible and unpredictable. But he had made what Meek considered a monumental breakthrough. Over and through his radio equipment, he had apparently established two-way communication with the dead. And Meek was about to present us with the evidence.

There are certain pronouncements that are difficult to know how to react to. This was one of them. Elizabeth was looking down at her Adidas, and didn't change her expression. I was trying to size up Meek, with his Brooks Brothers suit and foulard tie and dark socks and polished shoes that formed the shibboleth of the conservative business man. Yet here he was talking about direct electronic communication with the dead. There was a moment of silence after Meek dropped his bombshell, but finally Elizabeth got up and said, 'I've got to get a sweater. It's still chilly in here.'

She went to the closet, took out her sweater, and Meek continued. 'Meeting Bill O'Neil,' Meek said, 'began one of the most fascinating relationships I have ever had. But it is also one of the most frustrating. Jeannette and I have at times almost torn our hair out, working with his personality. But it has paid off.'

Meek explained that he had traveled around the world several times, and had studied many different mediums. Some appeared legitimate, some were borderline, and some were obvious fakes. But to him, O'Neil was the best clairaudient and clairvoyant medium he had come across. In other words, O'Neil showed clear evidence of being able to hear and see people in other dimensions. 'Like any good medium,' Meek continued, 'he could receive detailed information from those who were deceased – information that could be verified or that contained such elaborate detail that it was highly unlikely to be faked. But what interested me was that he combined mediumship with a startling amount of knowledge of electronics. Without going into details now, I'll just summarize by saying that O'Neil made contact first with a deceased doctor, a former ham radio operator who merely identified himself as "Doc Nick". The doctor claimed that he had died five years before, and gave instructions to Bill to show how certain audio frequencies could serve as an energy source. When these frequencies were combined with a tape recorder, voice contact could be made with him. In other words, clairaudient suggestions to Bill helped Bill modify his ham radio equipment so that the voice of the deceased doctor could actually be heard over the circuit, instead of through the conventional medium's voice channel.'

Liz, who had been quiet all through this, finally spoke up. 'Wait a minute,' she said. 'One person is alive and the other is dead?' Her tone was incredulous.

'That's right,' Meek answered.

Liz was still baffled. 'You mean you captured the voice of the dead person on tape?'

'And not through the medium's own voice?' I asked.

Liz continued to drive hard with her questioning. 'Hold everything,' she said. 'You mean this guy is just going to talk – I mean, which is the dead one?'

'Doc Nick is the dead one,' Meek said.

'Now who is this Doc Nick again?' Liz asked.

Meek smiled. 'I don't blame you for being confused,' he said. 'This voice that came through the speaker said he had been a doctor. But he had also been a ham radio operator. He said he had died some five years earlier.'

Across the room, Jeannette had dropped her head on the back of the sofa, and was looking up at the ceiling. Obviously, she had heard all this many times before.

'Of course Jeannette was not exactly thrilled when I decided to give up my career at 60,' Meek said, answering a question I had in my mind. 'In fact she felt I was acting rather stupidly.'

Jeannette smiled as he spoke.

Meek continued, 'It was rough on her, because I traveled across the world to make contact with physicians, physicists, parapsychologists and others who were deeply interested in researching the basic nature of Man. Jeannette had little knowledge or interest in paranormal research, and I couldn't blame her for her resistance to the idea. But now she is working with me full time.'

Jeannette nodded. 'George is very persuasive. I'm afraid he finally brought me around,' she said.

'What I want to do,' Meek continued, 'is to spread this story out to you so that you can get the overall picture. You'll have ample time later on to investigate any part of it. But you can take my word for the moment that the voice you are going to hear on the tape – subject to your later check – is the voice of someone who is dead, and has been working with Bill O'Neil clairvoyantly and clairaudiently.'

Meek went over to the tape deck and inserted a cassette. 'I have to explain one other thing to you,' he said. 'You'll hear loud humming noises in the background. These are the audio frequencies that Doc Nick suggested – it's a kind of sound energy against which he could bounce his voice, where his energy could interact to a point where it could be heard. It's a process that is similar to, but much more efficient than what is called Electronic Voice Phenomenon – or EVP. Have you heard of that before?'

I had, when I was researching psychic background material in England and Europe. They were called Raudive Voices, after the Latvian psychologist Dr Konstantin Raudive, who developed the process. By setting up certain radio frequencies and introducing what technicians call 'white noise', Raudive claimed that he could receive actual voices from the dead, although the phrases were short, cryptic, and disconnected. There was no two-way communication or continuity. I had listened to a short tape of them, and found them to be rather unconvincing. However, I never found time to follow them up, and had simply put them out of my mind. I had formed no opinion. I wondered if Meek were just repeating this sort of thing. But as he continued, it appeared that he wasn't.

'I researched all the EVP experiments in Europe,' he went on. 'All the so-called Raudive voices. I decided that the techniques they were using never had any possibility of achieving the kind of results I was looking for. But I did find that their use of the diode or interfrequency method was very important because whatever entities there were, were able to use this energy. We did a lot of experimenting to create these artificial background noises. They make it hard to hear, but they are critically important.'

I was still cautious. If the tapes were anything like the Raudive voices, I doubted that they would be persuasive. The key would be whether there would be a direct interaction between the voice of this Bill O'Neil and the purported Doc Nick.

'Our first breakthrough came on October 27, 1977,' Meek said. 'You might find some of the words difficult to understand over the background noise. So please listen carefully.'

Meek snapped on the tape deck switch. A weird high-pitched whine came on. Then a gravelly voice was heard, a voice almost too much like the sound track of a science fiction robot. Then Bill O'Neil's voice followed, clear and undistorted. There was no question about it, a two-way conversation was taking place. The effect was rather chilling.

O'NEIL: Try it again.
DOC NICK: All right. Do you hear me now, Bill? Can you hear me, Bill?
O'NEIL: Yeah, but you make it sound just like . . . oh boy . . . a robot on television.
DOC NICK: Yes, we always will . . . when we . . . we will . . . the one thing . . . you hear, Bill? You hear, Bill?
O'NEIL: Yeah, ok . . . uh . . . *(his voice is shaky)*. You have to forgive me but . . . uh . . . I know this is . . . you have to admit this is kind – of scary.
DOC NICK: *(Unintelligible)*
O'NEIL: It's all garbled. I can't understand you.
DOC NICK: I said why are you . . . leave it alone, leave it alone. Did you hear me, Bill? Do you hear what I say?
O'NEIL: Yeah, I got it now, Doc . . . uh . . . you asked what I was doing on the Vidicom, right?

It sounded for all the world like two ham radio operators in mundane chatter, the kind that could be picked up any time of the day or night. Yet if there were any basis to Meek's claim of communication with a deceased entity, the impact was startling. But this was a big 'if'.

We learned later what the reference to 'Vidicom' meant. Apparently Doc Nick had suggested some further electronic circuitry that might eventually bring in an image of the deceased communicant, if the system could be worked out. We also learned, as the tape continued, that another deceased, Dr George Mueller, had purportedly been in psychic contact with O'Neil. He was also said to be helping out in devising electronic communication. These two purported entities, Doc Nick and Dr Mueller, were allegedly competing for O'Neil's attention:

O'NEIL: *(Referring to the mention of 'Vidicom')* Dr Mueller wants me to get busy on this, you know.

DOC NICK: Oh, yes. *That* man.

O'NEIL: Yeah, that man . . . uh . . . uh . . . you'll have to forgive me, but this is not that easy, you know. It is not easy. *(The background humming shifts slightly in pitch)* . . . That frequency changed again.

DOC NICK: Yes, I know Bill. It is much better now . . . I feel more comfortable with this frequency . . . Don't change it any more. As I told you before, you must be careful of these frequencies. Mark the frequency change.

O'NEIL: *(A little testy)* Oh, yeah, yeah, sure. I'm supposed to guess what these frequencies are. I don't have any way of monitoring these frequencies!

The short specimen tape came to an end. Before either Liz or I had a chance to comment on this bizarre and other-worldly demonstration, Meek spoke again.

'Now I know you are probably still confused,' he said. 'I would be myself, if I were suddenly thrown into this picture. Here is a deceased human being talking in very prosaic terms with a living being through radio frequencies. It sounds utterly impossible. But I want you to hold off any opinion – one way or the other – until you have a chance to study the whole picture. Incidentally, we've named this project "Spiricom", for obvious reasons.'

At this point, I wasn't sure I wanted to study the whole picture. Nor did I like the term 'Spiricom'. Or 'Vidicom'. They sounded too corny. Also, the concept that a deceased entity could casually chat about radio circuits and frequencies with someone still living was too much to accept. I had run into a lot of incredible things in writing several books on the paranormal, but this one seemed to top them all. I have always tried to keep an open mind. But this situation made it difficult to do so. Meek was so matter of fact about it all, almost annoyingly so. I still had trouble connecting him with the subject matter. He looked and sounded as if he were addressing the New York Academy of Sciences, or the American Society of Mechanical Engineers – both of which he had belonged to.

'What complicates things,' Meek continued, 'is that Bill O'Neil had these two different types of contact with both Doc Nick and George Mueller. Bill would apparently receive long technical instructions from them through his mediumship, without the electronic equipment. These in turn provided him with the know-how to construct the proper circuits for the disembodied voices to come through. But we're still in a very rough stage. When I get discouraged, I remind myself of what one member of the French Academy of Sciences told his colleagues about Edison's phonograph: "Gentlemen, I have personally examined Mr Edison's phonograph, and I find that it is nothing but a clever use of ventriloquism."'

'How well do you know this Bill O'Neil?' I asked.

'We know him inside out,' Meek said. 'He's a complicated character. He's not the easiest person in the world to get along with. The strange part was that when Mueller began to come through in great detail, Doc Nick seemed to fade out of the picture. We gradually lost him. Mueller gave us enough information through O'Neil to enable us to track his career down. Mueller had apparently been a competent physicist. He told us through Bill where we could locate his death certificate issued in 1967. He gave Bill his Social Security number. He gave intimate details of his activities at the University of Wisconsin and Cornell. We traced all this detail and much more. And oddly enough, it checked out. So it was a weird situation. Here was this really learned guy talking to Bill, an eighth grade drop-out. But the main thing is that we were able to refine our equipment with Mueller's help. By September, 1980, we had our second major breakthrough.'

Still deadpan, Meek played another segment of the tape. There was much less background noise. Mueller's voice was loud and clear, but still in a gravelly monotone. He patiently instructed O'Neil, giving counts from one to ten, suggesting frequency changes as if he were tutoring a freshman engineering student. In some segments of the taped conversation, Dr Mueller seemed to go into infinite detail.

MUELLER: William, I think the big problem is an impedence mismatch into that third transistor.
O'NEIL: Third transistor?
MUELLER: Yes. The transistor that follows the input.
O'NEIL: I don't understand.
MUELLER: *(Impatiently)* The pre-amp, the pre-amp!
O'NEIL: Oh, the pre-amp.
MUELLER: Yes, I think that I can easily correct that by introducing a . . . by introducing a 150 or 100 ohm . . . I am not sure, William, a 150 ohm, one half watt resistor in parallel with a .0047 microfarad ceramic capacitor. I think we can overcome that impedence mismatch.
O'NEIL: Oh boy, I'll have to get the schematic back.
MUELLER: You'd rather have the schematic?
O'NEIL: I'd rather mark it on the schematic, Doctor . . .

I knew little or nothing about microfarads or schematics, but if there were anything to this strange mixture of living and dead, this technical detail had a strong sense of verisimilitude.

It was obvious that the implications were enormous. But, at the same time, the credibility was strained to the breaking point. It seemed that it would have helped if Meek were not so damned expressionless. He was throwing out theories and mega-theories as if he were running down a shopping list for the A&P Supermarket. I was half-mad at myself for listening to all this, yet something told me I ought to hang in there a while longer, since we had listened this far. There was a flood of additional questions in my mind, but Meek was intent on getting his story out. I was mostly interested in how he could confirm the data about these alleged electronic entities that seemed to be so co-operative.

I interrupted him long enough to get a question in. 'Tell me, George,' I said, 'what do you consider the best piece of evidence that O'Neil was really contacting Dr Mueller? In addition to his Social Security number, death certificate and that sort of thing?'

'There are so many bits of evidence that I can't cover them all in one sitting. Let me give you just one example right now. Mueller, who had top security clearance in the executive jobs he had before he died, gave O'Neil three unlisted telephone numbers. He suggested that we check them out to confirm that they were those of highest security officials. We checked them out. They were just what Mueller had said they were. More than that, all three were very upset and wanted to know how we got the numbers. I have all the details on this that you can review later.'

I would be learning more about this, but for the moment, I put it on the shelf. Everything depended on if and when I decided to go ahead with the story. All this material was coming so thick and fast, I was having trouble making any intelligent assessment at all. This mixture of science and technology and the paranormal was too much to absorb at once.

'There's another very interesting bit I'm trying to track down right now,' Meek continued. 'Not long ago, Mueller was talking to O'Neil and told Bill that he must get hold of a copy of a small book he – Mueller – had written back in 1947. It was an introduction to electronics. He specified pages 66 and 67, and told O'Neil that reading those pages would help him greatly to continue their contact.'

'You haven't found any such book?' I asked Meek.

'No, not yet,' Meek said. 'It was apparently an army publication. I'm checking everywhere, because this would make strong evidence. Library of Congress has no record, but I'm still digging.'

I made a mental note of this. It could be strong corroboration if Meek ever uncovered it. Especially if the specified pages applied directly to the subject matter. But I had traced obscure books before. The job was never easy and mostly fruitless.

Meek obviously had the persistence of a fox terrier in digging up details. It would be interesting to see how his search turned out. At the moment, it was getting close to dinner time, with no sign of Meek slowing up. I interrupted him long enough to see if he wanted a snack, but he and Jeannette politely refused, as he went on to prepare to show us a videotape of O'Neil working with his equipment in his lonely Pennsylvania farmhouse. Meek had supplied O'Neil with a video camera to attempt to get the possible 'Vidicom' system working. To test the camera, O'Neil had videotaped himself on camera during several sessions at his equipment panel as he talked with the alleged voice of Mueller.

Meek rolled the videotape, and the image of O'Neil, sitting in front of a disorganized mass of dials, speakers and switches, came on the black-and-white screen. O'Neil, with grizzled features and a shabby sweater, was twisting the dials as the scratches and screeches of background sound came over the speakers. The camera framed only a small corner of the room, which was in general disarray: tape cassettes in piles, a coffee cup on the table beside the radio equipment, a couple of books, pages open, and a dark ill-defined background where the light faded off behind the equipment. The scene had all the qualities of a Charles Addams eerie mansion. As O'Neil continued to vary the background noise on the speakers, Meek spoke to us.

'To go back,' Meek told us, 'we added this extra equipment for Bill. The video camera is off-screen, of course, but the cassette tape recorder you see there on the screen. You'll be hearing the voice of Dr Mueller when it comes in shortly on the tape. We haven't made any headway on our Vidicom experiments, so you won't see anything of Mueller, you'll just hear his voice. These segments you'll hear are just a smattering of hours and hours of conversations . . .'

On the screen, O'Neil seemed to be making infinite adjustments, but was still getting nothing more than static and background noises. Then the noise seemed to level off to a high whine, and quite suddenly the voice purporting to be Dr Mueller came in. It still had that gravelly, robot-like sound. As a sample, Meek had picked out a segment concerning those unlisted phone numbers:

MUELLER: By the way, William . . .
O'NEIL: Yes, sir?
MUELLER: Do you know those telephone numbers I gave you?
O'NEIL: Those are those unlisted numbers?
MUELLER: 'That's correct.
O'NEIL: If I — oh, boy — they may wonder . . . maybe there's another code or something. Considering what they're involved in. *(Apparently O'Neil was worried about the security clearances on the numbers.)*
MUELLER: You don't need to worry about that.
O'NEIL: *(Very respectfully)* I do worry about that, sir. Supposing they find out it was me – and they want to know how I got hold of the unlisted telephone number. *Now who would believe how I got hold of this number?*
MUELLER: Don't worry about that. There's nothing to worry about that in that respect.
O'NEIL: Well, I don't know, sir . . .

More conversation followed. It involved some sort of electrical device that O'Neil was attempting to develop for arthritis treatment. It was too complicated to understand in the brief mention on the tape. It would have to be another item to check later if I decided to follow up. I asked Meek to stop the tape.

'Now just what does O'Neil do for a living?' I asked. My confusion was still mounting.

'He tinkers around,' Meek said. 'Repairs radios and TV. He's very good at it, but very sporadic. We pay him a small fee to keep experimenting. Both he and his wife live very spartanly.'

'How old is he?' Liz asked.

'He's 64,' Meek answered. 'His wife is quite a bit younger. Recently he's been working on his own on an invention of a new type of antenna for radio and TV. It might just have some good marketing possibilities. I'm going to give him a hand on that. But I guess the best way to describe him is that he's an offbeat electronic mystic.'

Liz, who is never one to hold back her opinions, said, 'He sounds like a real odd ball.'

Meek smiled. 'Well, he leans in that direction. But he's not quite as bizarre as he sounds.'

'What does he want to get out of all this?' I asked.

'He sincerely believes, along with me, that this can be the greatest possible breakthrough for the human race,' Meek said. 'He certainly can't be in it for the money I can give him. It's minuscule.'

'How about ego?' I said. 'Would he expect fame or public attention from this?'

'The only condition he has asked from me is that he remain completely anonymous. I have only recently got him to agree that I could release his name when we present this entire project to the press, which I'm planning to do in the spring.'

Meek was obviously a man of strong persuasion and stubborn determination. I had no doubt about his sincerity and honesty. He was a credible man – but he was reporting an incredible story. He went on to say that he was in the process of setting up a major press conference in April at the National Press Club in Washington, and that he would present his findings to reporters there, along with a panel of his associates who had been working on the project with him. I wondered if Meek realized the possible reception he would get from a tough and cynical press corps that could laugh him out of town. The dailies and the weeklies would never take the time to explore Meek's project in depth. And even if they did, I was sure they would come down on it hard. In the past, I had found that some far-out stories checked out surprisingly well – but some did not. But

I had had the luxury of exploring them for a book possibility, not for a quick scratchy story in a daily paper.

By the time Meek had finished playing his sample tapes, I frankly didn't know what to make of it. It was obvious that only a long, deep probe would tell whether it was an important story or not. This would be a long and costly job, and I wasn't at all sure I wanted to tackle it. The only thing that would count would be the evidential material. Facts that could be traced, checked and verified. Resistance to such a strange phenomenon would be monumental. And yet in a way, Meek was right. If, by some rare and remote chance, the story was valid, there was no doubt it could be one of the greatest breakthroughs in history. But who would believe it? There was no sense in doing a story – even if it were true – if no one would be able to believe it.

I had more than a casual interest in the subject as the result of some of the previous books I had researched and written. I like to maintain an open mind, but certainly not a gullible one. My previous research had almost forced me to conclude that something was out there. It was still elusive. But the evidence – especially the cumulative evidence on the subject of life after death – was powerful. Of course I realized that evidence was not proof. But it possibly indicates the path to truth. If life is continuous, if we live after death, and if Meek's project could produce palpable evidence of this, it could have a powerful effect on the world.

Meek must have guessed what I was thinking. 'I've given a lot of thought to the long term benefits of proving Spiricom to the world,' he said. I still wasn't fond of that word. 'I believe, and I hope I can get others to believe, that we will have scientific proof that man's mind, memory banks and personality survive the death of the physical body. It can move us beyond mere belief, and into physical evidence. It can help reduce the sadness and anguish when a loved one dies. Knowing life is continuous can give an impetus to improving our own personal conduct. As communication improves, we may be able to draw on the wisdom of the ages. You've only heard a test smattering of what has come through in this early stage of Spiricom. It can help bring about the joining of religion and science. I hope it can eventually bring out the best of both.'

I told Meek that I agreed with a lot of what he was saying, but that this was all too much to absorb in a single sitting. He agreed. What he wanted me to do was to go through a large stack of transcripts, letters and background material that he would leave with me. Then if I were further interested, we might talk again. He also hoped that I would be able to come to the press conference in Washington the following spring at his expense.

'Well, obviously, George,' I said, 'the first thing I've got to do is sleep on this. The second thing is to go over your transcripts and other material here. Then we can talk.'

This seemed agreeable to both Meek and his wife, and they left. As far as I could figure out Meek was tenaciously determined to make an electronic breakthrough in communicating with those who had died. He was not satisfied with the conventional use of a medium to accomplish this. Yet he felt the use of reputable mediums could bring in the technical information needed. From this he hoped to build the equipment that would handle the job. The end product was most important: conclusive proof that death was merely a door to continuing life.

This was a big order. I had to admire his determination. But I couldn't help wondering about the roadblocks he was setting up for himself in the face of a materialistic world that worshipped science more than it did the 'nature of man', as Meek put it.

* * *

Liz and I didn't say much to each other as we scraped together our delayed dinner. A hearty extra-dry, materialistic martini was a welcome break after several hours of such a heady excursion into the outer reaches of human speculation. I finally asked Liz to sum up what she thought.

'It's either totally outrageous or totally awesome,' she said. 'Don't ask me which.'

I told her I was feeling the same way.

'I think Meek and his wife are very dedicated people,' she said. 'But I don't know anything about this Bill O'Neil. Except that it's obvious he's a maverick.'

She paused a moment, then added, 'But of course we've both come round to realizing that the question of life after death is at the top of the list.'

This was true. But how could Meek's ridiculous story be verified? And how could Meek and his story stand up in the face of a full-scale press conference?

I decided to suspend judgment until I had a chance to go through Meek's material. I had a lot of misgivings. But I also had a compulsion to dig deeper, even if my search would only lead to a blind alley.

# CHAPTER 2

# *Roadblocks*

The papers that George Meek had left with me consisted of a bulging file of assorted material. I started to wade through it the next day. I had had a restless night. The thought of a mechanical discarnate voice coming through a speaker was eerie. I allowed for the fact that it could all be contrived. But this didn't fit in with my assessment of Meek. Or even allowing for that, the incident was disconcerting. Recently some friends of mine had died. They were both vital and deathless. It seemed just as hard to accept that they had been wiped out like a magnetic tape as it was to conceive that their energies were still articulate and active. Not in the sense of somewhere 'up there' but 'through there', in another dimension, in a different set of molecules that were just as real as ours.

This is what intrigued me. Part of it, anyway. The other part was what the effect would be on people everywhere if Meek's claims came anywhere near checking out. I wasn't too optimistic, but I poured a cup of coffee while Liz was reading *The Times*, and collected the material in front of me on the table.

Much of it seemed to consist of Meek's reflections over the dozen or so years he had devoted to the subject of life after death. There were copies of several books he had written. One was called *After We Die, What Then?*. The title was appropriate enough in view of what we had heard the night before. A quick glance at the table of contents showed it to be a detailed study of evidence of survival after death. There seemed to be heavy emphasis on the relation between science and metaphysics, which reflected the name he was calling his foundation.

One book was the manual describing the Spiricom project which included a lot of formidable technical data. There were other papers, clippings, memos, and letters that would take considerable time to go through.

Liz looked across the table and said, 'Mr Meek seems to be very serious about all this.'

'Apparently so,' I said. 'But then so are we.'

'Anything look interesting?' she asked.

One thing that did catch my eye was several published articles on Thomas Edison and his attempt to create an electrical device that could receive evidential and verifiable messages from the dead. Until Meek had mentioned this, I had no idea that the famous inventor had turned his attention to such an elusive subject. What surprised me was the extent of Edison's interest. Meek's urge to develop his Spiricom project must have been actively propelled by Edison's little-known experiments.

Basically, Edison had tried to develop a mechanical device that would do away with the mysticism that surrounded much of psychic exploration. It appeared that Meek was following along this line. Allan Benson, a friend of Edison, finally revealed his talks with Edison over a 20-year span, up until Edison's death in 1931. Edison was an agnostic. He believed that life was energy, that intelligence was behind the universe, but that there was no personal immortality. But these views crumbled toward the end of his life. He told Benson that there might be a 50–50 chance that an individual's consciousness continued after death.

I skimmed over an interview with *Scientific American* published back in 1920. Edison was quoted as saying: 'I have been thinking for some time of a machine or apparatus which could be operated by personalities who have passed on to another existence or sphere. I believe that if we are to make any real progress in psychic investigation, we must do it with scientific apparatus and in a scientific manner.' Later on in the interview, he added that he hoped to be able to complete the machine 'before many months'.

'Wonder how he figured to do that,' Liz said when I read it to her.

I went down through the document. 'It says here that his theory was based on the fact that the body and everything else is basically electrical.'

'That makes sense, I guess,' Liz said.

'Then he goes on to say that some kind of sensitive mechanism, like a telephone, might be able to capture signals from this physical energy source.'

'Maybe Meek isn't as far out as he seems with his ideas,' Liz said.

I read further.

'Now the article is talking about Edison's friend, Sir William Crookes.'

'He's that famous British scientist who really got into the psychic, isn't he?'

'He was very distinguished,' I said. 'Invented the vacuum tube that made Edison's incandescent light possible.'

'Maybe that's why Edison got into the psychic himself.'

According to the article, Edison admitted that his light would never have worked without the pioneer work of Crookes in creating vacuums. Aside from that, Crookes had told Edison that he had taken over 40 photographs of a 'spirit' who had materialized during several seances he attended, and Edison was not one to doubt his word. Yet at the same time he found it hard to believe.

This was the same problem Liz and I had with our research. Even when the evidence was powerful and convincing; even when it came from reputable sources like Crookes and scores of other scientists who were willing to go out on a limb. The problem was weeding out the reputable from the disreputable, and there was plenty of the latter around.

There was another item in the material that was impressive. I discovered for the first time that Marconi, the inventor of wireless radio, had been working, up to the time of his death in 1937, on an unsuccessful attempt to capture supernatural voices.

It was apparent that Meek had again done his homework.

* * *

From the material in the file, I was able to trace in detail Meek's theories about the potential of life after death, and further motivation for his pursuing the issue. Because of his engineering background, his main objective was to bridge the gap between the living and deceased through electronic means. He realized that many would feel this was a crazy idea, but the group of associates he worked with lent mutual support to the idea that it might be possible. The group included electronic engineers and technicians, several professors in the fields of physics, sociology and journalism, plus international specialists in similar fields. Behind the search appeared to be an almost passionate desire on the part of Meek to bring together religion and science, not exactly an easy job.

Meek's confidence in the results of his plunge into scientific and metaphysical research was full blown, as his Metascience supporting papers reflected. He had also arrived at the conclusion that individual consciousness and personality not only continued to exist after death, but could be communicated with. And he was further convinced that the 'needless and destructive fear of death could be removed, as well as the deep concern over the loss of loved ones'.

He had other convictions as a result of his probings. He felt that cultural taboos on the subject of death could be removed; religious dogma could be replaced by a better religious faith based on hard evidence. His new developments, he hoped, could improve the outlook for both science and religion; living could become more enriched and on a higher moral plane with the knowledge that death could be transcended.

These were noble sentiments. But I had been going through a long struggle with myself, the result of my research on several books that reached out into strange and unusual phenomena that in the light of modern science were considered impossible. And although I was extremely cautious in my conclusions, I often found myself facing a barrage of criticism from obdurate scientific skeptics who claimed that the paranormal subject matter involved should never be examined in the first place.

Typical of these reviews was one from *Time* magazine about a book I had written in 1977 called *The Poison that Fell from the Sky*, the story of a town in Italy that was tragically doomed by dioxin. Although *Time* called it a 'first rate piece of reporting . . . an urgent, surprisingly muted, cautionary tale', the review was not so kind regarding some of my other books. The review began: 'There seem to be not one but two writers inside the prolific John G. Fuller. One has produced sober, responsible books on banking and medical research. The other is better known for his hyper-thyroid irresponsible studies of psychic phenomena. In 1965 Fuller, whose various incarnations include a stint as a columnist for the *Saturday Review* and Emmy Award-winning as a television producer, published *Incident at Exeter*. In it he concluded that the unidentified flying objects sighted and reported around the country were of extraterrestrial origin . . .'

There was one problem with the mixed review: I had *not* reached any conclusions about the strange events at Exeter; I had merely stated the facts and suggested in the book that the subject was one that cried out for scientific investigation. What was important to me was that the story opened up my mind to subjects that were being summarily dismissed by many scientists without any open-minded investigation.

In examining the George Meek material about possible electronic communication with the deceased, I was struck by certain similarities to the Exeter story, some 15 years earlier. At first glance, both stories seemed impossible. Both stories would be likely to be summarily dismissed by most scientists. If by any rare chance they were true, they would have a tremendous impact on history. But both stories would be extremely difficult to prove. As I checked through the Meek file, my mind went back over 15 years to the time when I was weighing whether or not to take on the book about the incident at Exeter. My concerns then were the same as my concerns now. I could recall clearly the problems I ran into then, and they would no doubt be around in the present.

* * *

I had checked into the Exeter Inn of the New Hampshire town of that name on a bright October morning in 1965. I had no idea that the rumbles from that visit would be echoing through the present and on into the future. What followed was a mystery as fantastic and sweeping as the legend of Sleepy Hollow, mixed with the most vivid trappings of science fiction. The story would jump from the pages of the august *Saturday Review*, to *Look* magazine, to the *Reader's Digest*, to a book called *Incident at Exeter*. It would become part of a controversy that seems to be coming to a head in the 1980s, and just may continue forever.

The story at Exeter was unambiguous. It was on the official records of the Exeter police, and reported by two officers of the department whose character, reliability and composure in crisis had been firmly attested by their superior officers. It was also reported on the record books of the Pease Air Force Base, the Strategic Air Command Post in nearby Portsmouth. The police officers were described by the Air Force as serious and capable witnesses. The incident happened at about 3 a.m. near Tel. & Tel. pole No. 668 on Route 150, as Patrolman Eugene Bertrand noted. The object hovered about 100 feet in the air, and was as big as a ranch house. It glowed brilliantly and rocked back and forth on its axis. Around its rim were pulsating red lights, flashing in a 5–4–3–2–1 pattern, and then reversing in sequence. It lit up a wide field and two farmhouses. Bertrand dropped to the ground, reached for his .38, thought better of it, and shoved it back in its holster. With him was Patrolman David Hunt and a young navy recruit named Norman Muscarello. Muscarello had seen the object, rushed to the police station, and begged the police to come with him to the scene. They did. It wobbled above, then came towards them. Then it slowly backed off to the east, towards the Atlantic, towards Hampton. Shortly afterwards Bertrand, a former crew member on KC-97 refueling flights, saw a B-47 come over. There was no comparison between the object and the Air Force jet . . . or a helicopter . . . or a balloon . . . or anything else in aviation.

This was the beginning of a six-week investigation for me. Two other incidents that same night were of interest. Just before 3 a.m., Patrolman Bertrand had come upon a woman in her car on Route 101. She was nearly hysterical. She said a huge, silent airborne object had trailed her car from the town of Epping, 12 miles away, only a few feet above her car. It had brilliant flashing red lights. She stopped her car, and the object took off with tremendous speed to disappear among the stars.

Just after 3 a.m. an Exeter night operator called the police station to report an hysterical call from a pay phone in Hampton. A male subject reported a large, unidentified object. Then the call was suddenly cut off.

In the six-week period, I unearthed over 60 such UFO reports from residents in a wide area around Exeter. They came from housewives, teachers, businessmen, Air Force pilots, coastguards, police, farmers and other solid New Hampshire Yankees. None were in the spook-and-kook category. But the most important thing about the case was that similar events were happening all over the United States, Europe, the Soviet Union, Asia, South America – in fact, the world.

What I didn't realize at the time was that whenever a story like the incident at Exeter was reported, it seemed to trigger an automatic response from a segment of the population who claimed, without direct investigation, that such events simply *could not happen*. Their counter claims were often accompanied by vigor and sometimes hysteria. The syndrome was not confined to UFOs. It seemed to apply to any paranormal event, from ESP to psychokinesis.

My first real encounter with this sort of thinking involved the Pentagon. Its press release shortly after the Exeter police sighting stated that a high-altitude Strategic Air Command exercise had been going on at the time. The release from Washington also said that the policemen and witnesses simply saw 'stars and planets in unusual formations'. There was no mention of the 60 other cases I had checked so thoroughly, nor why an ex-Air Force crew member would pull a gun from his holster at the sight of a star or planet. When the *Saturday Review* article appeared, the patrolmen received a letter from the Air Force indicating that their sighting on September 2 must have been a B-47 exercise conducted between midnight and 2 a.m.

There were problems with this Air Force letter. The sighting was at three in the morning, not two. And it took place on September 3, not September 2. The Pentagon appeared to be more interested in denial than facts.

In reply, Bertrand and Hunt suggested to the Air Force officer that it was urgent for them to clear up any possible conclusion that they (a) made up the story or (b) were incompetent observers.

When there was no reply several weeks later, the police officers wrote again, stating: 'We both feel that it's very important for our jobs and our reputations to get some kind of letter from you to say that the story put out by the Pentagon was not true; it could not possibly be, because we were the people who saw this – not the Pentagon.'

As part of my research, I called on Lt. Col. John F. Spaulding of the Air Force Community Relations Division at the Pentagon. I wanted to get further information, and to find out about the confusion in the Air Force records. The case was listed as 'unidentified', contrary to the official Air Force release. The Colonel said this must be a case of mistaken identity. That's why the Pentagon stories and releases didn't add up. Then I asked him if he were keeping an open mind on the case.

He reacted with unexpected fury. 'Are you saying that I'm lying about this?'

I told him no. I was just wondering how he was able to be so certain on the basis of second-hand reports. He took a sharp breath and said: 'Sir, you are talking to an officer of the United States Air Force!' Then he walked off melodramatically, and out of sight. His secretary looked a little embarrassed and said he had a lot of problems on his mind that day.

I couldn't blame the Colonel for being skeptical. Halfway through the research at Exeter, I couldn't believe what I was learning. Most of the 60 reports were of low-altitude objects, disc or round in shape.

They were almost universally large in diameter, 30 to 60 or more feet. At night they were brilliant; in daylight bright and metallic. They moved in non-aerodynamic patterns. The sightings were at different times and places over the six-week period, but the descriptions were amazingly consistent.

Then I saw one myself. I was glad I was with ABC-TV news cameraman Bob Kimball, even though there was no time to get his camera gear unpacked from his station wagon. We followed the running lights of a jet fighter from horizon to horizon. Its altitude was estimated at some 6,000 feet according to Kimball, who was a pilot. In front of it, moving at the same speed, was the object. It was a reddish orange disc about one-fifth the size of a full moon, glowing and incandescent. The plane seemed to be in hot pursuit, but it was not closing in on the disc. We were only able to keep it in view for some 20 seconds at the most. As it went across the sky, Kimball said: 'Check me. What do you see?'

'An orange disc,' I told him. 'Immediately in front of the running lights of an apparent jet fighter.'

'A little to the port of it, wouldn't you say?'

'Maybe. Not much to port.'

'Do you see any running lights on the disc?'

'No,' I said. 'Nothing but the orange disc.'

'Right,' Kimball said. 'What I'm trying to figure out is not *what* we saw, because there is no doubt about that. What I'm trying to do is to find any possible logical and familiar explanation for it.' We couldn't. And that's when I got on the phone to New York to ask *Look* to send up a senior editor and a researcher to check me out. I figured it was just possible that I might be going around the bend.

After reconfirming the interviews and research, the *Look* editors assured me that I wasn't. I was glad of that. As both a journalist and a documentary film producer on contract to NBC-TV, I had no intention of getting mixed up with the spook-and-kook department. But I began to discover that what I call the proponents of the Can't-Happen-Here syndrome can be just as ridiculous as the spooks and kooks.

Two things happened before my next encounter with the Can't-Happen-Here syndrome. One was that the day after the *Look* article appeared on the newstand in February, 1966, Lt. Col. Spaulding wrote to officers Bertrand and Hunt and apologized for the Air Force claiming their sighting was stars, planets, or B-47s. The other was that the late U Thant, then Secretary General of the United Nations, invited Professor J. Allen Hynek, head of the Department of Astronomy at Northwestern University, and me to meet him at his office on the top of the UN Building.

He had read the article in *Look*. He was struck by the fact that many almost exactly parallel stories had been reported to him from practically all of the UN member nations. We discussed the UFO situation for over an hour. I kept asking myself: 'Why the hell am I here in the office of the UN Secretary General discussing flying saucers, of all things?' But because there were so many world-wide reports from credible people, U Thant was intensely interested and serious. Professor Hynek came up with an interesting theory as to how a UFO could cover the problem of light-years' distances: since time is relative, a lifetime on another planet outside our solar system might be many times that on ours. An elephant lives thousands of times longer than a fruit fly. Our lifetime could be a fraction of a second to an extraterrestrial species. I was able to answer U Thant's questions on public reaction: intense shock at first, replaced almost immediately by healthy curiosity; there was no evidence of panic.

U Thant's attitude was in sharp contrast to the Can't-Happen-Here group. I was able to learn more about them on a TV panel show called *The Open Mind*. It was chaired by Dr Eric Goldman, on leave from Princeton to act as academic advisor to the President. On the panel of four professors was Dr Donald Menzel, head of the Harvard University observatory. I was glad to be able to discuss the incidents at Exeter with such a learned professor. Perhaps he could come up with some interesting insights. I described the case to him in detail, along with a striking UFO photograph I had tracked down and investigated for several days in Pennsylvania. Without waiting for me to finish the details, Dr Menzel said: 'I can tell you exactly what the situation was. These two policemen were hysterical subjects.' He went on to say how they were suffering from a form of delusion that was common to UFO sightings, and discussed the syndrome at length.

I asked him how long he had talked to the patrolmen, how far he had dug into their records and background as I had done. He didn't even know their names, and had spent no time in Exeter at all. About the photograph, he said: 'This is obviously a double exposure.' Yet he didn't know who the photographer was, had not examined the negative or talked to the expert photographers who had. When I asked him about the 60 other sightings in Exeter, he slammed his hand down on the table and said: 'Will you shut up! I didn't come here to go through an inquisition!'

I respected Dr Menzel's expertise in astronomy, but since most of the sightings were only a hundred feet in the air or less, it seemed that astronomy *per se* had little or nothing to do with the case. I was also startled that a man of Dr Menzel's standing could make such flat, unsubstantiated statements before a nationwide audience. It did not seem to be a scientific approach, especially from a scientist – and a good one.

I was soon to learn that the Can't-Happen-Here syndrome was not confined to scientists or the Pentagon. Shortly after the TV broadcast, I bumped into an editor on an aviation magazine named Philip Klass. He had read the *Look* article, which had now been reprinted in the *Reader's Digest*, and the book *Incident at Exeter*. 'You are a very good journalist,' he said, 'and I think I've been able to solve the mystery at Exeter for you.'

I told him I would welcome any explanation he had, that I was still puzzled by the whole event and almost wished I had not become involved in it.

'What the people saw,' Klass went on to explain, 'was either ball lightning or plasma. There's your answer.'

All I knew was that many of the sightings were carefully described by rational witnesses as metallic *vehicles*, and that ball lightning was a little understood phenomenon. It usually appeared with thunderstorms. Plasma was an intense electrical field researchers were trying to create and contain to produce fusion power. I said I would certainly check that possibility, but then I thought about the sighting with Bob Kimball. There was nothing gaseous about the disc we saw that was chased by the plane across the sky. I mentioned this.

'What you saw,' Klass said, 'was the afterglow of a jet engine.'

Aside from the fact that the object was sharply formed and well in front of the plane, I was surprised that Klass was able to tell me what I saw when he also had not been to Exeter. In addition, Kimball, as a pilot, had already ruled out the afterburner theory on several counts. Later, I looked up ball lightning and plasma to find that plasma needs some 10 million degrees centigrade to be created, it cannot yet be contained, lasts only a few seconds, and has never reached over a few feet in length. Yet Klass went on to write an entire book embracing this theory. He was later forced to back down from it by peer pressure. Klass, it seems, was branding everything to do with UFOs as pseudo-science, and in the process was developing some rather striking pseudo-scientific theories of his own.

Other evidence of the Can't-Happen-Here school of thought showed up at a Congressional hearing on the subject when an Air Force general was asked about my report of jets being scrambled after the UFOs. The general said that my report had to be inaccurate because there were no jet fighters based at the nearby Pease Air Force facility. There was a problem with his statement. In the book *Incident at Exeter* I had plainly written that there were no jet fighters at the Pease base, and that they would have had to be brought over from Westover or some other New England base.

By this time I was more than curious why there were so many attempts to discredit irrationally any straightforward attempts to explore the UFO phenomenon. Since this was my first attempt to explore a paranormal event, I had trouble understanding why the mere act of making a journalistic investigation should create what amounted to passionate scorn. The reaction to Exeter was only a symbol. I began to note that other aspects of the paranormal seemed to engender something of a frenzy on the part of critics who seemed rarely to bother to look thoroughly into the facts.

I was therefore delighted when I learned that Dr Edward Condon had been selected by the Secretary of Defense in the fall of 1966 to conduct a major study of UFOs at the University of Colorado on behalf of the Air Force. Condon was a distinguished physicist, a former president of the American Association for the Advancement of Science. He had grappled with and subdued the machinations of the House Un-American Activities Committee, and served as director of the National Bureau of Standards. To me there were the two clearly-defined elements that blocked intelligent investigation: the Can't-Happen-Here group of skeptical debunkers and the gullible advocates who would buy anything. Fortunately, Condon seemed to be neither of these.

But then some disturbing things began to happen. In a speech in Elmira, New York, Condon stated that UFOs were not the business of the Air Force. 'My attitude right now,' he announced to a group of scientists, 'is that there is nothing to it.' Then he added with a smile, 'But I'm not supposed to reach a conclusion for another year.'

This was hardly an auspicious start for a 'scientific' study that was to cost the taxpayer close to half a million dollars. Another rather ominous sign was that the Project Co-ordinator and key operations man, Robert J. Low, wrote a then-secret memo to the Colorado University officials explaining the program as he was going to direct it: 'Our study would be conducted almost exclusively by nonbelievers . . . (It) could and possibly would add an impressive body of evidence that there is no reality to the observations. The *trick* would be to describe the project so that, to the public, it would *appear* a totally objective study, but to the scientific community would present the image of a group of nonbelievers trying their best to be objective, but having an almost zero expectation of finding a saucer . . . I'm inclined to feel at this early stage that *if we set up the thing right*, and take pains to *get the proper people involved* and have success in *presenting the image we want to present* to the scientific community, we could carry the job off to our benefit . . .' (All italics are added.)

A half-million dollar *trick*? Presenting the image 'we want to present'? Making it '*appear* a totally objective study'? If this was the way that the study was predetermined, what possible use would it be? But beyond that, Condon began to point the study towards the crack-pot fringe of UFO believers. He went to a Congress of 'Ufologists' in New York, whom any sane observer could have told him were deluded and irresponsible. He showed every indication of concentrating on this fringe which would consist of straw men easy to knock down.

Condon's conclusions about the study were as negative as his expectations. Yet case after case inside the 900-page study is labeled as unidentified and without rational explanation. It was almost as if Condon failed to read his own material. Radar reports simultaneously confirmed by seasoned pilots are labeled by his own staff as 'unknown . . . no satisfactory explanation . . . no conclusion is possible'.

One of these was a clear visual sighting by a Capitol Airlines crew and that of a Northeast Airline DC-6 co-ordinated with ground radar. Others involve the 753rd Radar Squadron, a Western Airlines pilot with GCA confirmation, plus a Braniff and Continental combined sighting with ground radar confirmation. Scores more of such exact sightings are in the files of the Air Force, the CIA and several reputable UFO study organizations. The only explanation I could find for these cases being ignored was the desire to look the other way, or simply fear.

But I was still naive about this strange compulsion to avoid any careful exploration of the paranormal. I was puzzled myself about these strange phenomena and more curious than anything else. But the subject seemed more like an exciting challenge than fearful. To me, it wasn't a question of belief or non-belief. It was a question of exploration. I was glad, however, to get back to straight investigative journalism where there were plenty of interesting avenues to explore.

One story took me to a small village in France where a fascinating medical detective story had taken place. Oddly enough, a series of UFO sightings had taken place just before I arrived there that was almost identical to the Exeter story. I had to resist looking into it, and stay on the track of the medical story. But it indicated how widespread and persistent the phenomenon was – and how similar.

Another medical detective story took me to Africa to explore the new deadly disease called Lassa Fever that had stricken virologists at Yale, Columbia and medical missionaries in Nigeria as well as the African villagers. While there, I decided to circle back through Brazil, where I had learned of another strange story that seemed hard to resist. A peasant named Arigo had been reported to have performed successful psychic surgery over a period of more than 20 years. Both Brazilian and American doctors had verified his healings. President Kubitchek, a Sorbonne-trained surgeon and the man who created Brasilia, was one of his greatest supporters. There were more than six hours of 16 mm surgical film in color. Unlike the dubious healers in the Philippines, Arigo welcomed medical scientists and never charged for his services.

It certainly was a strange story. I wrote it cautiously in low key. Since the book was to be condensed in the *Reader's Digest*, the researchers there checked every fact, line by line, word by word, as they always do – probably more than any major magazine in the country. The book was to be published by T. Y. Crowell, a venerable publishing house of high standing. It was at this point that I ran into another expression of the Can't-Happen-Here syndrome.

The president of Crowell was a veteran editor named Lew Gillenson, an energetic and forthright publisher who rarely minced words. Just as the book was being prepared for publication, Gillenson was contacted by another Crowell author named Martin Gardner. Gardner was an erudite gentleman who conducted a column on mathematical games for the *Scientific American*. As a member of the Can't-Happen-Here school of thought, Gardner told Gillenson that if Crowell published my book on Arigo, he would never permit Crowell to publish another one of his books.

Gillenson was shocked. This was a threat of pre-publication censorship and the equivalent of book-burning. He told Gardner exactly that. When my book was published, Gardner countered by writing an emotionally-strung diatribe about it in the *New York Review of Books*. It was so strangely wild and frenzied and unscientific that it couldn't be called a review. Gardner seemed to react as if he had been stabbed by a poltergeist. I demanded equal space, and got it. But what bothered me was that Gardner was an otherwise witty and perceptive writer with a lot to offer. Why should he flare up with the intensity of a solar eruption at a book that explored a fascinating and compelling story that begged for an explanation? He must have known that I was at least a responsible journalist who made sure of the facts. At that time, I had just received an award from the New York Academy of Sciences for the book on the Lassa virus, and had received similar awards for other work. There was so much in the world that remained unexplained and needed to be rationally explored with a genuine sense of wonder. All through history, science had periodically tried to put a lid on itself. Every time it did, it blocked its own progress.

* * *

All these thoughts came to the surface in looking over the extensive file George Meek had compiled in line with his Spiricom project. Especially since Meek was intent on pulling science and the paranormal together. I was inclined to agree with him on this. But, equally, I despaired of ever seeing it accomplished, with the emphasis on *a priori* debunking on the part of so many, though by no means all, of the scientific establishment. The debunking group appeared to have lost sight of the basic nature of science. They seemed to have forgotten that the work of science is never complete, that good scientists are always open to fresh theories and contradictory evidence. Yet because science is a human enterprise, smugness was often easy to come by, as it is with any of us. Galileo's critics were certain they were right that the earth was the center of everything. The critics were certainly wrong. But strangely enough, Galileo had his own hang-ups. Speculating about the then-mysterious rise and fall of the tides, Galileo said: 'Everything that has been said before and imagined by other people is in my opinion completely invalid . . . The one who surprised me most is Kepler. He later became interested in the action of the moon on the water, and in other occult phenomena, and similar childishness.'

The important question is *why* many scientists react violently to any challenge to their current view of the universe. Fear apparently heads the list of those exaggerated reactions, creating scientific vigilantes instead of investigators. There seems to be a desperate insecurity reflected, a frantic reaching for a black and white explanation for everything. Not finding this, the debunkers have a tendency to proclaim a new religion of their own. John Wheeler, the Princeton physicist, tried to drive the Parapsychological Association out of the American Association for the Advancement of Science with the livid frenzy of a medieval pope. His actions were hardly a credit to his high academic and research credentials.

Rosalind Heywood, of the British Society for Psychical Research (which debunks as much as it investigates) answers the possible motivations with questions: 'Why are so few of us even interested that many people have experiences which current psychology cannot explain? And why are those people often too shy to mention them? Is it that the ordinary contemporary man has been brain-washed by yesterday's materialism to assume that here there *can* be no fire behind so much smoke?'

I had found that there was smoke and there was fire. The problem was to clear away the smoke. There was plenty of it. But most of the more intense critics brush the fire-hardened evidence aside, or come up with glib sophistry for answers. In doing so, the debunkers' activity can actually inhibit exploration, the function that brought science to where it is today.

There is no question that it is right to challenge paranormal phenomena, and to put any event involving it to a severe test. But since the subject is so fragile, the examination should be conducted with intensive care. There is no question that something is going on in the world that is not understood. It involves the mind, which is even less understood by science than the brain. The electronic equipment of our brain circuits is a marvel of design – but it is still finite and limited. We peek at the universe through a tiny slot between infrared and ultraviolet. The spectrum proceeds to infinity on each side of these wavelength gateposts. The problem is how to make intelligent observations on the part of either scientist or layman from such a limited and inadequate platform. For us to try to understand the full meaning of the infinite universe by science alone is futile. It's like trying to tune into a television broadcast with an AM radio. We have to reach out into the paranormal to probe, to get beyond the limited physical barriers.

George Meek's pilgrimage seemed to crystallize all this. It brought together in single focus the thoughts I had been struggling with over a long period of time. There was no question that he would be facing the same roadblocks I had faced. I admired his courage in being willing to meet the press head-on in the conference he was planning in the following April of 1982, barely five months away. It was a scene I couldn't quite picture, and I wasn't sure I wanted to.

* * *

In a way, I almost resented Meek's provocative challenge to me to get involved with his project. It would require digging back into my former frustrating explorations that often led to blind alleys. Yet in the several stories I had researched on the subject, I had found that I couldn't help becoming more open-minded. Reviewing my own reflections over the next few weeks after his visit, I found Meek's approach a bit methodical and ponderous, perhaps the result of his engineering background.

I had found that by looking at the subject of death squarely in the face, it didn't seem to be quite as big an ogre as I used to think, especially in the light of some of the interesting developments in psychology, medicine, parapsychology, theology – and even physics.

One problem has been terminology. There are certain words and phrases that are not inviting to the modern mind. They spring from the time when people wore togas instead of jeans. They have a tendency to turn off a mind that is saturated with moon shots, space shuttles, DNA, computers and Concorde jets.

*Spirit* sounds spooky, and some think that *consciousness* is more appealing. *Soul* sounds ominous; *extended self-awareness* could convey a more modern meaning. *Heaven* sounds so exalted and unapproachable that it seems out of reach; *extra-physical existence* would throw up less of a roadblock to the modern mind. Whether these are exact synonyms or not, they have a tendency to tame down that nasty fear that pops up whenever the idea of death comes up.

I'm convinced that the problem lies with both religion and science. Science has brought in a whole new vocabulary. It has tended to replace religious concepts rather than supplement them. At the same time, religion has clung to medieval words and images that simply don't communicate the way they used to.

The Age of Science came in on a tidal wave that by-passed many islands. Things that couldn't be conveniently measured were left to dry in the sun. There are signs now, however, that a few members of the scientific community are looking back over the islands to see what they have missed – including the distinct possibility of life after death. There are also signs that theology is not altogether averse to a rational exploration of the evidence of life after death. The two opposing camps might even find a few points of agreement. But in between the two camps is the perplexed individual who really doesn't know what to believe. Science has put a heavy dent in his faith, and he's still staggering under the impact.

The modern individual is pounded by both science and journalism. If there is a rational concept of life after death, he wants to know why, what, when, where and how. With his faith shaken, rational evidence – such as the possibility Meek's project suggested – might just be a way of getting back on the track.

I went back over my own probings into the subject. The first question that came up was this: how could we *possibly* exist after death? When we die, the brain, through which we seem to get all our impressions, emotions, thoughts, touch, sounds and feelings, is gone. No question about it. Physiologists have told us that when the brain is dead, there's nothing left for us to perceive with. This dictum has been the iron-bound shibboleth of science. And if this is true, the search for rational evidence of life after death is exterminated before it's even started.

But wait. Now science is coming along with some radically new concepts. They are almost literally mind-boggling. Recent neurophysiological studies of the brain by Wilder Penfield and Nobel Prize winner Sir John Eccles have revealed some startling probabilities: the mind is *separate* from the brain. This is not hazy thinking. Both Penfield and Eccles used the most sophisticated laboratory instruments over many years to reach this conclusion.

'If you can't follow me, believe me,' Eccles told a distinguished scientific audience at the University of Utrecht. 'The brain is only a useful instrument to serve the mind. This doesn't mean to underestimate the brain. The computer is a child's toy in comparison. The point is that the mind is superior to and entirely independent of the brain. This is essential to know for the understanding of life. The recognition of this creates the greatest frontier that science faces. This is a new outlook – the mind wandering over the brain to give it cognitive caresses. What happens at death is the ultimate question.'

I was interested to discover that Oxford's Sir Alister Hardy backs the theory up. 'Can we really believe that consciousness is but a by-product of an entirely physio-chemical brain?' he asks. 'In the field of consciousness lie all our feelings of purpose, love, joy, sorrow, *indeed all the things that really matter in life*. Why until recently has it been almost taboo in scientific circles to talk of extra-sensory perception, telepathy and the like?'

Still the nagging question that bothered me was: how can life be continuous if 'all this too, too solid flesh would melt'? Even if the mind was separate from and independent of the brain, what could hold the mind together if there were no brain or body hanging around?

But it is no secret to physicists that matter is mostly empty space. The nearest electrons spinning around the atom's nucleus are relatively as far away from it as the earth is from the sun. If you enlarged the nucleus to the size of a golf ball, the nearest electron would be over two miles away.

With the human body consisting mainly of empty space, it's a lot easier to picture the possibility of a mind continuing beyond its own physical limitations. What's more, there is a lot of serious scientific contention that the 'real' world simply doesn't exist without an observer around to look it over. As the Buddhists put it, the mind and the object of the search are one. If you look at a tree, you're only looking *through* and *at* a cluster of sub-atomic particles buzzing around like a cloud of gnats – again almost empty space. Perhaps totally empty space, because Einstein figured that energy and matter are the same thing, and concluded that the atom is only a concentrated energy field.

The sum of all this is that we are actually a *part* of what we observe, and inseparable from it. Since science has clearly pointed this out to us, the old limerick quoted by Alan Watts takes on a new meaning in this light:

On campus, a student said, 'God –
I find it exceedingly odd
   That a tree, as a tree,
   Simply ceases to be
When there's no one around in the quad.'

The answer the student received brought him out of his quandary:

'Young man, your astonishment's odd.
I'm *always* around in the quad.
So a tree, as a tree,
Continues to be
When observed by, Yours Cordially, God.'

The concept that matter, including people-matter, is a lot less mechanical than once thought was noted by Sir James Jeans, the Oxford-Cambridge-Princeton physicist, who wrote: 'The motions of electrons and atoms do not resemble those of the parts of a locomotive so much as those of dancers in a cotillion.' He observed that the universe appeared to be more a great thought than a great machine. Add to this recent advances in nuclear physics. They show that such sub-atomic particles as quarks and mesons and even electrons are as ephemeral and elusive as light itself. All these particles are only creating the *impression* of a mass. It seems that the material world is almost getting downright old-fashioned. Further, an instrument studying a sub-atomic particle can literally destroy the particle itself. With matter as flimsy as it is proving to be, there seems to be a new ball game in judging whether the mind or individual consciousness could exist apart from the brain.

But again, a big question came up that disturbed me greatly. The inquiring mind can ask: 'Great. Fine. But can anyone explain to me any possible way that I, as an individual, can actually exist in such a thin, formless and vague state? How can I *personally* be aware of myself in a pea-soup fog without form and substance?'

A professor of logic from Oxford, H. H. Price, has presented an interesting outlook on this. He felt it was useless to speculate on life after death unless you could *visualize* a clear picture of what it possibly could be like. You certainly needed memories, or you wouldn't be yourself. You certainly needed some form of a body, but the picture of floating on pink clouds with a harp would be murderously boring and unreal. You couldn't leave your own personality behind, or you'd be an anonymous blob. You also needed some kind of geography or real estate around you, or you might just as well sleep. But could any of this be possible after death, from a rational point of view?

Speculating on this, Professor Price came up with an interesting theory. There *was* a viable analogy to a place like this, where the mind and individual awareness could continue on without any physical baggage to hinder it. That analogy was our *dreams*. There is limitless real estate and geography there, without crowding. There is form, color, other people, buildings, landscapes, shops, clothes, automobiles and any other accoutrements of living you may or may *not* want around. There is even communication with others, and a vivid sense of self-awareness. You are 'dead to the world', as they say, but alive to your dreams. When you're dreaming, the dream is as real as real life. But it doesn't take up any physical space. Further, we can sometimes recall vivid dreams more clearly than many past real events of our lives. Professor Price looks at his dream theory this way: 'It might indeed *seem* to be physical for those who experience it. The image-objects might appear very much like physical objects; so much so that we might find it difficult at first to realize we are dead.'

This seemed very cogent to me. And then I discovered that the late William Ernest Hocking, once Alford Professor of Philosophy at Harvard, backs Price up. He reasoned we're all rather provincial in thinking there's only one kind of space. 'The dream world,' he says, 'is not somewhere in the waking world. The passage between them is as swift as the change in the direction of thought.' The imagery in this strange new world is very real, according to Hocking, but it only touches us at a tangent, and there's no way of measuring the distance between the two. For instance, if you dream you're in a canoe heading for a waterfall, you can't wake up and measure the distance from your canoe to the bed post.

In going over the theories of Price and Hocking, I reminded myself that the images of dreams are often as hard as concrete. I found a sample taken at random from the case-book of Wilhem Stekel, one of Freud's colleagues: 'I have passed the *examination* for a *driving license* . . . I stand in front of the *Opera House*. The *doctor* and my *brother* drive up in an *auto*. I get in and begin to *drive*. I cross the *street* just in front of another *car*. The *doctor's wife* shouts a warning . . .' (The italics are added.) In a matter of micro-seconds, the dreamer has created an examination form, a license, two autos, a street and an Opera House. He has also summoned three friends and communicated with them. On top of this, the dreamer has been 'seeing' all this *without using his retina*, and 'hearing' the warning *without using his ears*.

Forget about any Freudian symbolism here. Notice the clear, vivid physical places involving people, places, actions and things. The mind of the dreamer has built his own scenery, entirely absent from his body. We all do the same thing constantly, in far more detail than in this sketchy dream.

If the cool logic of Price and Hocking can be accepted, some basic questions about the nature of life after death can be answered. But not all. When I ran across Dr Raymond Moody and his million-plus selling book *Life After Life*, I found it highly persuasive. It brought serious medical attention toward that moment when a transition is made, as we go through that door that might well lead to continuous living.

There was a lot about Meek that reminded me of Moody. Both were approaching the subject from a clinical and objective point of view. Both were cautious and persuasive. Moody confined himself to the study of those whose vital life signals had stopped, yet had recovered to tell their experiences across the threshold in a different life. Meek was concentrating on the descriptions received from mediums about the nature of the afterlife. Yet they both coincided to present the same sort of information.

Moody's study of 150 near-death cases is drawn from a clinical medicine and human psychology point of view. The reports of those whose life signals had stopped, but were resuscitated from clinical death, showed striking similarities. According to Moody's compilation, the near-death experience nearly always involved a feeling of floating out of the body. There was most often a great sense of peace and wholeness. Frequently, there was an encounter with deceased loved ones, who appeared to help the patient make the transition to a new existence. Common also was the feeling of movement through a long, dark tunnel to a brilliant, comforting, joyful light. Consistently, there was a report of an instant replay of the whole life, as if the events were projected on color slides or film. In addition, there was reported the awareness of being in a body, but a different one from the physical.

One patient in Moody's book was typical: 'A brilliant white light appeared to me. The light was so bright that I could not see through it. But going into its presence was so calming and beautiful.' Many of Moody's respondents indicated that death no longer frightened them.

Moody was more than pleased when he discovered that the noted psychiatrist Dr Elisabeth Kübler-Ross was simultaneously conducting the same kind of research, and obtaining identical results. Neither knew of the other's work at that time. Meek, who was getting the same sort of result through mediums, was delighted that his results matched both those of Dr Moody and Dr Kübler-Ross. It clearly suggested that this similarity could not be brought about by coincidence.

In the wake of Moody's book, I came across several more medical and psychological studies and reports, nearly all of them clinically confirming Moody's findings. Dr R. L. Macmillan, of the Toronto General Hospital, reported on a patient who had been clinically dead: 'It is unusual for patients to remember the events following a cardiac arrest . . . This description is extremely interesting. The patient saw himself leaving his body and was able to observe it face to face. This could be the concept of the soul leaving the body which is found in many religions.'

Two major studies by Karlis Osis, the psychologist heading the American Society of Physical Research, have covered a span of 20 years. When one of several Gallup Polls showed that 73 per cent of Americans accepted the concept of life after death as a reality, Osis set out in the 1960s to explore the question on a large scale.

He questioned a total of 1,700 physicians and nurses in the US and India about their death-bed observations. 'My personal impression,' Dr Osis says, 'gained from wading through literally thousands of computer print-out pages, is that we have been seeing the real mountain, and not a Disneyland sort. There is little question that the data give support to the hypothesis of survival after death.'

But the impressive studies of near-death experiences still failed to bring full evidence that life is continuous. Nor do they examine the question of whether or not we can really *communicate* with those who have opened the door and shut it after them.

This, to me, was the critical stage. But it isn't actually much more esoteric than the quantum theory, where physicists are faced with paradox and the assumptions of probability instead of certainty. What's more, for those who feel that rational exploration here is treading on the toes of theology, a critically important event took place in March of 1979. It should have shaken the world a lot more than it did.

The six-column headline in the respectable British newspaper *The Guardian* did point up a certain importance to the story:

SECRET CHURCH REPORT OUT AFTER 40 YEARS
A Church of England Inquiry into Spiritualism Gives Guarded Support to Paranormal Phenomena.

Guarded support or not, the results created a time bomb. The report had been commissioned by the highest of the hierarchy, Archbishop of Canterbury Lang, back in 1937. The study had taken two years to complete. The panel of eleven was impeccable. It included everyone from the Bishop of Bath and Wells to the Dean of St Paul's. It was widely thought that the report of such distinguished theologians would put an end to the supposed threat to the Church by mediums, spiritualists, and those who believed it was possible to communicate with the dead.

Instead, the majority report from the seven most influential members of the panel was a shocker. It noted that 'Certain experiences with mediums make a strong *prima facie* case for survival, and *for the possibility of spirit-communications.*' (Italics added.) It noted that 'We think that it is probable that the hypothesis that they (the spirit-communications) proceed in some cases from discarnate spirits is the true one.' It noted that 'It is necessary to keep clearly in mind that none of the fundamental Christian obligations or values is in any way changed by our acceptance of the possibility of communication with discarnate spirits.' And it concluded: 'It is our opinion that representatives of the Church should keep in touch with groups of intelligent persons who believe in spiritualism.'

The report was stamped 'Private and Confidential' and put under lock and key in the confines of Lambeth Palace. It stayed there until the Church's 40-year embargo expired in 1979. When released, the document opened up the minds of many Church members who tended to avoid paranormal research because they felt it conflicted with Christianity. But there was reassurance for them in another statement by the majority panel: 'It is strongly urged that if we do not accept the evidence for modern psychic happenings, we should not, apart from long tradition, accept the Gospel records either.'

In spite of resistance from both theologians and scientists, the evidence from 'modern psychic happenings' has been growing. It provides the most palpable evidence yet of what life after death *might* consist of. Yet it is hindered by the high static noise level from the spook-and-kook elements. Scraping this roadblock away, and concentrating on responsible mediums, the only available detailed picture of an after-life emerges, aside from the medical studies of Moody and others.

Meek's studies of carefully-screened mediums and their parallel observations to those of Moody and Kübler-Ross went a step beyond the near-death experiences. Meek was digging into the *kind* of life that might be expected. The problem for me was that the results were hard to believe without studying the massive modern evidence that has been accumulating over the past ten decades, since serious psychic research began. It had taken the Archbishop of Canterbury's panel two years to make an assessment that radically changed its outlook. It would take at least that long for a serious student to grasp the significance of the work done by outstanding thinkers of both the British and American Societies for Psychical Research, who have spent as much time exposing frauds as they have verifying legitimate mediums.

There is a theory that everyone is psychic, and therefore we all have a touch of the medium in us in the form of hunches, foreshadowings, predictive dreams, and startling coincidences. Full mediumship appears to be a special talent that is developed just like the talent of an artist or musician. Some are better than others. The true medium seems to have the capacity to go beyond the five senses. Naturalist Stuart Edward White, whose wife was a remarkable medium, claims that a better word for a medium would be 'receiving station'. Whatever the name, there is massive independently-accumulated evidence that they have communicated with those who have died, as the Church of England panel almost reluctantly concedes.

This evidence consists of names, dates, places, relationships, and information that *en masse* could not be known other than through sources who are no longer living. On examination, it is so persuasive that it points to a rational conclusion that individual life is continuous, and that articulate communication is possible. One problem is that the evidence is piled so high that it is boring and tedious to go through it. Like the study of maths or chemistry, it requires painstaking labor to assess it. But without that labor, a natural tendency is to remain skeptical.

As Lawrence LeShan puts it in his book *The Medium, the Mystic, and the Physicist*: 'In the world as we commonly know it, it is certainly clear that clairvoyance and precognition are impossible. They surely cannot occur. The only problem is that they *do* occur.'

One of the mediums studied by LeShan was Eileen Garrett. She was so puzzled by her own abilities that she submitted herself to experimental testing at Duke, Columbia, Johns Hopkins, Oxford and Cambridge universities. But up until the time she died in 1970, she brought through a flood of directly verifiable information that convinced many leading minds in both Britain and the United States as to its validity.

One of the more interesting factors of the material Eileen Garrett 'brought through' was the description of the after-life purportedly described by the deceased Captain Raymond Hinchliffe, who disappeared in attempting an early transatlantic flight in 1928:

> What I want to tell you is what very few people understand: how it feels to go out of the body; what I personally have been doing ever since the realization of the fact came to me; and finally to acquaint you with the impressions I have gained in the new life here since.
>
> Transition from the physical body to the ethereal body occupies only a matter of moments. There is no pain in the severance of the two, and so alike are they that it is some days before the transition from one state to another is noticed . . .
>
> Actually, I feel no different. Nothing angelic. Nothing one would think of being connected with heaven or the hereafter . . .
>
> What do we do? We do everything for which we are fitted. There are huge systems of education, huge laboratories and institutions that deal with all the conditions for which man has fitted himself while on earth. Here our necessities are met by mental thought, and are organized and focused. Instead of taking anything away from the beauty of the picture, does it not add to it that your day of usefulness is only dawning when you come over here?
>
> What do we work at? We work mentally, and rejoice in so doing. Only now one desires to possess the gifts for the soul, and the gift of knowledge, and the gift to enable one to see more clearly, to understand and to realize the greatness of the universe.
>
> Do we eat and drink? That's another question people often ask. Certainly not in the way you sit down in your lavish restaurants. Such a pity, because I liked doing it. This ethereal body, so like our earthly body, has still some physical structure about it, and is therefore not perfected yet. It must retain something that is very akin to the physical state.

The information that came through Eileen Garrett included much more. The messages from Hinchliffe revealed that there were the malicious, the emotionally blind, the ignorant who were struggling for their own spiritual development and evolution, and who joined in the search for this objective. Apparently, this new stage of after-life was a refining process, with some mental, but no physical suffering.

I found it extremely interesting that Hinchliffe's description fits a universal pattern revealed in literally hundreds of similar case histories recorded by these 'receiving stations' called mediums. They are laboriously documented in similar detail. The consensus about this extra-physical world in which the individual personality continues on, is that there is no radical change except that the body shifts to a non-physical one, without the burdens of the flesh. The growth process is apparently just beginning; the world is left behind as a dream. Thoughts and aspirations are the things that become reality.

Over 50 years after Eileen Garrett's message from Captain Hinchliffe, one of Dr Moody's near-death patients reported, after he was brought back, an amazingly similar experience:

> Now I was in a school . . . and it was real. It was not imaginary. If I were not absolutely sure, I would say, 'Well, there's a possibility that I was in this place.' But it *was* real. It was like a school here . . . if you paid attention you would feel, sense, the presence of other beings around. I cannot describe it. You cannot compare it to anything here . . . Because this is a place where the *place* is knowledge. You all of a sudden know the answers. It's like you focus mentally on one place in the school and – zoom – knowledge flows by you from that place, automatically.

From 30 years of studying mediums on this line, Maurice Barbanell reveals in his book *This Is Spiritualism* that the overwhelming majority of mankind has nothing to fear from death. It's an awakening in which the newcomer is greeted by loved ones who have preceded him and help in the adjustment. There are houses, clothing and communication, but they are constructed of thought. There are no poor or rich, except poverty and richness of spirit. The geography and real estate is boundless because it, too, is created by thought.

The picture, if Barbanell's long research into the subject can be believed, is very much like that of the combined research of H. H. Price, Eileen Garrett, Dr Kübler-Ross, and Dr Moody. There is no Great Judge on a throne, but there is the indication that each of us has to review that instant replay of our lives. This could be a little rough, because self-judgment can often be harsh. But there is that full opportunity to develop. Murderers and suicides apparently have the longest way to go.

Swedenborg, the great Swedish mystic and scientist, echoed these conclusions back in the eighteenth century: 'The spiritual world,' he wrote, 'in external appearance is altogether similar to the natural world. Man, when he is loosed from the body, appears as a man in the world. He has senses, touch, smell, hearing, sight, far more exquisite than in the world . . . for life after death is a continuation of life in the world.' Swedenborg, incidentally, was most concerned with harmonizing his scientific brilliance with his religious yearning – which was quite similar to what George Meek was attempting to do.

Psychiatrists have found that one of the main causes of the dread of death is the 'dread of nothingness'. Man, it seems, can put up with almost anything except the thought of his own annihilation. The new ideas springing up about death in everything from physics to theology at least tend to neutralize this syndrome. They don't promise a rose garden, either. They suggest that there's a lot of work to be done. But this isn't such a bad idea. The worst part of the old flowery concept of heaven would be sheer boredom. There could be no concept worse than being bored to death.

In spite of the natural fear of death, many have found that this fear can be measurably reduced by probing deeply into these new ideas in the mood of adventure and exploration. Nearly all who have looked at the subject this way seem to agree with Carl Sandburg, who said: 'Death is merely part of life.' Or Teilhard de Chardin, who put it this way: 'Why should I be afraid of death, since it is only a mutation, a change in state?'

Of course the information about what kind of world we might move into after death is not final or complete. Nearly every study of available material suggests and clearly indicates that work is cut out for us to move on towards a higher plane of development. In confining the focus here, the complex idea of reincarnation is by-passed, and becomes a whole other story. Beyond the rational search inevitably lies the need for a quantum jump into faith – but the evidence that is showing up should supplement conventional religion rather than conflict with it. It might, in fact, send us scurrying back to learn more about what the ancients have been telling us all along.

As NASA's Robert Jastrow tells us at the end of his book *God and the Astronomers*: 'For the scientist who has lived by his faith in the power of reason, the story ends like a bad dream. He has scaled the mountains of ignorance; he is about to conquer the highest peak; as he pulls himself over the final rock, he is greeted by a band of theologians who have been sitting there for centuries.'

This of course was what Meek was gunning for, based on hard evidence, confirmed by electronics, and available for everyone to hear, a fusion of religion and science that would erase the barriers between the two. Although his tools were mechanical, his search seemed to be propelled by a passionate desire to bring what he was learning to the world. For me, what started to be a cursory review of his thoughts and his project turned into a much more extended search than I had planned. A month after his visit in the fall of 1981, I was continuing deep background research in wide peripheral areas that formed a link to the question of life beyond death.

In spite of all my research, however, I still envied Meek's confidence expressed in the books and papers he had left with me. The sum total of his opinion was simply that you cannot die. My feeling was that there was strong evidence that life continued, but I lacked that final conviction. One thing that my encounter with Meek did accomplish was to push me on to look for and review other sources of confirmation that I could understand and respect.

# CHAPTER 3

## *Behind the Man Named Meek*

George Meek's visit prompted me not only to reassess all my previous thoughts on the subject, but to examine certain points in greater depth than I had before. One problem in exploring such an elusive area is that your mind is likely to fluctuate constantly between belief and disbelief. At times, this can lead practically to an identity crisis. The story of Meek, O'Neil and Mueller would bring many facets of the paranormal into play, some of them painfully exotic. With his stubborn and determined mind, Meek had delved into psychic healing, the mysterious Electronic Voice Phenomenon known as EVP, materialization, including the baffling aspect of ectoplasm, and apparitions. I needed to examine each of these points if I were to make any kind of intelligent appraisal. The only one I knew anything about was the subject of apparitions.

The research that Elizabeth and I had done on the strange story of the ghost of Flight 401 had had a profound effect on us. In the process we had discovered that three veteran Eastern Airlines pilots and a Federal Aviation Agency technical officer were all serious psychic mediums. They had actively sought to help the reported apparition of their fellow airman who had been killed in the L-1011 Everglades crash of Flight 401, in what psychic researchers called a 'soul rescue'. This is considered to be accomplished by a seance that is purported to help an earth-bound spirit to move on to spiritual development. What intrigued me most was that these men were sane, competent and technically oriented. Yet they were absorbed in the elusive and ephemeral field of psychic research, and damned serious about it. They had no trouble in dealing with the concept of an apparition. I would have to delve into the subject again in considering the George Meek story.

One of the most difficult problems I had was trying to conceive how an apparition could possibly exist, especially one reported to be solid and clearly observable – and in this case, even speaking. I still clung to the concept that *if* there were such a thing as a ghost, it would certainly be something vague and misty, and on the stairs in a Victorian hallway. I couldn't picture an L-1011 flight deck with a solid form sitting in the cockpit jump seat, as the reports indicated. I had no idea whether apparitions had been studied seriously by responsible researchers, and if so, what the results were. I began to look for the most reliable scientific and credible sources I could find.

I was surprised at what I discovered. A leading British physicist and mathematician, G. N. M. Tyrrell, scolded science for dismissing apparitions as distortion of sense perceptions. He wrote that science itself depends on sense perception, and that his studies of apparitions showed that all sense-data of normal perception were present, except that there was no physically occupied region. There was, however, visual, auditory, and even tactile perception in many cases where apparitions or ghosts had been reported. He also pointed out that many cases were observed by more than one person, eliminating the possibility of subjective hallucination.

Back in the early 1900s, Professor James H. Hyslop, then a professor of logic at Columbia University, lamented the fact that millions were being spent to explore the North Pole and the stars, for deep sea dredging, and for studies of protoplasm, all of which searched for the origin of man. However, none was being spent to explore man's ultimate destiny. Yet wasn't this the question that really counted?

As a forerunner of George Meek and his theories, Hyslop felt that the psychic field could serve as a bridge between religion and science. He was convinced that the contempt of the skeptics for studying apparitions, for instance, was the result of the critics' failing to examine the evidence. At the same time, he acknowledged the reasons for their contempt. Some apparitions *were* the result of hallucinations. Some could start an irrational craze for the subject. Caution was important, but should not serve as an excuse for not investigating serious reports. Apparitions were noteworthy because, if true, they involved three very important conditions. (1) They provided evidence of the continuity of life after death; (2) They showed evidence of possible communication with the deceased; (3) They provided evidence that an articulate and even audible form could exist that did not involve 'matter' as we know it.

I was still trying to convince myself that Meek's idea of electronic communication with the dead could at least be theoretically possible. His story involved visual and vocal apparitions. I couldn't help feeling that this possibility was more a matter of modern physics than it was of parapsychology. If matter could be postulated as non-existent material, it seemed possible that many obstacles could be cleared.

The problem with modern physics is that it is having an identity crisis of its own. There is little question that it has replaced religion in the minds of a large segment of the population. But there is also little question that it has failed to supply the faith and comfort that is supposed to accompany a religion. Physical measurements and chemical laws are hardly able to compete with a baby's smile, a fugue by Bach, a Shakespeare sonnet or even a boring sermon that might have a few kernels of insight hidden in it.

I was surprised at how many scientific realists and tough thinkers suggested directly or indirectly that consciousness, awareness, memory and personality could theoretically be preserved after the death of the human body – and possibly communicate through some yet-to-be-discovered energy channels such as those postulated by George Meek.

Werner Heisenberg stated that atoms were not things; no distinction between matter and force could clearly be made. Max Planck felt compelled to assume the existence of another world of reality beyond the world of the senses. Alfred North Whitehead wrote that science was blind, that it dealt with only half the evidence provided by human experience. Einstein commented that the most beautiful and profound emotion we could experience is the sensation of the mystical. Thoughts like these again suggested that Meek was in good company.

* * *

Meek had found the views of Arthur Young both profound and provocative. Young is the inventor of the Bell helicopter, one of which has just been installed in the New Design Gallery of the Museum of Modern Art. He is a pragmatic realist who turned his entire attention to the study of the paranormal after decades of brilliant engineering success. His focus centered on blending quantum physics with modern mysticism, especially the mysteries of consciousness. In contrast to the cognitive scientists, Young believes that man can never be understood by examining the physical hardware that makes up a human being.

Young was intrigued with light. It is without mass, yet it can create protons and electrons that *do* have mass. Light has no charge, yet it can create particles that *do* have charge. For a photon, which is a pulse of light, time does not exist because Einstein has shown that clocks stop at the speed of light. Here we come to the concept that zero mass is equal to everything; that consciousness can exist without the mechanical brain. If so, self-awareness *could* continue after physical death, and it could be rationally conceivable that light in the form of radio waves could theoretically form a channel of communication between the two different worlds, a key to Meek's theory.

Without getting into the complexities of the Copenhagen school of quantum mechanics, Meek's viewpoint was that these flimsy and ghost-like elementary particles appear more like the fabric of dreams than substance. Since the elusive photon has zero mass, no electric charge, and an infinitely long lifetime, it has been called an amphibian between Being and Non-Being. It represents the threshold where everything can be compacted into an infinitely small mass, and in that way every particle in the universe could contain the seeds of everything else in it – including human consciousness: the way every particle of DNA contains the whole program for a human being, the way every part of a hologram contains the whole picture.

* * *

Trying to match up the paranormal with physics was frustrating, and Liz noticed my mood.

'Maybe you're trying to do the impossible,' she said.

'What I can't understand,' I said, 'is that if matter and energy are the same thing, why does science balk at the idea of looking into the possibility of life after death?'

'They're interested in mechanics. You're interested in trying to find out what goes on in the spiritual.'

'I don't like that terminology,' I said.

'All right,' Liz said. 'Call it consciousness.'

'My problem is that I'm still trying to convince myself that Meek's idea of electronic communication with the dead is at least possible. Theoretically, anyway.'

'Maybe you should just accept the possibility on faith.'

'That comes later. I want to get the logic first. The way I figure it, physics is now facing just as many paradoxes and contradictions as the psychic world.'

'How do you mean?' Liz asked.

I tried to review my jumbled thoughts on the matter, especially from Arthur Young's point of view about the photon. 'When you get right down to the one basic particle that everything is built on, it's the photon, right?'

'I'll have to take your word for it,' Liz said.

'Basically, Arthur Young is right,' I said. 'A photon has no mass, it's just light. So theoretically, anything could happen. Our physical bodies are simply forms of light, a whole mess of photons. And photons can take any form they want. Even non-solid matter.'

'I think you're losing me,' Liz said.

'I'm probably losing myself,' I said. 'What I'm trying to get at is that an apparition or one of Meek's radio communications might not be as wacky as it appears to be, as long as matter really amounts only to different forms of light.'

I seemed to be bearing a grudge against physics, but actually I respected it. What I didn't like was that it was failing to go beyond itself to embrace what really counted.

* * *

Being persuaded of the *possibility* of the continuance of the mind, memory banks and personality after death was one thing. Attempting to verify the claims of George Meek and his Spiricom project was another. Here was purportedly palpable evidence of articulate communication with someone who had died. Here was purportedly an audible voice, exchanging ideas and reporting facts about his life that could apparently be tracked down and confirmed.

There was little question that Meek was intent on having a book published that would get across the importance of the Spiricom project to the rest of the world. Not long after his 1981 visit, he sent me a summary of what he felt the long term benefits would be. He had obviously thought the whole thing through with his engineer's mind, and his communication reflected it:

I AT THE LEVEL OF INDIVIDUAL MAN

1 *Establishing knowledge of survival*

For the first time in the history of mankind we have scientific proof that man's *mind, memory banks, personality* and soul survive death of the physical body.

This at last permits the individual man to move beyond the two levels provided by his religions – faith and believing – and to ascend to the level of knowing that he as an individual will continue to live after so-called death.

2 *A reduction of sadness and personal anguish upon the demise of loved ones*

(There are many ramifications of this topic.)

3 *Improvement of personal conduct*

Provide insights and understanding which will vastly improve the quality of daily life here – and hereafter (creativity, joy, love, compassion, forbearance, freedom from many types of fear, etc.).

II AT THE LEVEL OF MANKIND AS A WHOLE

1 *Improved education*

When daily contact with clear, static-free two-way communication is ultimately established a few decades hence at the mental and causal levels, man will have access to the accumulated wisdom of the ages in all fields of knowledge. This will completely revolutionize and vastly improve all systems of education.

2 *Revisions in man's religions*

Nearly all of the creeds and much of the dogma which has accumulated around all of man's religions with the passing centuries will be outmoded. The central core of the great religious beliefs will be found to be scientifically justified and fully compatible with this greatly expanded comprehension of the Cosmos. Hence, in the centuries ahead, something of a marriage between man's religions and his science will take place.

Meek's deductions were probably correct *if* his assumption was justified that scientific proof of survival had been established. But I continued to feel he was jumping the gun in assuming that these strange communications had actually been proved. At best, it seemed, they were evidence, and the whole question of evidence versus proof came up again. There was one thing certain. His enthusiasm and dedication were boundless. It wasn't until much later that I was able to trace the roots of his commitment. When I did, it slowly became apparent that he had been on a collision course with William J. O'Neil, and the strange encounter that would develop from their meeting.

* * *

Springfield, Ohio, is a medium-sized city in the middle of Ohio that has spawned machine shops, foundries, Wittenberg University, and George Meek. With a passion for making scale models of everything from ocean liners to planes, Meek's scientific bent began early. He preferred this activity to sports, even though his father ran a successful sporting goods store. But he had an intense curiosity about life and the universe that grew alongside his mechanical abilities.

At the age of 11 he had an early brush with the marvels of radio that had a profound effect on the rest of his life. In those days, the crystal set, a fragile contraption, was just having its beginning. It utilized what was called a cat's whisker, a thin wire that tickled the crystal until, by magic, a radio broadcast would come through the earphones.

Meek bought a small Galena crystal and a cat's whisker, wound a coil around a Quaker Oats box and put in a variable resistor. The greatest thrill of his young life was hearing the call letters of station KDKA, 150 miles away in Pittsburgh. Although he turned back to the mechanical rather than to radio, his sense of wonderment increased as he moved into his teens.

What, he wanted to know, was man's relationship to the universe, and what was the purpose behind it all? Even as a youth, he wondered about life after death, and he began an intense extra-curricular study of all the world's great religions. Although he was not particularly theological, he took the Bible's admonition 'to seek, to knock, to ask' very seriously, parallel with his desire to do the same with engineering problems.

He had his mind set on going to MIT, but his father died and the funds simply were not there. It was also the time of the Depression. He took heart, however, when he learned that the president of Goodyear was offering two four-year scholarships to MIT on the basis of the candidates submitting any mechanical ideas they wanted to.

Meek immediately put his hobbies to work. He submitted a series of carefully-constructed scale models in the field of transportation: a large ocean liner, an all-metal tri-motor plane, a replica of the dirigible *Shenandoah*, and others. He was dismayed when he failed to win the scholarship, but consoled by the fact that the Chairman of the Board of Goodyear wrote to say he had come in third, and offering condolences.

Instead, Meek put in a year at Wittenberg, and then transferred to the larger facilities offered at the University of Michigan. He began working his way through with a combination of waiting at tables and driving himself through 12-hour days in the lab for five and a half days a week. It was an arduous program that he wouldn't care to repeat, including consecutive sessions in summer school. But he managed to complete his BS in Engineering in two years, graduating in 1932.

In the process, he encountered an attractive girl at a dance just before summer school was over. She was Jeannette Duncan, also moving swiftly through her undergraduate studies in two compressed years. She was somewhat embarrassed that she was under 21 when she graduated, skillfully avoiding a question by a classmate as to whether she had voted or not.

The love-at-first-sight syndrome went into immediate action. It resulted in their marrying two years later, as Jeannette went on to get her Master's in speech and linguistics, and to teach English and Drama.

But job prospects were not happy for Meek. In the Depression, engineers were a glut on the market. Unemployment was rife. Meek was desperate, but so confident of his abilities that he offered several companies to work one year free of charge.

Fortunately, he didn't have to. In 1933, Servel, Inc., offered him a job as an application engineer, creating designs for working models, and he moved up through the same job for General Refrigeration Corporation. This in turn led him to the job of Assistant Director of Research for the Carrier Corporation. Here his inventive career began to burgeon. His capacities caught the eye of Willis Carrier, Chairman of the Board. He was named engineering assistant, and together they developed the Weathermaster air conditioning system that is installed in skyscrapers all over the world. It was a major advance in the art, and Carrier inscribed a photograph to Meek: 'To George Meek whose perseverence, thoroughness and practical ingenuity made this notable achievement possible.'

Meek's design paid off dramatically when the then-named Statler-Hilton was being built in Washington. With a 120-foot height limit, the hotel was able to gain an extra floor through the space saved by the Carrier system which provided enough extra rooms to pay for the air conditioning installation itself.

When Meek joined the War Production Board in 1942, he again drew the attention of his superiors. One of them wrote an informal citation that read: 'More George Meeks and the war could be over much sooner.' As a further result of his work, he was asked to join the Embassy staff of Ambassador Averell Harriman in London.

After the war it seemed that Meek couldn't miss. Moving through various aspects of product development, patents, basic research, market and management consulting and industrial design, Meek worked with everything from frozen foods to heating systems for pre-fabricated houses in the Arctic. His work took him across the world, including over 40 trips to Europe for a large international and industrial banking conglomerate. For 18 years he supervised the new product development in its Swedish affiliate, the Munters Corporation. It specialized in thermal and air pollution devices. The devices Meek invented for the giant cooling towers of Munters are used to cool hundreds of millions of gallons of water each day across the world.

Meek was a workaholic. All through these times, he was driving himself relentlessly. At the age of 40 he went into a severe depression, and went to a psychiatrist. It wasn't long before he felt that he wasn't getting his money's worth. He found it better to work his own way out on a more spiritual basis – part of it through his studies in parapsychology. In fact, this spurred his intense interest in the field that never left him.

His work brought him into close contact with some of the highest figures in finance and industry. His new insights didn't particularly enchant some of his friends. At an important conference at Lehman Brothers, the prestigious banking firm at One William Street in Manhattan, some of his ideas appeared a little too idealistic for the three industrial leaders there, and Paul Mazur, senior partner of the Lehman firm. Mazur was so distressed that he interrupted the meeting and asked Meek to step out in the hall with him. His face was flushed and his gestures vehement.

'Dammit, George,' he said, 'if there's one thing you've got to learn, it's how to use OPM.'

Meek had never heard of the term. He asked what it was.

'It means one simple thing,' Mazur said. 'You've got to learn to use Other People's Money. You never use any of your own money if you want to get rich. It's the main rule of this business, and you'd better damn well learn it quick.'

Meek admired these men and their accomplishments, and appreciated that they had propelled him well along the way to business success. But he felt that their own lives were somewhat impoverished by their lack of spiritual insights – insights that had pulled him out of his morass.

One book that had a heavy effect on him was called *Breakthrough to Creativity*. It was written by a psychiatrist with high credentials named Shafica Karagulla, and explored the doctor's own efforts in reaching beyond psychiatry into psychic realms. Meek sent copies to his colleagues at the Lehman conference, with mixed results. It fell flat with the commercial giants, but he received grateful letters from their wives saying how much the book meant to them.

In 1965, at the age of 55, he paused and took stock of himself. All three of his sons had successfully completed college. It was at this point that his son George went to work for the Voice of America. Willis took a position with General Foods. James became a doctor, and joined the National Institutes of Health. Meek's long-term dream of turning all his energies to the study of 'the nature of man' was his goal – but he was determined to finance the project himself.

In spite of his business success, he did not have that kind of money. What he had in mind would take hundreds of thousands of dollars. On top of that, he did not want to begin such a project at a later age. His central objective was to create a method where living persons could use electronic instruments to speak directly to those who had gone on to the 'life-after-life'. Not through mediums or automatic writing or oui-ja boards, but electronically. Just as Edison and Marconi had tried – and failed.

This was his immediate magnificent obsession, and he went about it the same way he had conquered the business world. At the age of 55, he figured that it would take five years to accumulate enough funds. He resolved to terminate his professional career at the age of 60. He admitted that it would be called a crazy idea. But his mind was set on it.

It *was* called crazy – by Jeannette and his Swedish clients who were depending on him for the string of successful patents he was providing. When he first discussed it with Jeannette, she thought he had flipped his lid. She told him that his clients would feel the same, and that he would be writing off his entire career. The research involved would be monumental in time, money and travel. Meek was facing what he called a wrenching dilemma. The strain on the Meeks' 30-year long marriage was measurable.

He knew that the most creative years were supposed to dwindle after reaching the age of 35, but he refused to accept that premise. For the next five years, he dug in and created some of the most lucrative patents he had ever developed in the air and thermal pollution fields. It was a rush of inventive creativity he could not explain even to himself. His clients made millions from them, and Meek made enough to provide ample funding for beginning his new career.

His last project to punctuate his departure from the business world was an elegant finale. He had nine weeks left before his termination date in 1970. He quickly designed an invention for a complicated plastics forming system, designed the machine, put it in operation, took 16 mm movies of its performance, and flew 5,000 miles to show the film to his client, who then patented it in 13 countries. He had now successfully cleared the decks and was ready to step out into the mysterious world of the paranormal.

When he finally terminated his relationship with the Munters Corporation at the age of 60, Chairman Carl Munters told him he would regret the decision. Meek was unfazed. The deal with Munters would pay Meek a modest royalty on his series of inventions in the United States, and Munters would have full use of them in other countries. 'This put food on the table for the next 15 years,' Meek says, 'and provided the money for the worldwide travel and study.'

He went on a full-time library and literature research program at the scheduled age of 60. He made contact with several dozen medical doctors, psychiatrists, psychologists and scientists in many disciplines. He organized and led teams of his colleagues to travel to various countries to explore paranormal events in depth, not just the electronic idea, but the broad spectrum. Jeannette, reluctant at first, gradually came around to help full time.

* * *

Meek began his determined quest in 1970. He concentrated first on psychic healing. He co-ordinated the work of 14 prominent researchers. They included prominent professors like Dr William A. Tiller, Chairman of the Department of Materials Science and Engineering at Stanford, Dr Norman Shealy, Associate Clinical Professor at the Universities of Wisconsin and Minnesota, Sir Kelvin Spencer, former Chief Scientist in the then Ministry of Power in Britain, biologist Dr Lyall Watson, and others. With them, Meek scoured the world studying and observing healers, shamans, and spirit doctors from Europe to the USSR to the Philippines. The results were nothing short of astonishing. Something was there, something was going on that went beyond medicine, and could, if properly applied, supplement modern techniques with a powerful ally.

A belief almost universal among the healers was that man had both a physical body and an ethereal body. The latter was what counted most, where either health or illness was generated. The Russians called it the 'bio-plasmic body', avoiding the spiritual implications, but essentially it was the same thing. Another common belief was that the mediumistic healers (and most of them were mediums) felt they were assisted by a discarnate spirit or a band of spirits who infused them with energies or guided their hands in the healing process. Some claimed direct communication with apparitions over an extended period of time, both auditory and visual. Clairaudience and clairvoyance, the phenomena were called.

There were reports of possession, both benign and demonic, the type reflected by such stories as the *Amityville Horror* or *The Exorcist*. The benign were the most common, however. There were reports of the phenomenon described as 'materialization', where ectoplasm is said to form in the presence of certain trance mediums or healers who are reported to be exceptionally sensitive. This was the most difficult concept for me to accept. I had read sober discussions on all of these phenomena, but preferred to let the subject drop as far as I was concerned. There was no way available for me to check firsthand without extensive and time-consuming travel and study, as Meek was now able to do. I neither believed nor disbelieved the evidence. Both of these phenomena would come into play as Meek continued his search.

Meek's trip to Brazil, however, interested me. I have mentioned that I researched a book there on the psychic healer Arigo, known as the 'surgeon of the rusty knife'. There was no question to me that the evidence in that case was strong. A responsible team of American medical doctors and many Brazilian physicians testified to his remarkable powers. In fact, a two-hour interview with ex-President Kubitchek, himself a Sorbonne-trained surgeon, was one of the most impressive interviews I have ever had on the subject. I was surprised to learn from President Kubitchek that entire teams of fully qualified Brazilian physicians held sessions with skilled mediums once a week at the Hospital das Clinicas, the largest hospital in South America, where diagnostic information was elicited and utilized by the doctors. I was also aware of the many pretenders in this field.

One of Meek's discoveries, however, went beyond the phenomenon of psychic healing alone, and into the strange world of materialization. In Brazil, Meek had come across a well-documented case that involved a group of 15 doctors, psychiatrists and other researchers. They carried out a controlled test on a female medium who was reported to be able to produce materializations through ectoplasm produced from her own body. The medium was placed inside a locked cage and strapped to a fixed chair. As shown by a rather startling series of photographs, the standing figure of a nun began to form inside the cage. Gradually, the pictures show the figure forming and moving through the iron bars of the cage as if they were not there. All through the process, the medium remained in the cage. Careful examination of the photographs show the bars partly obscured as the figure passes through to emerge just outside the cage. The full scale figure was clearly recognizable as the sister of the medium, a nun who had died two months before. After a few moments, the figure had dissolved and disappeared.

Meek and the scientists who accompanied him on his trip were impressed by this case because the Brazilian research group was of high caliber and the photographs almost impossible to fake. As an expert photographer himself, Meek had once exposed a fake materialized figure in total darkness through infrared film. Through his own experience, he was convinced that the nun's figure could not have been faked. I examined both sets of photos, Meek's and those of the Brazilian doctors. I was impressed in two ways. First, Meek's exposure of the fake with infrared film demonstrated how easy it was to catch fakery. Second, I knew how difficult it would be to fake the figure of the nun emerging through the bars, with part of the bars obscured and part of them appearing to melt through the figure. I was fully familiar with film opticals and effects when I was producing documentaries for the networks, and felt reasonably convinced of the validity of the photographs.

But the reality of ectoplasm and the capacity to produce all or part of an apparent living form still eluded me. It would become, I was to discover, increasingly important in Meek's project. There is considerable literature on the subject. Wax impressions of fingertips have been reported by researchers in Poland testing a medium named Kluski. The same results were reported with a reputable medium named Margery Crandon in Boston. In France, the highly respected professor of physiology, Dr Charles Richet, had observed ectoplasm streaming from several mediums, and coined the word itself. Baron A. von Schrenck-Notzing, the noted German psychiatrist, conducted many experiments with mediums, and was able to capture enough of the elusive substance before it dissolved to analyze it. Under the microscope, he discovered 'numerous skin discs, numerous granulates of the mucous membrane, numerous minute particles of flesh, traces of potash and cell detritus'. The substance was slightly cloudy, colorless, fluid, with no odor. It left a whitish deposit, and was slightly alkaline.

Arthur Young, the Bell helicopter inventor, with about as practical an inventive mind as possible, looked on ectoplasm and materialization with a guarded view, but was not reluctant to examine the evidence. He points out that physical materialization by mediums has been repeatedly and dramatically confirmed by reputable scientists. In addition to Schrenck-Notzing, he reports that Gustav Geley in 1924 produced casts of ectoplasmic hands clasped in such a way that they could not be duplicated by any known means. Geley did so in the presence of 34 scientists and officials. Young also points out that this evidence is largely ignored, mainly because there is no theory to account for it.

Gustav Geley welcomed his own observations of ectoplasm because it seemed to remove a lot of mystical theories about mediums, and brought the subject to a biological and physical level. 'During a trance,' he wrote, 'a portion of the medium's organism is externalized. This portion is sometimes very small, sometimes very considerable – amounting to half the weight of the body in some of Crawford's experiments. Observation shows this ectoplasm as an amorphous substance which may be either solid or vaporous. Then usually, very soon, the formless substance becomes organic, it condenses and forms appear, which when the process is complete, have all the anatomical and physiological characters of biologic life.'

He goes on to add: 'The objective reality of these forms is proved by photographs, by their imprints on clay, on lamp-black, and on plaster, and finally, in some most notable cases, by complete casts. The phenomenon is the same in all countries, whoever the observer or the medium may be.'

What is said to be stranger yet about ectoplasm is that it is reported to appear in very large and very small forms, including identifiable miniature faces and other portions of a body, always associated with a very rare class of mediums who seem to be able to create the phenomenon. Because it is so rare and not repeatable on command,

I have felt that it is a drawback to the intelligent study of the paranormal, in spite of the scientists who have been involved with the subject. There was so much more evidential material in the mental area that could be assessed both from a scientific and a personal point of view, and without the sensationalism that accompanied the bizarre world of physical evidence. However, as I was soon to find out, I would be forced to come face to face with this sort of phenomenon in the case of Meek's exploration. Perhaps he, like Geley and Arthur Young, felt that it brought the focus down to a biological and physical level and more in line with an engineering approach to the paranormal.

Further, such a palpable physical manifestation of psychic energy might help explain some of the healing process that Meek had encountered in his world-wide investigation of healers, shamans and spirit doctors, many of whose powers have never been adequately explained or effectively discredited. With little or no education, many healers produced documented results with no real medical knowledge. Arigo, for instance, saw as many as 200 patients a day over a period of two decades. As *Time* wrote in October of 1972: 'He treated almost every known ailment, and most of his patients not only survived but actually improved or recovered. A few years ago, reports on the exploits of such miracle workers would have drawn little more than derision from the scientifically trained. Now, however, many medical researchers are showing a new open-mindedness toward so-called psychic healing and other methods not taught in medical schools.'

The most intriguing thing to Meek, in addition to the possibility of some sort of materialized substance acting like ectoplasm to bring about a physical cure, was that Arigo and many other healers he studied shared the common element that they were guided by a deceased personality or personalities who worked through them to bring about a healing. One of Arigo's guides was purported to be a long-deceased physician known as Dr Fritz, who brought immediate diagnosis and provided the actual energy for the treatment – including surgery in Arigo's case.

* * *

Meek was setting up a lot of targets for himself over a wide range of psychic activities. Together, however, they combined to point to his main goal – that two-way contact with the highest possible forms of consciousness by electronic means. Through mediums, he was hoping to reach discarnate scientists and technicians that could provide solid technical information to bridge the gap. The problem was to find a medium who not only was psychically sensitive, but had a technical background to match this rarefied field he was trying to explore.

There was already the Electronic Voice Phenomenon, with EVP researchers in Europe taking the lead to try to improve the quality of the voices mysteriously appearing on tape under certain conditions. Another one of his first probes, after he had pulled down the curtain on his business career, was to go to Europe to confer with the leading researchers involved.

Meek didn't doubt the validity of these apparent electronic voices from the dead. But he felt they were too faint, carried very few words at a time, were spoken too rapidly and were muddied by an enormous amount of background sound. They also did not permit any extended two-way conversation. The voices were heard through the use of a diode to generate the hissing sound called 'white noise'. This, as I explained earlier, was designed to act as a carrier wave for purported discarnate entities to bounce their energies from. An amplifier, microphone and tape recorder formed the basics of the rest of the equipment, although there were many variations used by the experimenters.

Many have accepted the unexplainable voices that have come through on tape as coming from paranormal sources. In fact, Professor Hans Bender, Director of the Institute of Parapsychology at the University of Freiburg in Germany, stated in 1968 that the discovery of EVP was probably as important, if not more so, than the discovery of nuclear physics.

Where Meek's approach differed with the EVP researchers was that he wanted first to get in touch with discarnate scientists he considered were living on another plane, communicate with them through mediums, and get direct information on how to build the electronic circuits to reach them. 'We wanted to join hands with deceased scientists across the dimensions that separate them from us,' was the way Meek put it. 'Hopefully the equipment we could jointly design would eliminate the need for a psychic or medium. We wanted to use a practical engineering approach because there was no supporting theoretical base to work from.'

It was an unusual group that George Meek set up to accomplish the all-but-impossible job of pulling in technical advice from discarnate scientists. But the earthling people he assembled, as always, were intelligent, knowledgeable, and of sound integrity.

What was most interesting was the make-up and composition of the research group. In addition to Meek, there was Melvin Sutley. He was a respected Philadelphia Quaker who was Chief Administrator of the highly-ranked Wills Eye Hospital, and one of the founders of the Spiritual Frontiers Fellowship.

Another was a close friend and associate of Meek named Paul Jones. Jones was a highly successful physicist, electronic engineer, manufacturer of computer devices and an inventor with over 100 patents. With Meek, he was interested in exploring not only the possibility of setting up electronic communication with other worlds, but in finding out whether inventions and discoveries could unconsciously be passed down to inventors from these other dimensions, just as healers were purportedly receiving direct aid.

Another associate in this unusual research group was Hans Heckmann. Heckmann had met Paul Jones when they were both taking a Silva Mind Control course, at a time when neither was convinced that any kind of communication could exist between the two worlds. Heckmann, a former German soldier who married the American nurse who attended him in World War Two, was now a computer specialist for Conrail in Philadelphia and an electronics expert who specialized in all forms of sound reproduction.

The ignition to form the group came from Melvin Sutley. He was startled when he learned through a medium that a deceased close friend of his wanted to work with qualified engineers to develop a communication system.

The apparent contact was a former cosmic ray scientist who had taught at Yale, Minnesota, Chicago and Swarthmore, Professor Francis G. Swann. Swann had died in 1962, over a decade before. Sutley had known Professor Swann when he was living. They had held long conversations about the possible continuation of life and individual consciousness after death. Through his studies in particle physics, the deceased Swann had been aware of the infinitesimal amount of 'material' that was included in what we think of as solid matter.

When he was alive, Swann told Sutley that he was convinced that there were interspersed planes of existence beyond our physical awareness, even though they would not mingle under ordinary circumstances. In fact, Swann had told Sutley that the chances of the two dimensions colliding would be about as little as 'two mosquitoes colliding in Grand Central Station'.

When Meek learned that Sutley had apparently communicated with the deceased Swann, he went into action. Meek was living in Fort Myers at the time, but he set up a small lab in Philadelphia where his colleagues could work during evenings and weekends, and where he could fly up and join them. The lab where they carried out their other-worldly experiments was simply a rented room, sparsely furnished and dominated by the electronic gear Heckmann had built in an attempt to capture any kind of signal they might get through from Professor Swann.

Meek would arrive on a Saturday morning. The group obtained the services of a medium, the executive I mentioned earlier from N. W. Ayer. The method used to set up the communications through the medium was relatively simple. The medium sat in a chair at the head of the table. Meek, Heckmann, Jones, and Sutley took their places around it, after making sure that the electronic equipment was properly set for the remote chance they could capture Professor Swann's voice from the other side of the cosmic fence – not only through the medium, but through the equipment as well.

Paul Jones, with his cool, logical, pragmatic mind, had little trouble in expanding it to embrace such an exotic scene. His studies into the paranormal had convinced him how logical it was to realize that the mind was separate from the physical brain which in turn only served as a communication link to the physical world. He liked to point out how 'unsolid' the body really was. 'If you stretched a solid steel rod from coast to coast,' he once said, 'and removed all the space between its elemental particles, the rod would only be about an eighth of an inch in length.'

Heckmann, too, had little trouble adjusting his technical mind to the process. Tall, Germanic and stolid, he watched as the medium brought through the thoughts of Professor Swann in hours of sessions without a break in the style, form or diction of the technical messages. Melvin Sutley, the graying and distinguished administrator, marked how accurately the messages received reflected Swann's personality and thinking.

When the sessions started, Heckmann or Meek would open with a brief prayer. The medium would slide quietly into a self-induced trance. Before long, his voice would change into the deeper tones of his 'control', and the voice would say: 'I am Swann.'

But Swann indicated that he was not alone. He stated that he was joined by several other discarnate entities who were anxious to develop this new form of communication. The Swann group was reported to include the late Lee de Forest and Reginald Fessenden, both outstanding radio pioneers. Various questions would be posed by the research group. In answer to a technical question from Meek, the voice of Swann answered through the medium: 'We are not dealing with sound frequencies. They are acted upon by various other factors. Also, where you live, there are modifying factors. For instance, in the experiments with taping voices, the voices are ordinarily very faint. They must needs be amplified by certain experiments such as the diode and radio connection used by Dr Raudive. There is also the matter of a little higher radio frequency of radio equipment which helps those communications exceedingly. The dedication of those who listen is equalled only by our dedication here, which is as it should be. You have not much to work on except the equipment as yet. You can not accomplish everything because the active application of the energies must come from us . . .'

At this point, the Meek team of technicians were working with equipment they designated as Mark I. It was far more complicated than that of the EVP researchers, consisting of a 300 megacycle generator (now designated as megaHertz, replacing the previous designation of 'cycles' and 'megacycles'), an antenna, pre-amp, and a radio signal generator. But in their sessions, to date, no communication had been received through the equipment. Only the human medium provided the communication. Through the medium, however, they received more encouragement from Professor Swann: 'Your signal is clearer and more powerful . . . The problem is to put the energies we work with together to produce the voice sound. Our work is done mainly through thought or mind energies . . . There can be the combination of certain energies to create voice.'

It was a laborious process. Each session was taped and analyzed. The responses that came through were at times technical and at other times broader and more philosophical. And like their earth-bound technicians, the purported spirit group apparently had their own problems. As so many communications of this type have indicated, life in the next world does not automatically endow the participants with universal knowledge or skills. If what has come out through psychic messages is true, each individual has a long way to go, depending on the stage of evolution he had reached at the time of his death.

Questions were asked vocally, and the voice would answer through the medium. At times, the purported voice of Professor Swann would pause to explain the development process his discarnate group were going through in attempting to make actual radio contact: 'We have left behind, shall we say, on lower levels much of the use of the so-called voice,' Professor Swann said. 'Our work is done mainly through thought or mind energies. We will call it "thought" because that is how you understand it. But let us say that these are mind energies directed in a certain focus or a certain pattern. There can be the combination of certain energies to create what you call voice. And that is the problem we are dealing with right now.'

At other times, the voice of Professor Swann would elaborate on the available spirit energies: 'From the standpoint of comparison with the energy of the electrons that you are working with we would say that it would run perhaps 20,000 megacycles. We cannot designate it that because it is not the type of electrons you are familiar with . . .'

And at times, Professor Swann would give a suggestion of what it was like in the next world: 'Since we have undergone a second death and rebirth to our present level of consciousness, it is natural that our philosophy has been expanded. Here work is for the joy of accomplishment and for the good it may be for those on the lower planes.'

The progress was painfully slow. Meek's team logged scores of hours of such communications, picking up clues that might lead to the two-way electronic communication they were searching for. In the process, Meek felt that there was strong evidence of a scientific basis for the central core teachings of all the world's great religions from Christianity to Judaism to Buddhism to Islam and the others. The goal was to reach up to the mental-causal plane where Professor Swann's higher forms of after-life could offer wisdom and assistance to help solve the problems of modern civilization.

Although the group – now calling itself Metascience Associates – was receiving copious and illuminating messages through the medium, there were still no signals received directly through the electronic apparatus. The job was described by Swann through the medium: 'It's like trying to hit a small target out in the ocean with a rifle bullet.'

There was a flutter of excitement when it appeared that Swann pinpointed a signal, leaving an audible 1 kHz impingement on two tape recorders in the lab, one of which was not connected to the equipment at all. But Swann spoke through the medium to say it might be possible to locate their signal more easily if the higher harmonics extended above 1,000 MHz. The Metascience group immediately went into action to design Mark II, at 1,200 MHz. Meanwhile, Meek took off for Europe to explore the new developments in the EVP research, where he hoped to find further clues.

One problem with the ordinary EVP experiments was that some of the crude, brief messages received suggested that messages were coming from the lower astral planes where purportedly poorly-developed individuals remained earth-bound, without the desire to move on to higher planes. Beyond that, some highly undesirable characters were considered to be among those who attempt to 'possess' others or create violent poltergeist activities in the *Exorcist* or *Amityville Horror* style.

Meek was aware of the possibility that possession could be a very real thing. He was concerned about it in relation to his electronic experiments. He considered entirely possible the theory that those on the lowest astral planes search out and try to possess a person whose energy field is similar to theirs, whether for the purpose of high-voltage lust, crime, or alcohol. Enough cases of this kind had been reported to make it a distinct potential. To by-pass this theoretical situation, Professor Swann's recommendations to use the higher wave lengths or frequencies might help to reach the more highly evolved levels of consciousness, and avoid the pitfalls of contact with the lower planes.

* * *

By the spring of 1973, Jeannette Meek was still not altogether content about the pilgrimage that her husband had set for himself, and still wondering about the wisdom of breaking off a brilliant and successful career in international consulting as an engineer and inventor. As Meek described it, it was obviously very hard on Jeannette as he travelled over the world to contact technical and scientific people – 'odd balls like myself who wanted answers to questions for which no information could be found on the shelves of university libraries or anyplace else in the world.' The insights acquired, however, came directly home when several acquaintances of Jeannette's were markedly improved by the holistic healing Meek was uncovering.

Gradually, she again came round to Meek's point of view and felt that 'this far-out research that her husband was engaged in' was opening up exciting new frontiers. Once a reluctant observer, she now became a complete co-worker and began to put in 10 to 12 hour days without complaint.

Returning from one of his many trips abroad, Meek was hopeful of finding a medium to study, preferably a healer who had the rare capability of materialization, and was closer to home than those he had been examining. He spoke to Henry Nagorka, an editor of the magazine *Psychic Observer*, about this possibility. He told Nagorka about some of the healers he had studied who had shown evidence of materializing ectoplasmic forms of various kinds.

Nagorka mentioned that he had been in correspondence with someone who might just fill the bill. His name was William O'Neil, and although Nagorka knew of him only through the 'letter to the editor' sort of thing, his correspondence suggested that O'Neil might have this ability.

Meek, as usual, lost no time in going into action. He sat down to write to O'Neil on March 27, 1973. Although Meek didn't know it at the time, he was about to embark on one of the strangest series of experiences in his quest. The relationship that followed would mark the beginning of a long and turbulent sequence of events for the tall and dignified George Meek and the rough-hewn, brilliant, and irascible Bill O'Neil, in a search that was to carry them both into unknown and sometimes frightening territory.

# CHAPTER 4

## *Behind the Man Named O'Neil*

Born in the small town of Dubois, Pennsylvania, in 1917, William J. O'Neil had gone on to combine his technical and electronic career with a broad spectrum of natural talents that he never seemed to be able to develop fully. The atmosphere of his town, lying to the northeast of Pittsburgh, was industrially bleak and oppressive. The railroads and the coal mines were constantly undergoing labor upheavals and recession. There were frequent economic convolutions. In spite of this, O'Neil loved the rugged hills and countryside where the Seneca and Delaware Indian tribes once thrived. He sensed a very real attachment for them. The fact that his mother was descended from the Senecas brought him a great deal of pride.

There was nothing in his early years that suggested he had any particular leanings toward the psychic. There was one incident that puzzled him, even frightened him, both at the time and in later years when he often thought about it.

It happened when he was about 12 years old. He was standing in the doorway between the dining room and the kitchen. His mother was in the process of making bread. On the table was an old earthenware crock she used to keep the salt. He always had a fondness for that crock, and as his mother was using it, a scene flashed back through his mind. He recalled vividly when his baby sister, two years younger than he, had placed the crock on the floor and was pushing it around like a toy, and babbling with pleasure as she did so.

'Remember that time, momma?' he said. 'How we all laughed at her as she slid it across the floor? She was such a cute little baby.'

His mother stopped mixing the batter, and said, 'That wasn't your sister, William. It was *you* who did that. Don't you remember?'

'You're wrong, momma,' he answered. 'I watched her do it, and remember just how she acted.'

'William,' his mother said. 'Your sister wasn't born until two years later.'

'But I *know* it was my sister. I know it. I remember it.'

'You'll have to ask your grandmother. She remembers it, too. You're getting things mixed up.'

It was simple, even silly little incident. But William couldn't get it out of his mind. How could he remember the scene so clearly, seeing his sister there when she had not been born until two years later? It would only be far into the future, when he was an adult, that other scenes would happen that would have a much greater impact on him, far beyond this simple event.

Much as he loved the region, O'Neil constantly rebelled against his schooling. When he quit high school as a freshman, he punctuated his departure by slamming his football helmet on the field, and never returned. From then on, his life was never without a struggle, in spite of his talents that embraced all the raw materials for a potential rough-hewn Renaissance man: sculpture, oil painting, music, cartooning, photography, botany, hunting and fishing. With his obdurate stubbornness and unpredictable flashes of temper, he often hid his genuine longing for mental and spiritual development, especially his idealistic and sometimes unrealistic desire to work for the betterment of his fellow man.

Starting as a civilian technician with the US Navy Radar-Radio laboratory at Pearl Harbor in 1939, O'Neil put his technical genius to work. In spite of his lack of formal schooling, he was awarded enrollment in a course of advanced electronics at the University of Hawaii under Navy Department sponsorship. After a spell in the Army in the Intelligence Section of the 22nd Infantry Brigade, he started his own two-way radio communication shop in Media, Pennsylvania. This marked the beginning of a long chain of electronic jobs. They ranged from that of an electronic tube foreman for RCA in Cincinnati to a computer technician in Florida working with telemetry devices used in the rocketry program at Cape Canaveral. His military clearance status was 'secret'.

Following this, he worked at Hughes Aircraft on the West Coast, and later as an owner-operator of his own sales and service company both in California and back in his own home grounds in western Pennsylvania. Through all his career, O'Neil kept up his extracurricular activities. He managed to conduct a children's program at WKRC-TV in Cincinnati, and to work spasmodically at his art, music and poems, all of which were of the folksy sort and not likely to attract sophisticated critics. His avid reading, however, made it possible for him to overcome many of the disadvantages of his truncated schooling.

Although O'Neil didn't consider himself psychic at all, he began reading books on the subject from his youth on. He was intrigued, and his interest began to grow slowly, especially in the area of healing. He recalls his early days with his mother, where telepathy was more or less taken for granted. Further, because of his mother's Seneca Indian lineage, he grew up in the Indian lore of the area. It included legends and folk medicine that he became convinced would work under the right circumstances. This was further fortified by very subtle signals that he might be developing into a psychic sensitive, almost against his wishes.

It was in fact this development that brought him and Mary Alice together. In 1972, at the age of 55, O'Neil felt that he had to take positive action to satisfy his almost missionary zeal to help people who were less fortunate than he was. He knew nothing about George Meek, but his urge happened to come at the same age that Meek had made his decision to finish off his business career.

O'Neil's impulse to take a direct step took the form of applying for a job with the Peace Corps, in spite of his age. To qualify, he checked into a local hospital for the complete medical the Peace Corps required. Sharing his room was the father of one of Mary Alice's friends. Mary Alice came to see him, but ended up with a long talk with Bill in the hospital lounge area. When they learned of their mutual interest in psychic and holistic healing, they were quickly drawn together. When the time came for the final decision about joining the Peace Corps, O'Neil knew he wanted to marry Mary Alice and decided to cancel his plans. Perhaps, he thought, he could help others in a different way at home in Pennsylvania.

Their interest in psychic phenomena began to grow steadily. They experimented with hypnosis, sometimes a risky thing, and there were indications that Mary Alice might be psychically sensitive herself. Neither, however, was aware of the possible dangers involved in an undisciplined and untutored approach, especially when it turned out that both were susceptible to a trance state.

O'Neil, with a muscular five-foot four frame, had been married before. He had fathered six children ranging in age from 6 to 25. Mary Alice had also been married and had borne two children. Both were worried about trying marriage again. However, they finally decided to move into a trailer home in the town of Kittanning, as Bill planned to build up his general electronic and repair work in the community. Since they shared a common growing interest in holistic healing and the paranormal, they looked forward to mutual development in that area.

Mary Alice, a soft spoken, mild mannered and quietly intelligent woman in her early 40s, admired Bill for his determination to bring healing to those who needed it after conventional medical methods failed. She finally said to him, 'Look, Bill, I'm afraid of getting married again. But you must be somebody very special. I'm losing my fear.'

Bill, also wary, said, 'So am I.'

They married. Mary Alice continued with her interest in handicrafts and in her aspiration to help Bill in holistic healing, even though she felt inadequate for the job. Bill was convinced that she would be of great help if she were willing to try. As with many such healing teams, one member acts as a 'battery' for the other, which is regarded as helping along the healing process.

They had some success. Bill used the conventional method of the 'laying on of hands'. Or at times, he would use some of the folk medicine techniques that had come down to him from his mother through her Seneca Indian lineage. Other times, he merely said, 'Please, God, help this person with Thy love.' In one case, a neighbor had a large ulcer on her leg that had resisted conventional medical treatment for months. O'Neil placed a bay leaf over it, and the woman reported that the ulcer healed up completely within 24 hours. In keeping with the tradition of many serious holistic healers, the O'Neils never accepted money, even though it was often pressed on them. O'Neil stated that he considered it a privilege to be able to help the sick, and resisted all offers even though he had little income.

Mary Alice continued to admire him for this, and never pressed for him to accept either a fee or a gift. But she remained tentative in her feelings about the psychic process. It seemed so alien and improbable. It wasn't until a neighbor dropped by one day to have Bill fix a portable TV that she became less hesitant. His name was Benton John, who lived about a mile away. With him was his daughter, Susan. At the age of 14, she had to use crutches, and both her legs were in removable plastic casts. Bill asked her father what was wrong with her.

'Well, I'm afraid she was born this way,' Benton answered.

'Why does she wear the casts?' O'Neil asked.

'Every night we have to put the casts on, and sometimes during the day. If she doesn't have them on, and she bends her legs during the night, she wakes up screaming. If she doesn't have them on in the day, she has to use her wheelchair. And take medication.'

'I see,' O'Neil said. 'Well, come on in and have a cup of coffee.'

O'Neil felt deeply for the little girl. He pointed to the casts and said, 'Those things really bother you, don't they?'

When she answered yes, Bill said, 'Can you stand up without your crutches?'

She again answered yes, and Bill asked her to do so. She could stand all right, but she couldn't walk. With a nod from her father, Bill went to her and put his arms around her. 'God love you,' he said, 'and make you better.'

Then he asked her father to take off the braces. He did. Surprisingly, the girl walked across the room. Four years later, she was training to be a cheerleader. There was no more need for the casts, crutches or medication.

Since the results were immediately observable, Mary Alice's reservations diminished, even more so after what followed. The John family had more than its share of troubles. Benton's wife developed a lump on her breast, and, with some embarrassment, he asked O'Neil if he could help. With any of his healings, O'Neil always insisted that other members of the family be present, and he did so in this case. He had Benton put his hand on top of his own, touched the lump, and offered a brief prayer. Within a day the tumor was gone.

All of this smacked of miracle work, and though Mary Alice had to believe what she saw, her credulity still remained strained. Especially when a third event took place with the John family. To add to their enormous problems, their small son was a deaf mute. Unable to talk or hear, he could not respond to any sounds or voices. In appreciation for what O'Neil had done for his wife and daughter, Benton John brought over a truck full of firewood. With him was his deaf son. O'Neil, unaware that the boy was deaf, warned him to stand back from where they were stacking the firewood. Benton explained to O'Neil that the boy couldn't hear at all, and could only respond to gestures.

Without hesitation, Bill went to the boy and touched his ear, murmuring a prayer as he did so. Then he asked the boy if he could hear. The boy immediately answered, even though he was only able to mumble. O'Neil covered his mouth so the boy could not see he was talking. Again the boy answered. O'Neil went behind the truck for a third test, where his lips could not be observed. An immediate vocal though inarticulate response came. Benton shook his head in disbelief and continued unloading the truck. Although the boy never was able to speak, he was able to listen and take simple commands from then on.

Instead of being fully elated by his capacities to help, O'Neil shared Mary Alice's concern about the bizarre quality of these experiences. As yet, there was no medical confirmation of the results that were fully documented, and O'Neil continued to be frightened by his apparent abilities. Whatever they were, he considered they were a gift, and resolved never to abuse it. He hoped to be able to combine whatever talents he had with his electronic experience, perhaps to develop instruments that could be tested by the medical profession and put into professional use.

His experience with the John boy prompted him to explore what could be done to assist deaf mutes in hearing through an electronic device, perhaps a new form of hearing aid. With luck, and with his past experience in everything from Sidewinder missiles to telemetric devices for rocketry, he felt perhaps that he might be able to create a device by which a deaf mute could monitor his own voice as well as the voice of an instructor or a therapist.

He started by building several radio frequency oscillators in an attempt to find the frequency most appropriate for the deaf to detect by the tactile senses. With this equipment, he found he was able to generate frequencies ranging from the sub-harmonic to ultra-high. Sandwiched in his small lab among the oscillators, pre-amps, relays and other equipment was a small five-gallon aquarium with various species of tropical fish he enjoyed watching while he worked.

One winter evening in early 1973, O'Neil started to operate two oscillators that sat on each side of the aquarium on his work bench. It was late at night, Mary Alice had gone to bed, and he was tired. He began what is called 'beating' the oscillators together to experiment with and to log various frequencies. As he did so, he began to notice some kind of movement within the aquarium, other than the movement of the fish swimming about. He couldn't quite define what kind of movement was going on, and ascribed it to the figment of a very fatigued imagination.

Two nights later, he tried the same experiment. *Something* was swirling within the waters of the aquarium again, but it was fleeting and vague. In the next step, he disposed of the fish, and began beating the same frequencies together. The same strange swirling occurred as he went through the same series of experimental frequencies. In addition, there were swirls of color within the water.

Now O'Neil was puzzled, somewhat afraid, and not a little curious. He became intrigued with a phenomenon he had never seen before, never heard of, and which was impossible to explain. He continued the experiments, beating a series of frequencies against each other through the water-filled aquarium. What happened next almost left him in shock.

As the water and the colors swirled again, he noticed something he couldn't possibly believe. Some of the swirls actually began to take various shapes, miniature shapes. There was a hand in miniature size, part of an arm, even part of a head with long hair. They were there, all inside the glass enclosure. There was no question that they were there. But he could not believe it. He immediately shut down the system and leaned back in his chair.

He came up with an answer he didn't want to admit to himself. He was hallucinating. He was insane. There was no question about it, he said to himself. Insanity was the only answer because he was convinced that it was no longer a tired mind seeing the apparent materializations. Yet somehow he doubted his own conclusion. He didn't feel insane, and his deepest feeling convinced him that he was not. He said nothing to Mary Alice about it, and nothing to anyone else, content to sweat it out by himself – and even try the experiment again.

He waited for two weeks, taking the time to cool down and go about his ordinary routine. He tried to resist the urge to experiment with the same process. Finally, he decided to approach one more attempt with a clinical and open mind. Late one night, he summoned his courage, turned on the oscillators. Perhaps, he thought, the phenomenon was an inexplicable result of reflection or refraction of some kind. Perhaps he had produced a false imagery within his own mind.

He started all over again, changing the oscillator frequencies as he beat them against each other. He looked for any additional movement or materialization that might occur. Then at one point, while he varied the frequencies of the oscillators, he began to shake violently. He could not control the convulsive movement of his body in any way.

He had to struggle to turn off the equipment. He couldn't sleep the rest of the night. During his wakefulness, he turned over every possible explanation in his mind. His main thought was that he might have ventured electronically through a frequency or frequencies similar to X-rays, possibly gamma rays or beta particles. Perhaps they had a destructive effect on the tissues or the nervous system of his body.

After a sleepless night, O'Neil went to see his doctor. He told him nothing about his experiments and the subsequent results. He was afraid of either ridicule or being regarded as mentally unbalanced. He simply explained that he was very jittery and had been under strain for some time. The doctor prescribed a tranquilizer, which he took for a month before the nervous condition abated.

When he felt better, he couldn't resist the temptation to try the experiment once more. He did. He repeated the operation exactly as he had done before. The swirling and the colors appeared in the water. The miniature materializations began to form. He began shaking violently again. This time he took immediate and conclusive action. He shut off the equipment, dismantled the oscillators and threw away the aquarium. He was not going to take such a risk again.

But the experience haunted him. He convinced himself that he was not insane, but if he wasn't – what was the explanation? He knew of no one to turn to, with whom he could share the experience intelligently, no one who could explain it to him. He still didn't confide in Mary Alice, afraid that her growing faith in his ability as a healer might again be set back.

To try to get some possible kind of explanation, O'Neil went to the reference section of his library and looked up publications that dealt with the paranormal. He found the name of Henry Nagorka, editor of the magazine *Psychic Observer*. He sat down and wrote him a letter, explaining in detail what had happened, and almost begged for a reply that would set his mind at rest.

He waited for several weeks. No reply came from the magazine. He began to give up hope that he would ever get a reply – or ever hope to find an explanation for the strangest and most frightening experience he had ever faced.

But at the end of March, 1973, a letter arrived in his post office box. It was not from Henry Nagorka or the *Psychic Observer*. It was from someone named George Meek. The letter was postmarked Fort Myers, Florida. As he opened the letter and began to read it, the convergence of the two men, so vastly different in background and character, was now ready to create a most startling and puzzling series of events that may – or may not – remain forever inexplicable.

# *PART 2*

# CHAPTER 5

## *The Making of a Medium – 1973*

George Meek's letter to O'Neil was brief and to the point. Meek had not expected Nagorka to come up with the type of medium he was looking for so quickly. To find a medium relatively close to home who had the rare capability of materialization would be of great advantage. What Nagorka and Meek failed to realize was that O'Neil did not consider himself a medium. He had no previous experience of what he had encountered in his lab, and feared for his own sanity.

In his letter at the end of March, 1973, Meek wrote:

> Dear Mr O'Neil,
>
> Some weeks ago, when visiting Henry Nagorka, we were discussing materialization phenomena and my deep interest in this subject. I told Henry of a recent trip I made to Brazil with a group of five scientists from the United States and England, specifically for the purpose of observing either partial or full body materialization.
>
> The trip was not successful and I asked Henry if he knew of anyone in the US who was seriously interested in the subject. It was at this point that he mentioned your name. We are convinced that only by a careful study of materialization phenomena can we begin to understand some of the very subtle forces involved in man's relation with all-pervading Spirit . . .
>
> This letter is for the purpose of asking whether you do or do not care to share some of your experiences with us and tell us enough about your activities so that we can see whether or not any joint research study might be undertaken . . .

When O'Neil opened the letter, he was filled with relief. O'Neil had been unable to get the picture of what had happened in his aquarium out of his mind. Here was someone who seemed to understand a little of the agony he had experienced. Whoever Meek was,

O'Neil was hoping that he could get at least some kind of explanation as to what had happened.

He wrote Meek back in great detail, revealing that he was in his mid-50s, that he had been an electronics technician over the previous 15 years, and that he was about to re-marry in the near future. He explained that both he and his fiancée had been exploring parapsychology and the physical sciences. O'Neil added that he was trying to combine his technical inventiveness with his belief in the power of psychic healing, even though he had no formal training in medicine or psychic studies. Then he spilled out the whole series of strange events, from the moment that there were disturbances in the waters of the aquarium to the great fear and anxiety that developed afterwards. The letter provided a catharsis for O'Neil, and he held nothing back.

In the last part of the letter, he revealed the motivations that were propelling him in the search that had carried him into this strange series of events:

> I have no desire to repeat the experiments outside of supervised and laboratory controlled conditions. However, since that time I have conducted extensive study and research into the possibility of the effects of radio frequencies on human tissue, and, further, the possibility of the existence of other 'dimensions' if you will – factual, spiritual or whatever that may exist and which may or may not be cognizant of our own (human) and known existence on this planet. I am continuing to approach the 'all' of possibility with an open mind, making no statements or conclusions that will not be in keeping with honest and sincere scientific practices. Any theories that I might put forth will of necessity be substantiated by continued experimentation and research by myself and hopefully by others.
>
> I am no longer frightened by thoughts of that which I know exists. However, knowing is – without concrete evidence of that knowledge – insufficient to be shared by my fellow man. Nor should I wish to spend my remaining years behind the unfeeling walls of a mental institution. I'm sure you will understand.
>
> Should you, Mr Meek, be numbered among those who would think me somewhat less than sane, I shall not be offended. Suffice to say that truth is the one tranquilizer of spirit's ailing existence.

Thanking you again for your most impressive letter and a sincere wish for continued success in your future endeavors . . .

* * *

When Meek read O'Neil's letter, he was startled at what he found. It was almost as if O'Neil was made to order to help in his search. Here was a potential, if undeveloped medium, apparently with a profound interest in probing and linking both mechanical and metaphysical regions. O'Neil was actually experimenting with radio technology, just as Meek's Philadelphia group was doing. Further, he was showing direct evidence of being able to create the materialization phenomenon.

But Meek was also concerned. O'Neil was obviously inexperienced. It was doubtful if he was aware of some of the dangers involved in launching into untutored mediumship. There was always the possibility of uncontrolled possession in this type of case. Some materialization mediums had been reported to be extremely vulnerable to psychic forces of a negative cast. They often needed expert guidance until their development was considered complete. Before O'Neil got too deeply into further research, Meek wanted to assure himself that O'Neil would take extraordinary care before plunging further into the type of research he had embarked on.

On the other hand, Meek was convinced that whatever progress he and O'Neil might develop could be widely beneficial, and would override the negative aspects that might come up. As a combined medium and electronic technician, O'Neil's contribution could be invaluable in working towards the electronic breakthrough Meek was determined to find.

This was the beginning of a correspondence that would continue for more than a decade. It was a long while after it began that I had a chance to review the massive file of the Meek/O'Neil papers. When I did, I found them to be among the most unusual I had ever encountered. Between the lines, the characters of both O'Neil and Meek emerged, both determined to remove all the obstructions in the universe, each in different yet somewhat similar ways.

Although O'Neil showed a tendency to be carried away by hyperbole, it was obvious that his first letter to Meek was directly along the line Meek was following. It also demonstrated several other things. One was that his lack of formal education beyond grammar school was not much of a drawback as far as his diction and knowledgeability were concerned. Another was a passionate drive to experiment with and learn more about the paranormal. A third was that here was a very complex character who was willing to share his bizarre experience even though he was aware that his sanity might be questioned. The fact that he *did* question his own sanity, however, was a good sign.

If I had not made it a point to learn about the historical track record of the materialization phenomenon, I would have dismissed O'Neil's letter abruptly. But I had gradually been learning that abrupt dismissals form a roadblock to further discovery. Meek of course had far fewer reservations than I had, because his direct research into the phenomenon of materialization was what had prompted him to write to O'Neil in the first place.

It was fortunate that they were both almost passionate letter-writers. With Meek's constant travel all over the world, and his preoccupation with the Philadelphia research group, he and O'Neil did not actually meet face to face until more than two years later. What followed was to be a long-distance post office relationship that made up in intensity what it lacked in face-to-face meetings. Perhaps if Meek had been able to advise O'Neil more directly at the start, he could have prevented some of the terror that followed shortly after the first exchange of letters between the two.

* * *

The unusual qualities that O'Neil displayed in 1973 prompted Meek to discuss his apparent capacities with his colleagues in the Metascience group in Philadelphia and with other associates interested in deep psychic research. He respected O'Neil's request for anonymity, and in July forwarded only unsigned portions of O'Neil's letter to associate scientists in Brazil, Germany and Switzerland. Dr Hernani Andrade, President of the Brazilian Institute for Psychobiophysic Research, was especially interested and sent a five-page questionnaire to Meek to forward to O'Neil.

Meek briefed O'Neil fully on the work of the Metascience group in Philadelphia. O'Neil welcomed the idea of the electronic approach they were using. He was wary and skeptical about his own developing mediumship. He wrote to Meek to tell him that he felt the radio and even television spectrum might create a 'mediumless' way to hear and even see proof of survival after death. It might, he hoped, remove the spooky aspect.

O'Neil was skeptical about spiritualism of any kind, and joined Meek in feeling that electronics were the best way of bringing proof positive of survival if it were scientifically authenticated.

But he remained anxious and curious about the aquarium incident. He wrote to Meek that he wanted to get to the roots of the accidental and alarming results of his experiment. He added that he was planning to try a different approach by beating two oscillators against each other on opposite sides of a vacuum chamber.

Meek was getting ready to leave on one of his frequent and lengthy research trips with Jeannette at the end of August, 1973. He had no time to follow up O'Neil's idea, but urged him to get in touch with Paul Jones in Philadelphia with the idea of setting up a test program when he returned. It would, Meek planned, dovetail with the Swann sessions in Philadelphia, adding O'Neil's electronics expertise to that of Jones and Heckmann. Meek was concerned, however, about O'Neil continuing any further experiments of beating the oscillators together without other experts on hand in case the process went out of control, as it had done originally. This was not a trivial concern. In addition to the shock to his nervous system that O'Neil had reported, there were credible reports of one known suicide and two cases of possession among EVP researchers in Europe. In drawing up a schematic for further oscillator experiments, O'Neil himself showed an awareness of the dangers growing out of his own neophyte experience. He labelled the drawings with a notice: *It is suggested that extreme caution be exercised when operating this equipment above 300 MHz, since associated harmonic frequencies in excess of the suggested 20 watts power output may have an adverse effect on human tissue (nerve). Such caution can be implemented by shielding (lead, etc.).*

* * *

When I read O'Neil's cautionary note on his drawings several years after the fact, I began having my own misgivings. Both Bill and Mary Alice seemed unaware that psychic sensitives throughout history often experience clairaudient and clairvoyant encounters that appeared as vivid realities. I had interviewed Douglas Johnson, one of Britain's most noted mediums, one time when I had been in England. He told me about a young child who came to him with her mother who was scheduled for a reading. Johnson was cautious because sometimes children grow either restless or concerned during a reading. Johnson suggested to the mother that she take her daughter downstairs to the library until the reading was over. The mother was startled. She failed to see any little girl at all. Johnson, who could see her plainly, described her in detail, including an exact description of the clothing she was wearing. The mother burst into tears. Johnson was giving her a detailed description of her daughter who had died the year before. Only then did Johnson realize that he was dealing with a materialized projection. Real as the solid, three-dimensional image of the girl seemed, she was not in the room at all. Many other similar cases are constantly reported by psychics, whose vision and hearing apparently go far beyond the normal to become clairaudient and clairvoyant.

The typical imaginary playmates that children converse with and play with for hours on end are a phenomenon that has drawn recent psychological attention. Not only is the syndrome considered to be normal and healthy; there has been some speculation that some children might be clairaudient and clairvoyant and are seeing and hearing things that might be out of the range of adult eyesight and hearing.

But Johnson was a highly developed medium who could take these strange encounters in his stride. As I read on through the Meek/O'Neil letters, I had the uneasy feeling that the O'Neils were plunging too far ahead of themselves in this unpredictable region. My hunch was not unfounded.

* * *

One evening after Meek had left on his journey, O'Neil and Mary Alice were sitting in their trailer home talking over their plans for further research in healing. Mary Alice was sitting in the living room section, and Bill had gone to the bathroom. On his way out, he saw a pretty five year-old girl standing between him and Mary Alice. Thinking that she and her mother had come to visit Mary Alice, he said, 'Hello. What's your name?'

The girl suddenly began crying. 'I want my mommy,' she said.

Bill looked over to Mary Alice. There was no mother or anyone else present. Bill turned to the girl again and tried to get her to talk. She only repeated that she wanted her mother and continued crying. Then he noticed that Mary Alice was shaking. She seemed to be in a trance. She finally came to, as the girl continued to cry for her mother.

Bill rushed to the phone and did the only thing he could think of: he called Paul Jones, who in Meek's absence was the only person he knew who was knowledgeable about such phenomena. Jones himself was frightened. He had no direct experience of this sort of thing beyond the experimental work the group was carrying out in the Philadelphia lab. He did, however, switch on his tape recorder, and asked Bill if he could put the little girl on the phone.

He did so, as the tape indicates, but all she could do was say her name was Lorna, and continue to call for her mother. Both the O'Neils were in a state of panic as Jones tried to placate the little girl, but suddenly there was silence on the other end of the line.

In the trailer, the girl disappeared as suddenly as she had come, and the event was over. The O'Neils remained shaken for many weeks, as was Paul Jones. What none of them knew was that the incident was only a prelude to another episode that would take place in the weeks to come.

* * *

During his trip to Europe in the summer of 1973, Meek had O'Neil very much on his mind. He was not exactly sure of the best way for O'Neil to handle this apparent capacity for materialization, which remained one of the most baffling elements of mediumship. He wanted to define the parameters for further research with O'Neil when he returned. The consensus was that such experiments were not harmful, but they should only be conducted by serious researchers who were aware of possible dangers and could take effective measures against them. Meek had not yet learned about the episode with the sudden appearance of the little girl who had materialized in O'Neil's trailer home.

One of the first items on Meek's agenda when he arrived in England was to confer with a British medium named Bertha Harris. She was well versed in the problems of extra-sensitive mediums, and had worked with a physician, Dr Carl Wickland, in one of London's psychiatric hospitals where they treated schizophrenics as cases of possession rather than disease. Although this method had been followed successfully in Africa and South America, such treatment was unusual in developed countries. A large percentage of patients had been able to leave the hospital after this bizarre treatment.

Mrs Harris, the medium, would go into a trance to make her vocal cords available to the possessing entity. Dr Wickland would then interrogate the entity. Then, as in exorcism, he would persuade it to depart. His medical reports on this method were sober and convincing.

Guarding against this sort of intrusion was a high priority for Meek. He was determined to attempt to reach only those discarnate personalities on the higher levels of spiritual development, avoiding those on the lower levels who were constantly reported to interfere with serious researchers reaching for wisdom rather than psychic static. This appeared to be a major problem with the EVP experiments, where the two cases of possession had been reported.

Writing about possession in his own book, *After We Die, What Then?*, Meek states:

> It has been observed that death does not make a saint of a sinner, or a sage of a fool. The individual carries over all the old beliefs, the old habits, the old desires and all of his faulty techniques and religious dogmas. Those who believe there is no after-life are not at all prepared for what they find.
>
> Those departing souls who arrive on the lowest of the astral planes find that they lack physical bodies and are bewildered by the total darkness that seems to surround them. Some may be attracted by the magnetic energy field that emanates from nearby mortals, and which is seen clairvoyantly as light. Consciously or unconsciously a few of these attach themselves to the magnetic auras of those still in the flesh, thereby finding an avenue of expression by obsessing human beings. In such cases they will influence the possessed person with their own thoughts, impart their own emotions to them, and weaken the will power of the possessed person. In some cases this takeover can be so complete that they will actually control the possessed person's actions and often produce great distress, mental confusion and suffering.

When Meek returned from his trip to Europe, he learned from Paul Jones about the appearance of Lorna, who had apparently materialized out of nowhere in the O'Neil trailer home. Although

Meek had not met the O'Neils in person, he felt a personal responsibility to see that they avoided the pitfalls developing mediums often faced. When in England, Meek had made it a point to elicit and record on tape some very strong advice from the medium Bertha Harris about the problems of the low level sort of entities she had encountered in her work in the London hospital with Dr Wickland. Since both of the O'Neils had become involved with the paranormal as a result of their strong desire to carry out holistic healing rather than pure mediumship, Meek figured that the more informed they were, the safer they would be. He lost no time in forwarding the Bertha Harris tape and other research background to the O'Neils on January 24, 1974, with an accompanying note:

> Dear Bill and Mary Alice,
>
> To give you still more knowledge on materialization matters beyond the tape I had Bertha Harris make for you, I send you the attached material.
>
> You should begin to see that the phenomenon is nothing harmful in itself – IF – IF – IF – you do it under controlled conditions.
>
> Under no circumstances should you let this come about when you are home alone!
>
> If you do not heed the above advice you have a good chance of getting possessed by a low level entity who can cause you the same kinds of troubles which some of those people had experienced in this book by Dr Wickland. You are *very* receptive.
>
> It is safe to do these things only with close and understanding friends who can help control the situation.
>
> Sometime this spring I very much want to meet you both personally. In the meantime I suggest that insofar as possible you politely decline any offers to get involved in 'materialization' research.
>
> Sincerely,
> George

It was obvious from the tone of the note that Meek was developing an almost paternal attitude toward the O'Neils. He already sensed Bill's proclivity towards jumping impulsively into an action without thinking through its consequences. O'Neil's native but untutored brilliance, coupled with his lack of formal education, seemed to have left him with a sense of frustration, in spite of the fact that his voluminous reading had tended to overcome much of the education gap. His letters to Meek already revealed that he was subject to tidal actions and emotions, some of them naive, some emotionally immature, some poignant – but all tending to reveal a deep philosophical concern for the planet. 'Needless to say,' he told Meek in one letter, 'I am a very happy man at this writing. Especially since Mary Alice is also deeply interested in my work and has already been a most wonderful helpmate in my research and experimentation, both in the area of the physical sciences as well as possessing an inborn understanding of the spiritual or parapsychological endeavors in which I am presently engaged. Since it is my conviction that love is the one prime motivating factor in man's relation with the All, I feel that it is with love first that I choose to approach my subject whether on the physical or spiritual plane . . .'

As Meek was to learn as their relationship went on, O'Neil's thoughts and feelings were intense, transparent, and volatile. Along with expressions of humility and gratitude there were also traces of stubborn haughtiness and fierce pride. These would bubble to the surface in the middle of contradictory protests of inferiority that possibly stemmed from his failure to complete his education. All through his life, this appeared to bring about intense frustration.

* * *

As I continued reading through the enormous stack of correspondence between Meek and O'Neil, the events that were foreshadowed with each letter assumed the proportions of a strange mystery story. O'Neil's letters revealed a puzzled but determined personality with alternate moods of elation and frustration. He and Mary Alice remained shaken by the all-too-sudden apparition of the child, and her equally sudden disappearance. I had learned enough about apparitions to know that their effect on those who reported them was profound.

The simplest way to explain ghosts and apparitions – whether they appear as solid materialized form or as ephemeral shadows – is to pass them off as hallucinations, and let the subject go at that. But this is the easy way out. With thousands of cases reported by credible people, anyone who wants to examine the paranormal is forced to look at the evidence. Another poll taken by George Gallup, Jr.

indicates that 11 per cent of Americans believe in ghosts. Twenty per cent of the British do so, and of those, seven per cent reported they had actually seen an apparition.

But none of this makes it easier to comprehend the reports of those apparitions described as materialized projections, such as the one experienced by the O'Neils with the child who called herself Lorna. Unlike the ectoplasmic form of apparition, this type is solid in appearance and movement. Although audible conversation is said to take place at times, the image – like a modern holograph – is only a very realistic phantom. There is rarely a tactile contact recorded in most cases, but O'Neil was convinced that he felt the pressure of the child's hand on the phone when, in desperation, he had called Paul Jones.

All O'Neil and his wife knew was that together they had witnessed an unknown child who suddenly appeared out of nowhere. She then disappeared as suddenly as she had arrived. Both remained visibly shaken. For Bill O'Neil it was as much of a shock as the time of the aquarium incident. Two such events within a relatively short period would be enough to shatter the complacency of even a veteran psychic researcher.

In spite of the fact that Meek and the O'Neils had not yet met, Meek had become something of a father figure to O'Neil, and the only one apart from Paul Jones to whom he could turn to get some kind of explanation of what was happening to him. Meek in turn saw in O'Neil the means to combine psychic sensitivity with electronics expertise, a condition he had never encountered before in all his travels. What was disturbing to Meek however, was that the appearance of a 'materialized projection' sort of apparition, such as Lorna, also occasionally foreshadowed the possibility of possession. If so, the only protective device recommended by experts like Dr Wickland was the technique of creating a two-way conversation with the possessing entity through a skilled medium, and persuading the purported intruder to move on to its spiritual development. In the small community and lonely home in the mining hills of Pennsylvania where O'Neil lived, there was little likelihood that such help would be available, and Meek's letter of warning took on a special importance as 1974 began.

* * *

My own travels had opened up my mind at least to look at what was to follow in a clinical way. It would also have been hard to do without the deep background research I had done on the subject. Like many others, I had been inclined summarily to shrug off possession and mediumship. What I discovered in researching unrelated stories in Nigeria, Brazil, Nepal, Indonesia, and other developing countries was that both of these phenomena were universally taken for granted. From the Asmat tribes of West Irian to the Sherpas of Nepal to the Seneca Indians who contributed to Bill O'Neil's lineage, the reality of the spirit world and shamans and ghosts are taken seriously. They are also likely to be respected by anthropologists and explorers who have had the chance to witness first hand the direct evidence of the power of the shaman-medium in dealing with this invisible world.

The Western world espouses for the most part two major religions – Christianity and Judaism. Historically, the two religions also have a healthy respect for seers, soothsayers, prophets, visions, and spirit visitations and possession. However, these are now mostly consigned to the world of mythology at least. Although spirit possession still continues to be reported in practically every culture in the world, including the Western countries, it is often described in different forms, creating considerable confusion. As John Beattie, the cultural anthropologist of Oxford University, states, it is important to make a clear distinction among the different types.

Not all possession is supposed to be bad. The spirit guides of the mediums are considered creative and helpful, and thought to be on the higher astral planes when they are *controlled*, and are intentionally summoned by the medium to convey wisdom or healing from a higher level. But the spontaneous invasion by the low level entity is considered dangerous and to be urgently removed.

The primitive shaman is credited with great success in accomplishing this removal. The process appears to be that of fighting fire with fire, since the benevolent possession by his spirit guide is thought to take over and to accomplish the job of removing the disturbing entity. All cultures seem to utilize the same technique for exorcism: talking directly to the invading entity, invoking the help of a god or gods, and commanding or persuading the unwelcome force to leave.

In many cases, the entity is reported to speak through the vocal cords of the possessed person with vicious and salacious language totally uncharacteristic of the subject. Jesus was said often to rebuke 'foul spirits'. In medieval Europe Christian priests employed two-way dialogue and 'bell, book, and candle' to combat the evil force. Modern priests employ similar tactics. Beattie reports that the African shamans of Nyoro cajole a possessing spirit with soft words and send him away. The Sherpa spirit doctors carry on an elaborate ritual with butter lamps and drum beats, tongue-lashing the invader and dramatically expurging him from his victim. Dr Wickland, in his case, worked indirectly through a medium who carried on lengthy conversations with the entity before persuading it to leave the body of the victim.

There has been a growing realization that possession is not confined to tribal cultures, and is often mistaken in Western countries as schizophrenia or paranoia, either because a person is developing into a medium without being aware of it, or because he or she is the victim of a low level entity possession. Present day psychiatry is just beginning to recognize this possibility. In some techniques, the psychiatrist enters into his patient's delusion, and converses with his delusional companions. Aside from the clearly prescribed procedures of the exorcism rites of the Catholic Church, there is apparently very little that can be done to help a victim of possession, and very few people capable of doing it. One of these was George Meek's friend, Henry Mandel. At the time of the stress both the O'Neils were experiencing in February of 1974, neither Mandel nor Meek were aware that the theories of possession were about to turn into fact.

* * *

Meek was living in Fort Myers, Florida, at the time, aboard a spacious 50-foot houseboat he had designed himself. With an office on shore, he and Jeanette lived comfortably in between the times they were traveling over the world in their research. His 77 year-old friend Henry Mandel lived more than 100 miles away in St Petersburg.

Mandel had been a successful electrical contractor, who, at the age of 64, was startled to discover that he had extraordinary healing powers. Like Edgar Cayce, he had no background in medicine, yet he could diagnose and treat people holistically in a similar manner.

Meek considered him one of the finest healers he had encountered in all his travels. He had taken several friends and relatives to him, with striking results. One of the most successful was a scientist friend who had a severe spine problem that doctors in the best hospitals in New York and Boston were unable to help. Meek brought his friend to St Petersburg in a critical condition. He could only walk bent over, and in great pain. Mandel took the friend to a small sanctuary room in his house, and within 30 minutes he could stand up straight and kick his leg up as high as his shoulder.

In spite of his age, Mandel was continuing his holistic healing work, with patients flying in from widely scattered parts of the country. He had particular success with cancer patients, working in conjunction with medical doctors treating them. But since Mandel was a trance medium, he was ideally qualified for cases of possession.

As with most trance mediums and healers Dr Mandel had a spirit guide. Also, as reported very frequently, his guide purported to be an American Indian, in this case named Tall Oak.

This factor of healers and trance mediums has always bothered me. I have never been able to understand why the guides – also known as 'controls' – had to have such exotic names and nationalities. Eileen Garrett, one of the most famous of modern mediums, had a guide called Uvani and another called Abdul Latif. Arigo's had the unlikely name of Dr Fritz – among several other guides who were purported to assist him as a 'spirit guide'. But as Maurice Barbanell pointed out in his book *This Is Spiritualism*, the American Red Indian is frequently reported to be a spirit guide, even though the medium is European. Estelle Roberts, a highly esteemed British medium, has a guide named Red Cloud. Others have similar American Indian names. Barbanell does not find this surprising. He states that in the days of their prime, the North American Indians were the masters of psychic law with profound knowledge of supernormal forces. They have also been considered to be in advance of their times. The totem poles of the Cherokee Indian, among other tribes, clearly represent three levels of mind, the lower, middle and higher selves. Two wings separate the two lower segments from the top segment, representing the flight of the higher self after the body and lower levels of the mind are discarded. Naturalist Ernest Thompson Seton, a renowned authority on the American Indian, extols their psychic power at length in his book *Gospel of the Redman*.

Whatever the theoretical or actual case about psychic guides, neither Meek nor O'Neil had any hint of how Dr Mandel and his Indian guide Tall Oak would become involved in the nerve shattering trauma that was to follow.

# CHAPTER 6

## *Unwelcome Encounter – 1974*

It happened on the night of February 4, 1974. In Fort Myers, Meek was asleep on his boat at the dockside. The phone rang at about three in the morning. It was Paul Jones calling from Philadelphia.

'My God, George,' he said. 'I just got a frantic call from O'Neil.'

'At this time of morning?' Meek said. 'What seems to be the trouble?'

'It's like the Lorna case, only worse,' Jones answered. 'I tried to calm him down, but it was no use.'

'Sounds like this is a job for Mandel,' Meek said.

'I know I couldn't do anything to help,' Jones replied. 'Mary Alice seems to have gone into another trance, and O'Neil seems to be going in and out of one.'

'Sounds like a case of possession,' Meek said.

'That would be my guess,' Jones said.

'Look,' said Meek. 'I'll try to get hold of Mandel right away. Maybe he can do something by long distance.'

'It's worth a try,' Jones answered.

'I'll let you know what happens,' Meek said, and he hung up the phone.

He had only hung up for a few moments, when the phone rang again. It was Bill O'Neil calling from his home in Pennsylvania.

'George, George!' O'Neil said. He sounded as if he were in a panic.

'Tell me what's happening,' Meek said. O'Neil was now breathing heavily on the other end of the line.

Suddenly a gruff, harsh voice cut in. It was cursing and screaming.

'Who is this talking?' Meek asked. There was a moment of silence, then more cursing. 'Answer me,' Meek added sharply.

'My name is Phil, goddam you,' the voice said.

Then O'Neil's voice came back on. 'Tell him to go away, George. Please God, tell him.'

'Who is it?' Meek asked.

'I don't know, I don't know,' Bill's voice said. 'I don't understand what's happening.'

'Where is Mary Alice?' Meek said.

'She's here. But she's in a trance.'

'Listen,' Meek said. 'Remember when I warned you about possession?'

O'Neil ignored the question. 'I don't know anything. Please help, George.'

Now Meek spoke firmly. 'Listen carefully, Bill,' he said. 'Do exactly what I tell you.'

'I'll try, I'll try,' O'Neil answered.

'I want you to hang up the phone, and keep it *on the hook* – you understand?'

'Keep it on the hook,' O'Neil mumbled. His voice was fading out.

'As soon as you hang up, I'll get an expert to call you right back. His name is Henry Mandel. He knows just what to do in cases like this. Do you follow me?'

But there was a click on the other end of the line as Meek spoke. O'Neil had already hung up. Meek did likewise. Then he suddenly realized there was a problem. Mandel's unlisted number was in his office, several blocks away.

Meek threw on his clothes, rushed to his office, and found the number. Then he realized that he did not have O'Neil's number. There was another delay as he called Information to get it.

But there was still another problem. Mandel made it a habit not to answer the phone at night. It was now nearly 3.30 in the morning. Meek decided to try anyway. He was surprised when Mandel answered it promptly. Mandel had been on his way to the bathroom when the phone rang.

'Henry, I hate to do this to you,' Meek said, 'but I have a friend who seems to be in terrible trouble. I think it's a pure case of possession. Would you call him for me?'

'If you think it's necessary, George, I will,' Mandel said.

'Both Paul Jones and I think it's urgent,' Meek answered. 'I wouldn't bother you otherwise.'

Mandel agreed. Meek gave him O'Neil's number, and told Mandel he'd pay for the bill. Mandel immediately dialed the number.

Within a few moments, the situation became clear to Mandel. O'Neil was alternately rational and reflecting the entity who called himself Phil and another apparent entity who called himself Richard. There were sounds in the background that suggested that little Lorna had returned to the scene and was speaking through Mary Alice at times. She in turn had moments of lucidity and stretches where she was apparently unconscious.

For ten minutes, Mandel made little headway with Bill O'Neil and his two alter egos. He decided to work with Mary Alice, and began persuading Bill to turn the phone over to her. As he did, Mandel remembered to turn on his recording equipment to track the scene as it unfolded.

'Whenever you get ready,' Mandel said to Bill, 'I'll talk to your wife there. She'll be all right. We'll get things straightened out.'

There was a pause on the other end of the line. Then Mandel said, 'Are you there, Bill?' Then there was a strange voice in the background that said 'Hello?'

O'Neil then spoke down the phone in his normal voice to Mandel: 'Are you still there? Please hang on.' His voice sounded fully rational now. But it changed to desperation when he added, 'I'll pay for the telephone bill.'

'That's okay,' Mandel answered, and at this point he decided to bring in his spirit guide as he always did in a crisis. 'Now I'm bringing in my spirit guide, Tall Oak,' he said. 'Tall Oak is there with you. He is taking over there.'

Mandel listened for a response. He heard a strange voice that seemed to come through Mary Alice. It sounded like a little girl.

'Yes?' Mandel asked. 'Lorna? Are you the little girl?'

But Bill now spoke. 'No. Not yet. She is in a trance.' He paused, then: 'Here we go.'

'Now you wake up,' Mandel commanded. 'You wake up and talk to me now!'

Bill responded. 'Okay. Here is Lorna. This is the little girl.'

'The little girl? Or is this your wife?' There was another pause. 'Hello?'

Lorna's voice, which seemed to be coming through Mary Alice, came on. 'Hello.'

'Who are you?' Mandel asked.

'Lorna,' the voice answered.

'Lorna,' Mandel said. 'Are you the little girl who is possessing this woman?'

'I am Lorna,' the voice said. 'Where is my mommy?'

'All right,' Mandel answered patiently. 'Now Tall Oak is there. You see the Indian who is there? He wants to take you, Lorna, to your mother.'

'I want my mother,' the Lorna voice said.

'Yes, I know,' Mandel answered. 'He will take you there. Do you want to go with him so you get to your mother?'

'There's a tall man here . . .'

'Yes,' Mandel said. 'Now you go with Tall Oak and he'll take you to your mother. Okay? He is a very fine Indian boy and he is very pleased to help you.'

'That's nice,' the apparent voice of Lorna answered.

'Will you go with him?'

'All right,' the girl's voice answered.

'Now, Tall Oak,' Mandel said. 'Lorna wants to go with you so you can take her away. Thank you, Lorna. Thank you, thank you.'

After a pause, Bill's voice came on again. 'Hello?'

'Bill? Lorna is gone now.' Bill could be heard sobbing. 'Take your time,' Mandel added. 'Is your wife all right now?'

There was a mumbled reply, as Mandel said, 'Come on, Bill. Straighten out. I'll straighten you out, too, Bill. Everything is going to be all right.'

'My wife just said to come over and see what is the matter.' Bill was mumbling. 'Here is my wife.'

'What's her first name?' Mandel asked.

'Mary Alice,' Bill said.

'Mary Alice. Oh, yes. Let me talk to her.'

In a moment, Mary Alice came on the line.

'Hello, Mary Alice. How are you?' Mandel asked.

Her voice was casual. 'Hi. I'm okay. Who's this?'

'I'm Henry Mandel.'

'Mandel?'

'Yes. George Meek called me and told me to call you. You needed some help.'

'Oh.'

'I just sent Lorna, who is bothering you, to meet her mother.'

'Well I'll be darned,' Mary Alice said. Now she sounded confused.

'So you are no longer going to be bothered by her.'

'Oh, thank heavens,' Mary Alice replied.

'Yes. You feel all right now?'

'Yes. I feel great.'

'Sure,' Mandel said. 'So just let me talk to your husband Bill. We'll take care of him.'

'All right,' Mary Alice said. Then she added with some alarm, 'He's falling into a trance. He's gone into a trance.'

'I know that,' Mandel said. 'Now we are going to remove the problem from him. You stay on the phone now, Mary Alice.'

'All right.'

'Now Tall Oak is going to be back in a few minutes . . . he's going to take away from Bill what's troubling him.'

Mary Alice seemed relieved. 'Oh, I hope so.'

'We know so,' Mandel assured her. 'This is my work. George is a good friend, and he called me. We will handle this all right.'

Then Mandel addressed Tall Oak. 'Tall Oak, as soon as you are back you get to work on Bill, and remove from him this excess baggage.' He was referring to the apparent entities Bill was burdened with.

Mary Alice asked, 'Shall I hold the phone to him? Shall I give Bill the phone?'

'No,' Mandel answered. 'You hold the phone so I know what's going on. Now – you've been in trance before? Were you troubled with this girl before?'

'Just a few times, I guess.'

'All right. You are okay now. Now I want to straighten out Bill. But first, can you put the phone to his ear so I can talk to him – and then take it back so I can talk to you?'

'All right.'

'Now hold it there for a while.' Then Mandel addressed Bill as Mary Alice held the phone.

'Now, Bill, I want you to wake up.'

Bill could be heard to be moaning. 'Wake up, Bill,' Mandel continued. 'You're all right. Tall Oak has got some boys there. They're going to help you. They're going to remove that person. We are going to be kind to him and put him in progression.' He was referring to the term used by mediums for dissatisfied entities who refuse to move on to their spiritual development. 'It's a beautiful place where he won't bother you any more.'

Then Mandel addressed Mary Alice. 'Now, are you back on, Mary Alice?'

'Yes.'

'Is he awake?'

Suddenly, however, a loud gruff voice came on the wire: 'Go to hell!'

'What did he say?' Mandel asked Mary Alice.

But the voice repeated itself. 'Go to hell!'

Mary Alice spoke. 'He is not himself.'

'I know,' Mandel said.

'He's swearing again,' Mary Alice said.

'That's okay,' Mandel replied. 'That's not him, Mary Alice. That's the entity. Now we are going to move that entity out of him just as we moved Lorna out.'

Mandel took a deep breath, and spoke firmly. 'Now Tall Oak, you see now that this individual is taken out and put into – I say in the name of the most high God, remove this disturbance from this man. Get him out of there . . . get him out!'

Mandel paused a minute, then continued. 'If he doesn't leave by himself, then we'll have to pull him out and put him in jail. Pull him out of there, Tall Oak!'

Mary Alice's voice was heard speaking to Bill. 'Bill, Tall Oak is helping you . . .'

Mandel continued. 'We call on all our help to intercede here . . .'

But then the voice of an entirely new entity introduced itself on the phone line. 'Richard,' it said, then repeated, 'Richard . . .'

Mandel brushed the voice aside. 'Hello, now, Bill. You feel all right now? This is Mandel talking.'

Again the other gruff voice spoke. 'You know me. Richard.'

'Oh? Who are you?'

'I am Richard.'

'Richard who?'

'I don't know.'

'You are disturbing Bill. Do you know that?' Mandel said sharply.

'You know me. I am Richard. You know me.'

'Richard,' Mandel said. 'I want to help you. Do you want help?'

Richard spoke again. 'You son of a bitch!'

Mandel remained calm. 'Richard, do you want some help? You can get help if you want it. I don't want to put you in jail. You wouldn't want me to do that, would you?'

'I am Richard,' the voice repeated.

Mandel raised his voice again. 'I want you to leave Bill's body. Do you hear me? You are occupying someone's body! I want you to leave that body. Do you hear me, Richard?' He paused, then added,

'Tall Oak? Clean that body out and take him wherever he needs to go . . .'

Then suddenly, Bill O'Neil's normal voice came back on the phone. 'Hey,' he said. 'Paul. Can you hear me, Paul?'

'Yes?' Mandel answered.

'Is that you, Paul?' O'Neil asked.

'No,' Mandel answered. 'This is Henry Mandel still on the phone.'

'Henry who?' Bill asked. His voice was puzzled.

'Henry Mandel.'

Now Bill was bewildered. 'I called Paul Jones.'

'I know, I know,' Mandel replied. 'But he and Meek called me.'

'Oh?'

'Bill, are you listening to me?'

Bill's voice suddenly turned respectful. 'Yes, sir.'

'Now,' Mandel went on. 'You are Bill O'Neil. Okay?'

'Yes, sir.'

'And I am Henry Mandel.'

O'Neil still couldn't get things straight. 'I called Paul Jones.'

'I know. But Paul called George Meek, and Meek called me. Now we have removed these entities that have been bothering you and your wife.'

'Yes, sir,' O'Neil replied.

Mandel was beginning to feel that he was over the hump. 'You feel clear now? You are all right now?'

A long pause followed. Then Mary Alice spoke. 'Bill is holding his stomach here.'

'Yes,' Mandel said. 'That's because they hurt it. Now, I am taking away that pain from his stomach. That pain will go away. I am holding his stomach, even though I am not there.'

There was the sound of Bill's breathing heavily on the line. 'Bill, just take your time,' Mandel urged him. 'You'll be all right.' After a pause, he added, 'Feeling better now?'

Suddenly, O'Neil's voice became serene. 'How about that,' he said.

'Just talk to me now,' Mandel said.

Bill still didn't have his bearings. 'Paul . . . oh my God.'

'What's the matter now, Bill?'

'My God, I am very tired.'

'Well, you are all right. You just had a terrible ordeal. Just calm down and talk to me now. You see your wife is all right, too, now.'

'I've never experienced this before,' Bill said.

'Well,' Mandel said with reassurance, 'Very few people do. And there are not many people in the world who can do what we are doing.'

A light touch broke the somber occasion. 'Can I blow my nose?' Bill asked.

'Sure,' Mandel said. 'Blow it all you want to.'

'Oh, thank God,' Bill said in apparent relief. 'Where is Paul Jones?'

'Well, Paul is not around. He can't do anything about this. George Meek called me, and I am taking over. I want you to listen to me closely. You are not bothered by anyone now?'

But suddenly, Bill began breathing heavily again. His voice became rasping. Then there was a hissing sound. 'Yessssss-sirrrrr!'

'No!' Mandel commanded. But the order had no effect. One of the entities appeared to be coming through again. 'I don't want no part of this,' it said.

'I'll take care of this,' Mandel said. 'We have an Indian guide who is doing this work, and he is taking all this over . . .'

The entity spoke again. 'She is a son of a bitch, you know that, don't you?'

In spite of the jumbled continuity, Mandel was not fazed, being well versed in the vagaries of this sort of possession scene. There was rarely any sustained continuity, with the apparent entities fading in and out as in a bad dream. This was no exception.

'Who are you talking about?'

There was another long pause. He could hear Mary Alice trying to talk to Bill in the background. But only the entity came through again: 'She is a whore!'

'Who is?' Mandel demanded. 'Who is?'

Mary Alice spoke into the phone. 'He is gone again.'

'I know,' Mandel said. 'There is another one in him.'

'It is Philip, I think,' Mary Alice said. 'His name is Philip.'

'All right,' Mandel commanded. 'We'll take that one out and –'

The voice that sounded like Philip spoke again. 'My God, I don't believe this. I don't believe this shit.'

Mandel remained unfazed. 'Now you want help, too? What's your name? What is it?'

But now the voice shifted back to that of Bill again. 'I'm tired. I'm so very tired.' But the tones changed back again quickly. 'My mother is a whore! You know that, don't you?'

'It's Philip again,' Mary Alice said. 'Yes, it's Philip.'

'His name is Philip?' Mandel asked.

'Yes,' Mary Alice answered.

Mandel addressed Philip. 'Philip, I want you to listen to me. I am Henry Mandel, and I have the power to put you into jail for a thousand years if you don't want to do as I tell you to do. Is that what you would like to do? Would you want to go to jail? Philip? Do you hear me talking to you? Well, Tall Oak is there and he is willing to take you to a place called progression where there is love. But you must leave Bill's body and his home. It is not for you. There is a better place for you.'

'I'm having fun,' the voice answered capriciously, then added an eerie chuckle.

'Yes, I know,' Mandel said. 'But you are going to go to jail, and you will not have fun there. Now which do you want? I have the power to put you there.' There was a pause, then: 'Philip, do you hear me?'

But Bill's rational voice answered instead. 'Oh, my God – Paul? Is this you, Paul?'

In the background, Mary Alice explained again that this was Henry Mandel. Bill responded on the phone.

'Henry Mandel?'

'Yes, I am here, Bill. I am here.'

'I called Paul Jones,' Bill repeated.

'I know you did,' Mandel said. 'But how do you feel now?'

'Oh, kind of tired,' Bill said. 'How the dickens did they get hold of you?'

'George Meek called me. You know George Meek.'

'Oh, yes,' Bill said. 'The gentleman from Florida.' He still seemed dazed. 'Well, I called Paul about my wife. Now how the dickens did he get hold of you?'

'He called George Meek, and George knows and understands that this is my work.'

But after this brief interval of quietness the heavy breathing started again, followed by more harsh mumbles.

'Bill! Tall Oak – remove that!' Mandel said sharply. 'All right. My hands are on you, Bill. Take him out, Tall Oak. Yank him out of there.'

Bill was mumbling again. 'I close my eyes. I don't see any . . .'

'I don't care whether you close your eyes or not.'

'Oh dear,' Mary Alice interrupted. 'He's crouched on the floor.'

Mandel spoke quickly. 'That's all right. He will get rid of it.' Then he addressed Mary Alice. 'Are you all right now?'

'Thank heavens,' Mary Alice said.

'Mary Alice,' Mandel instructed. 'I am going to put around you a new aura and new vibrations so they can't disturb you again. Now I am going to ask this in the name of Jesus of Nazareth. As I put my hands surrounding you, I am asking that blue and gold colors surround you in light. And I say that in the name of Jesus of Nazareth. And my hands are His and His are mine, as I am touching you now on the head. So be it.'

For a moment there was calm on the phone line, and it appeared that the long struggle was over. But the calm did not last long. 'Philip' returned, and Mandel repeated the same exorcism process again, until at last the ordeal was over.

Restored to normal, Bill did not seem to remember what had gone on. He finally brought things into focus when he was able to grasp that Mandel had called at Meek's urgent request. Bill was embarrassed and remorseful.

'Please forgive me,' he said.

'That's all right,' Mandel replied. 'You feel all right now?'

Bill sobbed quietly for a moment. 'Forgive me for crying. I can't help it.'

'You're not bothered by anybody now?'

'No,' Bill said. 'My wife had gone into a trance. That's why I called Paul Jones. And George.'

'I know. But then you were in a trance also.'

'Me? You're kidding. Are you sure?'

'Ask your wife. She will tell you.'

'My wife is a medium,' Bill explained. 'But she doesn't know it. Lorna, the little girl, came through, and I thought I had to call somebody.'

'Well,' Mandel said, 'we took Lorna and took her back to her mother. She is no longer bothering your wife.'

Bill answered in great relief, 'Thank God Lorna is gone.'

'Now – are you both all right? And can I say good night to you?'

'Yes, I think so,' Bill answered. 'I don't even know what's going on.'

'You don't have to, Bill. You will know about it later. But now I want to put a new aura on you . . .'

Mandel repeated the same process as he had done with Mary Alice earlier. Then he said good night.

'Thank you and God bless you,' Bill said, and they both hung up.

With the session over, Mandel called Meek on the phone to report the results. It was then almost dawn. He was happy that the long-distance informal exorcism appeared to be successful. He would furnish Meek with a copy of the tape, and hoped that the experience would fortify the O'Neils against any future problems. Meek and Mandel agreed that as highly sensitive mediums, it was likely that the O'Neils would encounter further apparitions, but under controlled circumstances at a higher level, and without the anomaly of possession.

* * *

When I reviewed the transcript of the long-distance telephone exorcism, I found it hard to believe. Later, when I listened to the actual tape of the session, I found it impossible not to believe. The voices were there, clear, strong and impassioned. It would have taken the most skilled actors of the Stanislavsky school of acting to create such a scene, if they could have created it at all. I had to remind myself that exorcism has a long history, and that *The Exorcist* was based on an actual documented case. Meek's warnings had been well taken before the episode. They would be even more important as the bizarre story continued to unfold.

* * *

The incident took place in early February, 1974. Meek reflected on the best way to handle the situation as far as the O'Neils were concerned. He finally decided to send them a copy of the tape so that they could understand better what had happened. He figured that the more the O'Neils knew about the phenomenon, the less chance there would be for such a terrifying experience ever to happen again. Such an intrusion by low level entities was the exact opposite of what he sought in trying to reach up for wisdom and enlightenment. It was also a setback for O'Neil who was reaching for the same thing.

Meek received a prompt letter from O'Neil thanking him for sending the tape, and noting how appalled he and Mary Alice were on listening to it. All through the ordeal, neither had been at all aware of what had been going on most of the time. Meek wrote back to reassure O'Neil that there was no need to feel ashamed, and that they had been unconscious victims. He suggested that it might be wise to refrain from psychic activities for a while, and to call on him for help at any time.

Throughout the rest of 1974, contact between Meek and O'Neil was sporadic. Occasionally, Bill would put his thoughts on tape, and send the cassette to Meek. But it was not until the latter part of the year that another series of episodes began to unfold. It was to baffle not only the psychically inexperienced O'Neil, but Meek and his associates as well, as they continued to work in the small Philadelphia lab on the quest for the hoped-for electronic breakthrough that still eluded them.

# CHAPTER 7

## *Healing Grace – 1975-76*

The unfolding of the mediumship of Bill O'Neil through the mid-'70s formed the whole history of psychic development in capsule form. Although it is theorized that everyone is in some way psychic, there seems to be a threshold where the true medium makes a quantum leap that goes far beyond the average person's awareness, intuition, and sensitivity. The result is hard to visualize, understand or explain.

These were the conditions the O'Neils faced in the early days of 1975. Bill O'Neil was going about his none-too-profitable electronics and service repair work, and conducting his own experiments. Things had calmed down since the traumatic night of the possession and exorcism, and O'Neil and his wife were getting ready to move from the trailer into a rented farmhouse that would provide more space for Bill's equipment. They hoped, in fact, to get an option to buy the property if all went well. It was an old white clapboard house that sat on a lonely winding road, up on a rise that overlooked a segment of the Allegheny valley. O'Neil welcomed the loneliness. He claimed it gave him time to think. A gnarled apple tree to the rear of the house, barely alive, appealed to O'Neil. The orchard it was in would provide enough shade for a place to meditate which he liked to do in the open, as close to nature as possible.

It wasn't long after the O'Neils moved into their new home, when the next in the series of shocks took place. O'Neil was in his new laboratory on the second floor of the house. He was taking a break from electronics, and relaxing with his guitar, putting together a folk tune. The musical and poetry ideas had been flowing freely over the past year or so, and Bill wondered if this might be a positive aspect of his newly developing capacities as a medium.

He had noted in some of the books he had been reading on psychic subjects that several mediums had been able to write voluminous books through automatic writing – where the hand moves almost swiftly across the page to write, completely independent of conscious thought. There was also the phenomenon of Rosemary Brown, the British widow who, with little knowledge of music, began composing more than 400 compositions in the style of Liszt, Beethoven, Chopin and other great composers without conscious use of her own mind. Highly praised by many music critics, some of her compositions were played by the London Symphony Orchestra with great acclaim. Her only explanation was that the composers appeared before her visually, as apparitions, guided her hands on the piano, and then dictated the compositions note by note.

O'Neil had not encountered any composers face to face, but he felt he was getting help with his music from beyond himself. What he did encounter late one night in January, 1975, however, was of a different order. He was sitting in his upstairs lab, a log fire burning in his fireplace, surrounded by a maze of wiring, stacks of pre-amps, generators and radio equipment, and a couple of ashtrays spilling over from his chain-smoking hours of the day. Next to him was a pot of coffee, which he chain-drank.

As he plotted a melody on his guitar, he happened to look beyond his work bench, towards a darkened corner of the room. At first he couldn't believe what was happening. A vague shape was beginning to form, but it was hard to tell what it was. With the memories of his recent sequence of traumatic events still fresh in his mind, he tried to deny what was happening. Finally, he was unable to do so.

Now he could clearly see the full, rounded form of the head and face of a man, along with his right shoulder and right arm. O'Neil was gripped in fear. All he could say was, 'My God, who are you?'

He was more than surprised when the figure answered, in fully audible speech.

'They call me Doc Nick,' he said. 'I was a ham radio operator, too. What are your call letters?'

Dumbfounded as he was, O'Neil gave them. 'They're N3AZQ,' he said, hardly realizing he had spoken. 'But who are you?'

'Used to be a doctor,' the figure said. His voice remained fully clear and audible to Bill, although his body was only partially materialized. 'And I just want to let you know that you can become a really rare and unusual healer.'

'I want to be that,' Bill replied. 'But who are you? Where did you come from?'

'We can be getting into that later,' the figure said. 'Meanwhile, I'm going to guide you along on a regular basis. Detailed suggestions. On a regular basis.'

Bill was trying to fight back panic, but he managed to keep himself calm. Even though he was stunned by the strange and unbelievable conversation with what he was sure was a partial apparition, he told himself that this must be another sign in his psychic development that he would have to deal with. Just as he was about to speak again, the mysterious Doc Nick disappeared as suddenly as he had appeared.

Bill assured himself that this was at least a benevolent form of encounter, one that might reinforce his desire to be able to help people through the healing work he had been determined to do before the unexpected visit. By the time he had calmed down, he found himself looking forward to a future visit from the strange entity, where he could do some further 'reality testing', and try to check the validity of his experience.

He recovered enough to tape record his recall of what had happened, and to wake and tell Mary Alice about the incident. They were both relieved that the visit had none of the ugly overtones of the night of the possession encounter, and prayed that if it happened again, it would remain benevolent. If the apparition were really in the nature of Arigo's 'Dr Fritz' or Eileen Garrett's 'Uvani' or Dr Mandel's 'Tall Oak', O'Neil felt some very strong good could come of it.

But then of course there was the problem of credibility. Who could possibly believe any of the phenomena that had been happening over the recent months? Some comfort came from the knowledge that mediums like those above had undergone similar experiences. However, a broad spectrum of the public had trouble believing them and the strange names of their purported spiritual guides, to say nothing of the whole concept of clairaudience, clairvoyance, apparitions, possession, and all the evidence of life continuing after death.

* * *

I tried to picture the stress O'Neil must have been under in this second major incident. In several interviews with mediums, I had attempted to figure out what made them tick. I had always ended up profoundly puzzled. Furthermore, they were usually puzzled themselves. Almost universally, mediums are alarmed and frightened when they encounter the first signs of psychic development. The worst is the fear of insanity.

The vivid encounters with clairaudience and clairvoyance, with precognition, with pictured scenes that form mentally and are confirmed by facts later – all create a sense of fear and isolation when they crop up spontaneously. Yet there is no evidence that developed and established mediums are in any way paranoid or schizophrenic, once they come to terms with the fact that they are psychic sensitives. Most often, they have no desire to be sensitive in this way, and simply resign themselves to accepting the inevitable. Most do not like it at first. Some fight against it. They make intense efforts to find out why they are endowed with such strange gifts, and many do not consider it a gift at all, but a frightening hindrance to living a normal life.

When, as a child, Eileen Garrett found herself communicating in both sound and image with her deceased aunt and uncle, she sought help desperately. As an adult, after years of overwhelming experiences of this sort, and others that in turn brought great help and guidance to hundreds of people, she became even more determined to get to the root of these strange surging powers that set her apart. They continued to nag and worry her. They were anything but cerebral. They came from her guts, her solar plexus, through her fingertips or the nape of the neck. She would see scenes in the lives of people she knew – her friends and associates read like a list from *Who's Who*, from George Bernard Shaw to James Joyce to Aldous Huxley to Carl Jung – as if they were projected on an inner screen in living color.

She submitted herself to studies and experiments with Dr J. B. Rhine at Duke University, with the noted Dr Alexis Carrel, with psychiatrists at Columbia, Johns Hopkins Medical School, Harvard, Oxford and Cambridge. She went through blood tests, electroencephalograms, electrocardiograms, personality, Faraday cage, and word association tests.

But the results were inconclusive. Scientists were simply not equipped to handle a phenomenon like this; it was beyond the scope of science, but no less real. Her authenticity was never challenged, but the capacity to define and measure the phenomenon was. What made the situation tolerable was that, like all accomplished mediums, she was able to gain full control over her mediumship, and turn it to constructive and creative use.

* * *

If Eileen Garrett, a cosmopolitan at home anywhere in the world, was baffled, Bill and Mary Alice O'Neil were even more so. They could only lean heavily on George Meek and Paul Jones, but were still isolated from them by many miles. In fact they had not met either personally, in spite of their voluminous correspondence. What the O'Neils had to do was convert their spontaneous psychic experiences into fully controlled ones involving the higher level entities that would be constructive and helpful. This sort of development was, of course, unpredictable. The conflict within the minds and emotions of an inexperienced medium who is forced to accept what is happening, and in many cases fighting against it, is difficult to picture.

The O'Neils felt comforted by the knowledge that they had George Meek to turn to so that they could protect their own sanity. Bill lost no time in sending the taped report of his new harrowing experience to Meek.

Meek was not surprised. There were too many cases of mediums encountering not one, but several sorts of guides. In fact, he would not be surprised if O'Neil ran into more incidents as he developed. Meek was relieved, however, that the so-called Doc Nick appeared to be benevolent and controlled. This was the most critical point, as revealed by the scores of case histories of mediums that Meek had reviewed.

Meek wrote on January 27, 1975, to reassure O'Neil, although he suggested that one development in a family should be enough and that Mary Alice should be discouraged from any further attempts to develop mediumship at this time. She might assist and support Bill in his healing, but that should be the limit. He also warned Bill that he should limit his efforts to produce automatic writing or automatic composing.

These phenomena, while often creative and capable of producing good works at times (one of the greatest literary figures of Brazil had produced over 20 highly acclaimed books through automatic writing), had at times resulted in the personality-takeover process of possession. Meek suggested that Bill gradually shut it off. He also reminded the O'Neils of the importance of prayer in engaging in any psychic activity. It was claimed by experienced researchers in the field that prayer would prevent the traumatic experience of possession, and would encourage entities of a higher level to make contact.

* * *

Meanwhile, Bill O'Neil continued to have sporadic contacts with the ephemeral Doc Nick. Sometimes, he would be fully audible and visible. At other times, Bill could only hear him speaking.

But the visits of the doctor continued to be constructive and instructive. Although Bill frequently called Mary Alice into the laboratory, she was unable to see or hear the elusive doctor, except for a fleeting moment on one occasion. It seemed that Doc Nick was giving Bill a complete course in holistic healing, including instructions for 'the laying on of hands' and possible electronic devices that he should design for the treatment of arthritis, leukemia and a wide range of disorders. Bill felt some of the suggestions amounted to nothing more than 'ritualistic hogwash', but he was willing to give them a try.

One obvious target for healing was the six year-old daughter of a neighbor, named Tracy Stover. She was receiving full medical treatment for leukemia, but the prognosis was not good. Her doctor had to tell the family that her life expectancy was three more years at the most, or shorter if she did not respond to treatment. Bill was deeply grieved by her condition, but didn't feel that he could intrude on the case and was not certain as to how to treat it anyway. He knew only that it would be a form of mental healing. Doc Nick was not always specific, and he used complicated medical terms that were difficult for Bill to understand.

One night in April, 1975, Bill was in his laboratory on the second floor of his farmhouse, pondering what steps he should take in the face of the bewildering series of circumstances that had been developing over the past several months. He did not want to attempt to help little Tracy unless he was asked by her parents. He decided to wait until the moment seemed right, and went on to reflect on his current circumstances.

Whatever this impulse was to attempt to heal others, he felt, it was a mixed blessing. His big fear was the fear of ridicule. These strange appearances of Doc Nick were intriguing, but if he ever told anyone about them, ridicule was all he could expect. He was grateful for George Meek to confide in, in spite of the fact that he had to depend on correspondence to do so. Meek could at least understand his concern for his own sanity.

To his despair on this April night, he suddenly saw that another shape was forming in a shadowy corner of the lab. It was another figure, and it was not Doc Nick. It appeared to be a crusty gentleman of uncertain age, just as insubstantial as the form of Doc Nick, but just as audible when he spoke.

'I want to assure you, William,' the figure said, 'that your concern about death is unfounded.'

Dreading the appearance of another materialized form, O'Neil said: 'You've got to explain this to me. Who are you?'

'My name is William Kincaid,' the figure said. 'I am willing to help you, and understand your concern.'

Bill felt his only hope for his own sanity was to establish who the figure was. Perhaps, he hoped, he could document facts and locations, and later track them down to prove the man had actually lived and was not a figment of his imagination. 'You say your name is Kincaid,' Bill spoke. 'If so, give me some facts about your life. Where are you from? What did you do when you were alive?'

'I am from Natchez, Mississippi. I once worked for a food and grain store there. You can verify that if you wish. But what I am here for is to assure you that there is no such thing as death.'

'I am coming round to believe that,' Bill answered. 'But you've got to give me more specifics.'

'That will come later,' the purported figure of Kincaid said. 'But I want you to realize that death is just a word spoken by the ignorant to describe that part of existence that is on a different plane. Remember that. There simply is no such thing as death.'

Bill became more curious. 'If there is not, and I don't disbelieve you, what is it?'

'Fear and ignorance about this transition from here to there,' Kincaid answered, 'is the one fact standing in the way of your knowledge and understanding of all things. On the present level and all other planes of your existence.'

Bill nodded. Then he said, 'What more can you tell me about this transition?'

The figure didn't answer right away. There was a long pause.

'Can you tell me?' O'Neil repeated.

The pause continued, then the figure said, 'I am thinking.'

For O'Neil, this was a baffling reply. How could a figure on another plane of existence have to take time to think? Didn't he have greater comprehension so that he didn't have to pause, as humans had to do?

But O'Neil didn't get an answer. The figure seemed to melt away in front of his eyes. Again, Bill was dumbfounded. Completely unnerved, he went to his battered typewriter to write Meek a letter recounting what had happened.

* * *

In Fort Myers, Meek received O'Neil's letter on April 24. With his in-depth knowledge of the development of a medium, Meek was again not surprised. Every one, from Edgar Cayce to Jane Roberts and her experiences with the 'Seth papers', reported the appearance of a series of different apparitions, often in long sequences. What Meek was pleased about was that the quality of the apparition was improving. Kincaid was apparently on a much higher level than the low-caste entities that had invaded the O'Neil home during the Mandel episode.

O'Neil's letter reflected his intense desire to try to nail down the identity of this strange visitor. Only in this way could he assure himself of his sanity. Meek made a mental note that he would try to trace back such a possible person who had once lived in Natchez, and then sent O'Neil a long letter to reassure him that his psychic development was improving, and he was not to worry about this new visitor, or Doc Nick. Both appeared to be trying to help Bill in his understanding of death as a transition rather than a termination of consciousness.

He also urged O'Neil to try to help the Kincaid entity to move on to higher spiritual development, and to discontinue his earth-bound activity. Meek was anxious to get across to O'Neil the essentials of what he considered to be the documented evidence of what took place after the transition called death. He reminded O'Neil that he was certain that the sole purpose of existence was the spiritual evolution of each individual. Bill could help Kincaid by convincing him of this. At the same time, Bill must guard against slipping into a possession situation again. He concluded his letter to O'Neil:

> If there is ever the slightest doubt as to the correctness of a course of action which you think is generally okay, be certain to sit down with Mary Alice and (1) Discuss it aloud fully and (2) Sleep on it for one or two days and discuss it again.
>
> You are both extremely sensitive, you are both mediums. Moreover, and this is something very rare – you are both materializing mediums. Hence you have to be absolutely resolute

in making certain that you do not allow anyone – I repeat *anyone* – to take over your minds and bodies.

Remember you are not 'crazy'. You have achieved a level of attunement with the cosmos that is possible for very few human beings. In the centuries ahead this will become very common. Now it is rare and anyone who stumbles into this condition naturally thinks he is ready for the nut house.

By constantly attuning to the Master Nazarene, you can be certain your house is built on solid ground. William Kincaid or anyone else can well turn out to be shifting sand . . .

Regardless of whether Meek's theories and convictions about life after death were correct, they were of immense help to the O'Neils in their continuing puzzlement. What Meek had said in his letter was a condensation of the consensus of paranormal studies over the years, drawing on the best sources. Although Kincaid became a very rare visitor, the ubiquitous Doc Nick did not. Because of this, Meek sent O'Neil a medical dictionary so that he could make a strong effort to find out what the ephemeral doctor was talking about.

* * *

The subject of holistic healing is so complicated, it would take a series of text books to cover it. It has been slowly gaining in acceptance by the medical profession, although cautiously. Even more confusing is the variety of ways it is practiced. At its best, it does not conflict with the brilliant accomplishments of modern medicine. Instead, it serves as an adjunct to it. In 1973, an article in *Medical Economics* began:

> A scientific basis for spiritual therapy has not been found, but more and more physicians are becoming interested in the healing touch of a woman credited with cures in hopeless cases.

The article was about the noted healer from Baltimore, Olga Warrall, who had gained respect over many years for her healing work. She used varied techniques, from the 'laying on of hands' to prayer to absent healing sessions. Her track record has been documented, and is excellent. She finally began working with the Johns Hopkins Medical School, in conjunction with conventional treatments there and with marked success. Because she urged co-operation with doctors, and used her healing work as a supplement, she has the full co-operation of the staff.

Among the theories of the effectiveness of 'laying on of hands' by responsible healers is a suggestion that undefined energy forces emanate from the hands to bring a direct physical effect to the cells of the patient being treated. This is not as fanciful as it seems. Kirlian photographs have shown energy streaming from a healer's finger tips, and at the end of the session, the energy has faded from the healer, and has been transplanted to the patient. Words and suggestions are employed, which have shown documented results, especially in improving the patient's attitude. Hypnosis is sometimes utilized with success and, for many, prayer is considered indispensable.

Cancer and leukemia patients have not only been treated successfully by these methods, but by a whole new approach on the part of the medical world through treating the body with the co-operation of the mind. Dr Carl Simonton, the California radiation therapist, utilizes three meditation periods a day for his patients, where they are encouraged to tune into the cancerous areas by visualization to see the white blood cells destroyed by the concurrent radiation treatment he is rendering. Statistically, the results with his patients are impressive. Contrary to general belief, much of the holistic healing process is mental healing rather than faith healing. Many procedures require no faith at all, although healers like Olga Warrall employ it.

* * *

Bill O'Neil was as confused about the subject as he was about his unexpected mediumistic development. He was employing bits and pieces of all the techniques, depending on his inner conviction that he could and must heal. This sort of compulsive drive was typical of many healers who were never able to explain their motives rationally. Money was rarely an object for any of them, even if they made modest charges simply to stay alive. In O'Neil's case, he needed money desperately in the face of little work and no steady income. But Mary Alice agreed with him that any such charges would defeat the purpose of his objectives.

Meek, interested in O'Neil's electronics interests for his psychic research, found this attitude a stumbling block when he wanted to provide some modest funds for equipment for O'Neil's lab. O'Neil balked at the idea, even though the electronics research would require a few days of labor each month. When O'Neil resisted taking any fee because it might be considered as payment for his holistic healing work, Meek finally persuaded him, on the agreement that what little he did send was for electronics equipment, and not for any part of his healing activity.

In addition to holistic healing, Meek and O'Neil were still seeking the same objective: to eliminate the medium as a 'middleman' and replace this channel by direct electronic communication with higher planes of existence. They agreed that audio communication was the first to strive for, with video contact, a much more ambitious enterprise, a possible future goal. Although Meek had achieved some impressive results with infrared photography, capturing strange forms that were not visible to the naked eye, the long term goal of video communication was still a long way away.

What was emerging was a picture that revealed O'Neil as stubborn as Meek when it came to whatever goal either was seeking. Although O'Neil refused ever to take money for healing, he was not without his dreams. He hoped that some day his music or poetry or artwork or inventions would bring him in enough money to be financially independent, even though the results to date showed no such promise. Many of these dreams were unrealistic: it was questionable whether his art, poetry or music could break through the tough realities of the commercial world, where selling material was much more difficult than creating it. In music, you had to be in the right place at the right time. With poetry, a robust market was almost non-existent. With art and sculpture, success only came with the combination of concentrated exclusive dedication and talent, and with enormous good luck. The same with inventions. The problem was that O'Neil was dividing his energies and spreading them over such a wide and diverse spectrum that his chances diminished with each new enterprise. In addition to that he was paying scant attention to the practical service and repair work that kept him alive.

In spite of this and his incurable idealism, Mary Alice remained devoted to him, putting up with mercurial shifts of mood, and supporting him in his desire to work in so many different and disparate areas.

* * *

Strangely enough, Meek and O'Neil did not meet in person until August, 1975. But their voluminous correspondence had actually created a stronger bond than if they had worked together face to face. In spite of their hyperbole, O'Neil's letters were articulate and often profound. They belied his lack of formal schooling. Meek's letters were analytic and painstaking, constantly taking measure of O'Neil's problems and the vast complexities of the paranormal. Both were idealistic and sometimes over-sentimental when their enthusiasms ran away with them.

O'Neil had actually forgotten that Meek was coming to see him, and was working in his garden when Meek drove into the driveway. Since O'Neil had moved to the remote farmhouse because he wanted privacy, he was at first annoyed that a visitor was arriving. Meek stepped out of his car, the impeccably dressed business executive, a sharp contrast to the coarse-grained homespun surface of O'Neil.

When Meek introduced himself, O'Neil welcomed him cordially, and since Mary Alice was not at home, the two went to the upstairs lab, where Bill's scattered equipment smothered the room. It was obvious to Meek that the house was shabby and critically in need of repair. He wondered how the O'Neils kept warm in winter, with only two fireplaces to supplement a stove and some oil space heaters. O'Neil's passion for electronics was evident from the amount of equipment that was scattered throughout the crowded laboratory.

Meek filled O'Neil in on the work in the Philadelphia lab. He also filled him in on the details of the Mark I equipment, and the higher wave lengths of over 1,000 MHz they were using with Mark II. Working with a new gifted medium, Sarah Gran, they were receiving many instructions from the discarnate Professor Swann, but still had no direct voice impingement coming through the speakers, to say nothing of the direct electronic dialogue they had hoped for.

O'Neil had several ideas to contribute, and outlined to Meek ways in which he thought he could improve on the equipment which might possibly lead to a breakthrough. Meek felt the desire to offer further financial help to O'Neil for the exploratory work he was doing on behalf of the Metascience group, but he realized that, in doing so, he would have to be careful not to offend O'Neil's mulish and stiff-necked pride. He held back any suggestion at this time.

Although the meeting was mainly technical, Meek felt that they had come to a better understanding of each other, and that somehow O'Neil's mercurial genius would lead to significant progress to supplement the Philadelphia experiments.

* * *

In early December, 1975, Sarah Stover, the mother of little Tracy who was suffering from leukemia, stopped by the O'Neil house to see if he would check a faulty TV tube in the Stover set. The news she brought about Tracy was not good. She had been going downhill from the time the O'Neils first heard about her case earlier in the year. Mrs Stover had never requested any healing help from Bill before, but the situation had now become so serious that she felt she had to.

O'Neil was still wary of becoming involved with such a serious advanced case. Not only had the six-year-old had leukemia since birth, but she was receiving blood transfusions and medication on a regular basis. On seeing the child in her house, Bill decided to drop his caution. At least, he felt, he was not interfering with her medical treatment in any way. His work would only be a supplement, although he was not sure whether he could get into trouble in the face of the general attitude of the medical establishment.

With words, prayer and the laying on of hands, O'Neil worked with her parents on treating Tracy almost every day during December, until the day she was due at the clinic for her periodic check-up. O'Neil felt convinced that something was happening as the process went on, although he had no idea how, or if it actually was. He was also afraid that, if by some miracle the evidence of a cure was found, he would somehow be in violation of the law for carrying out the treatment. He asked Mrs Stover not to mention the fact that he had been involved, even if it turned out to be effective.

Tracy arrived at the clinic on schedule for her examination and check-up on Monday, December 15. The Stovers did not have to wait long for the results. The white cell count was completely reversed. Other tests indicated that there was no need for a blood transfusion, and there were no other signs of the disease. The doctor and the technicians at the clinic could not believe what they were finding. They assumed the tests were in error, and immediately set up a complete schedule of further tests. When pressed by the doctors as to what routine Tracy had followed over the previous month, Mrs

Stover kept her word to O'Neil, and merely told them that a group from her church had been praying for her and Tracy, and that by some miracle that might have helped. On December 29, the whole battery of tests was repeated. A cure was confirmed, and further transfusions were cancelled. Although the doctor felt the cure was complete, he scheduled another check-up a month later. The results were again confirmed.

The Stovers were elated and, nearly a decade later, in 1984, Tracy was robust and healthy, at the age of 15. At the time of the healing in 1975, they were delighted, but frustrated that they could not openly show their appreciation to O'Neil, who would accept no money or gift, and would not permit them to reveal what he had done. The Stovers, however, not only brought O'Neil firewood, but went privately to their attorney the following year, and swore out an affidavit that chronicled the entire case history. It read:

HENRY GRAFF
Attorney
Terminal Bldg
Bradford, PA

COMMONWEALTH OF PENNSYLVANIA SS }
COUNTY OF McKEAN " }

MARK STOVER and SARAH STOVER of RD No. 1, Adrian, PA 16210, parents of TRACY STOVER, being duly sworn according to law, depose and say as follows:

1. Our daughter, Tracy Stover, is six (6) years of age.
2. That she was diagnosed as having leukemia.
3. The prognosis was that her illness was a terminal one and that her life expectancy could be determined at approximately nine (9) years of age but could be shortened at any time, depending upon her response to treatment.
4. We solicited the services of William J. O'Neil, RD No. 1, Adrian, Pennsylvania, for the purpose of obtaining a psychic healing for our daughter, Tracy.
5. Mr O'Neil visited our home daily from December 7, 1975, to December 28, 1975.
6. On December 29, 1975, she was examined by her attending physician and, after a complete physical examination, includ-

ing blood tests, was diagnosed as cured and no longer requiring blood transfusions or any medication whatsoever.

7. The said William J. O'Neil did not ask for any fee or payment of any kind in return for the attention he paid our daughter, nor was there any promise of any fees to be paid in the future.

8. The said William J. O'Neil did not administer any medication whatsoever or perform any ritualistic services during any of his visits to our home.

9. We are not cognizant of psychic healing or its ramifications.

10. We know that our daughter was diagnosed as being afflicted with leukemia at birth and that she was subsequently diagnosed as cured on December 29, 1975.

11. We are grateful for the interest shown by William J. O'Neil in our daughter, Tracy, and would not agree to ever bringing any action, of any kind, against him for the services and attention we sought from him.

(Signed) *Theodore M. Stover*
(Signed) *Sarah R. Stover*

Sworn to and subscribed before me
this 19th day of January, 1976.

*Sydney F. Toy*
Notary Public

My commission expires June 21, 1977.

O'Neil was grateful for the affidavit for more than one reason. First, he felt it showed that a major healing had actually taken place, confirmed by medical testing. Second, it forestalled the possibility of his being accused of ritualistic hocus pocus and of interference with the doctor's medical treatment. The affidavit also impressed Meek. In spite of O'Neil's volatile unpredictability, Meek had great faith in him in both the electronic and healing areas. As Meek wrote to him: 'In my opinion you are working on a subject of untold potential value to future generations.'

# CHAPTER 8

## *More Strange Encounters – 1976-77*

Because the progress was slow in trying to reach the electronic breakthrough, Meek determined to learn more about the EVP experiments continuing abroad. He was still not satisfied with the monosyllabic phrases of EVP, even though thousands of messages had been recorded by the European researchers. But perhaps there were clues he had missed. In December, 1975, at about the time that Tracy Stover's healing was being confirmed, he took off for Germany, Sweden and England to compare his developments with the research there.

Although Konstantin Raudive, of Germany, was considered the father of EVP, he was no longer living. Meek's chief target was Friedrich Jürgenson who was now considered the leading exponent of EVP. He was greeted by Jürgenson in his home at Höör, Sweden, a tall, energetic man in his 60s, with a shock of graying hair and pleasing, aimiable features. Jürgenson had been born in Russia and migrated to Sweden, where his painting, singing and documentary film producing had brought him considerable acclaim. Two of his films had received awards at the Cannes Film Festival, and his painting skills had brought him commissions from the Vatican to render three different portraits of the Pope in 1969 at his summer residence, Castel Gandolfo.

Meek took an instant liking to Jürgenson's warm-hearted and compassionate demeanor. He welcomed Meek cordially, explaining that he was not a scientist, but had devoted most of his recent years to probing these disembodied voices that were most baffling.

'You have to have great dedication for this work,' he said. 'And there are four basic requirements. First, you must have time – plenty of it. Second, you must have patience – an incredible amount of it. Third, you must have money, money to assemble equipment, discard what doesn't work, and buy more to replace it.'

'I've been experiencing the same thing,' Meek agreed.

'But,' Jürgenson added, 'the most important thing of all is the willingness to take ridicule and slander.'

With this, Meek was in total agreement.

Meek found that Jürgenson's dedication to the EVP puzzle was intense. Like Meek, he felt that an electronic voice bridge would solve the puzzle of death for the first time in history. Jürgenson had succeeded in recording hundreds of voices on tape that clearly stated they were 'the dead ones', and brought enough direct personal information to rule out completely the theory that they were stray radio voices. When the message was for Jürgenson, he was clearly addressed by name. When others were present, their names, too, were mentioned. He had also recorded question-and-answer responses, although the answers came after long delays, and were short and fragmentary. Predictions were recorded that turned out to be accurate. These were strictly personal messages of advice, and hints of where to find important lost documents or valuables that turned out to be correct. But no clear, lengthy dialogue had been established on the tapes.

Jürgenson knew three successive Popes personally, Pius XII, John XXIII, and Paul VI. They indicated that they were interested in EVP, and asked him about it many times, in addition to listening to some of the recordings. But the exact reaction of the Catholic Church was muddy. There was difference of opinion all through the hierarchy. One bishop reported that 'my reaction would be as if I was making a rather badly connected transatlantic telephone call, and I could not quite make out what the voice was'. Another bishop told Peter Bander, a British publisher who had brought out Raudive's book *Breakthrough*: 'I am definitely impressed and willing to be impressed by this phenomenon. The point is made by the author that this is an additional proof of life after death . . . I welcome the book for this reason alone.'

Meek was impressed with Jürgenson's 16 years' worth of experiments, but was inclined to agree with the bishop who felt the recordings were too much like a badly connected transatlantic call. His research trip was, he felt, ultimately a failure, although he agreed that the state of the art of EVP at the time was persuasive in showing definite evidence of life after death. But it was not, Meek thought, sufficient to impress a wide general public. Most important, he found no evidence in the voices that indicated that high quality discarnate researchers were attempting to provide technical information to bridge the gap between the two worlds. He wrote in a summary of his trip: 'At this time it would appear likely that some of the voices come from disembodied spirits, some from the consciousness of persons still alive . . . While some of the recordings can be quite properly explained as imagination, hallucination and radio interference effects, there remains a vast body of voices that cannot be explained by any of these.'

Meek's report went on: 'The quality of the reception is not such that the world at large would develop any conviction of life after death from listening to them . . . Personally I am inclined to believe that Jürgenson may well be correct in maintaining that conviction on a substantial scale will come only when and if it is possible to have a video image of the communicator.'

This video image was, of course, Meek's ultimate goal, but it seemed a long way off. 'I feel I do not have a lot to show for a considerable expenditure of cash and a month of work,' he wrote to Paul Jones. 'But as a little sign says on my cabinet, "To get somewhere, you must follow many paths which lead to nowhere."'

* * *

All through the year 1976, O'Neil was barely eking out a living with his radio and TV service work. Much of the reason for this appeared to be his lack of attention to practical matters and his continuing pursuit of ephemeral dreams. He was scattering a lot of energy on rather exotic stuff, some of it on the continued prodding of the mysterious Doc Nick who was still showing up in audible and sometimes visible form. He apparently gave O'Neil strong approval after the successful report on Tracy Stover.

In between periods of alternating conviction and doubt, O'Neil translated what he felt were audible instructions from Doc Nick into recommendations that embraced folk medicine in the style of Edgar Cayce. For a patient with a foot problem, he recommended: 'Secure bay leaves, fresh if possible. Not ground, not the powder used in spicing, but whole bay leaves. If you can't get them fresh, then use the whole dried bay leaves which I understand can be secured from a pharmacist. Boil these leaves violently until the water is very dark. Add more water and bring up to a heat where it is hot, but not too hot to soak the foot comfortably . . .'

In contrast to the folksy tone of these instructions were those O'Neil suggested to Meek for the experiments with Professor Swann: 'Voltage amplitudes obtained with my own limited equipment and facilities ranged from 10 to 80 microvolts RMS. DC voltages are specified as those necessary to fire solid state circuitry of audio oscillator and switching relay . . . In lieu of a millivoltmeter during experimentation I would suggest a microvoltmeter instead – for a more accurate monitoring network . . .'

The contrast between O'Neil's homespun and technical material was striking, but the upshot was that neither of the two styles of information was worth anything unless palpable results followed that could be thoroughly tested. Further, the whole exploration was so bizarre that more than ordinary confirmation would be required to establish any sort of credibility. The problem was especially severe with holistic healing. There was evidence that it worked effectively in many instances, but the results were hard to pin down even in the face of so much evidence. On the other hand, it was worth trying, but *only* after the point where medical science had done everything possible. The Tracy Stover case was strong evidence – yet it could be said that the results were merely a spontaneous remission, with no direct proof that the healing had done the job.

There were further problems when the purported Doc Nick came through with directions that stepped on actual medical practices. According to O'Neil, Doc Nick had pressed for the use of iron oxide, orally or by injection, for the treatment of cancer. A daily intake of small amounts was specified. Any such research was obviously a job for professional pharmaceutical laboratories, and Meek was quick to remind O'Neil that no experimentation of this sort was permissible. The folk medicine of topical application of bay leaves, or the suggestion of raw honey and vinegar, was one thing. Going beyond that was another. In addition, Meek had found occasion to believe through his research that it was the healer-medium himself who actually did the healing; any physical device employed was probably a placebo, although often a dramatically effective one.

Although Meek appreciated O'Neil's desire to carry out his healing efforts, they were still off the major track of breaking through the communication barrier. Joining with an electronics expert named Will Cerney, Meek had now set up an additional laboratory in Fort Myers, to carry on concurrent experiments with the Philadelphia lab and O'Neil's work in western Pennsylvania. O'Neil was now showing strong evidence that he was as passionately dedicated as Meek to the cause. He wrote to Meek on July 27 that he continued to be uninterested in any monetary rewards or fame, stating, 'My only desire is that I be kept free of any publicity or personal or monetary recognition in order that I remain unhampered to carry on any additional research, both in the area of electronics and availability of being used as an instrument of healing activities.' He added that he was ready to push for trying to develop the possible visual contact through television channels while he continued to carry out the voice experiments.

O'Neil also kept sending periodic reports on the frequent visits of the persistent Doc Nick. Some of them were on tape, and Meek reminded him they were too rambling and urged him to write more disciplined letters. By now, O'Neil had become so used to the visits that he hardly gave them a second thought. He was no longer shocked or disturbed by the phenomenon, and claimed he was getting precise technical information on a regular basis. He continued to see the full visual form of Doc Nick, but more often he communicated by conversation only, which O'Neil claimed was heard in his inner ear. O'Neil took copious notes that he frequently sent off to Meek for perusal. On one occasion in the early fall of 1976, O'Neil wrote down some verbatim philosophical observations from the elusive Doc Nick:

'Spontaneous materializations are more likely to occur between those who are incarnate and discarnate, when brought about by a common love for one another, e.g., husband and wife, mother and child, etc. This is not to say such communication can not be accomplished if approached in a sincere, prayerful and loving manner, unlike the fraud perpetrated by 90 per cent of all so-called mediums. Genuine spirit communication can and will be accomplished when science and religion eliminate the mystery that has involved the subject for thousands of years. Emphasis must be placed on the reality of natural, rather than unnatural, aspects of the multiple planes or dimensions of existence . . .'

* * *

As I continued poring through the voluminous Meek/O'Neil papers, I was amazed at the wealth of observations O'Neil had written and recorded, and at the meticulous detail in Meek's responses. Meek had presented me with a dossier of over 500 documents, each carefully indexed and arranged in chronological order. Because of this the strange story unfolded to me like a bizarre novel. It was hard to stop reading them, wondering what was going to happen next.

Many questions came up in my mind. Did O'Neil really hear this figure of Doc Nick uttering rather profound observations on life, death, and the hereafter? Were they merely projections of his imagination? What were these 'multiple planes and dimensions of existence' that the alleged Doc Nick talked about?

To accept O'Neil's report of these encounters in the darkened loneliness of his lab strained credulity to the breaking point. Acceptance required a belief in communication with a discarnate personality which few people are able to accept. I had the same trouble in spite of the research I had done for other books. Even researchers in the paranormal find this process difficult to visualize, although the record books are full of such reports from credible people. I remember an Air Force officer commenting to me about the UFO phenomenon. 'Credible people are seeing incredible things,' he said. This seemed to be a general rule about anything that had to do with the paranormal. Yet the subject of life after death, and all its supporting phenomena, were too important to ignore, and too challenging not to examine.

Only recently has the Pentagon reluctantly leaked the fact that up to $6 million a year has been spent on psychic research that included the use of psychic mediums for research on the placement of MX missiles, and the employment of psychics to determine the position of Soviet submarines. The Navy, for instance, is reported to have employed some 34 psychics, according to the *New York Times*. The CIA is reported in the same article to have consulted a leading parapsychologist to try to determine if psychics could jam computer systems by psychokinesis. Providing the ignition for such activity is the fear that the Soviets are far ahead of the United States in such research. Many feel they are.

In O'Neil's case, there is some evidence that he had been or is in touch with Army Intelligence, although he will not discuss this point. The Doc Nick encounters apparently involved only the philosophical and technical detail as far as healing or the Spiricom developments were concerned.

Although Meek's long study of the paranormal enabled him to accept the apparent two-way traffic between O'Neil and his visitor, he was aware of the resistance of the layman even to consider the concept. Because Meek had found that the presence of a clairaudient and clairvoyant spirit guide was an integral part of nearly every trance medium he had studied, he was sanguine about the probability that O'Neil was reporting the facts. But it was imperative to Meek that his eventual goal of two-way communication, that could be heard aloud by anyone and recorded on audio and/or video tape, be accomplished. In the meantime, he had little trouble accepting the reports from O'Neil about Doc Nick as a forerunner to the time when such conversation could be directly captured and registered on tape for all to hear.

Although neither O'Neil nor Meek was active in any formal religion, they considered that their research was closely linked to God and the Universe. They utilized that belief in guiding their efforts, as well as in screening out the lower level of what they referred to as earth-bound entities. In fact, O'Neil wrote in the fall of 1976, on receiving a book from Meek called *Ghosts in Solid Form*, that he was gaining confidence that he was not hallucinating, and added: 'I'm finding prayer more and more important as a part of my own daily activities. I honestly don't think I could get through the day without an early morning walk in the orchard, and a prayer for continuing strength, physically, mentally, spiritually and emotionally . . .'

* * *

O'Neil faced the beginning of 1977 in a mood of confidence and elation. His prayers seemed to have been answered, in that his job with the electronic repair company was burgeoning. Several reports from his healing work indicated that the results were beyond expectation. One involved the family of a professor from Johns Hopkins, who wanted to fly both the O'Neils to Baltimore for a weekend to help a friend there and another in Washington. The American scientist Itzhak Bentov, author of *Stalking the Wild Pendulum*, referred several cases to O'Neil with excellent results. Sarah Gran also reported recovery from a chronic ailment that had failed to respond to medical treatment. O'Neil continued to turn down any payment, although several large checks were offered to him. Acceptance, he explained, would be sacrilegious.

Bill's routine was not a common one. He worked in his lab much of the night, and slept much of the day. His early morning walks in the orchard were taken before he went to bed, not when he woke up late in the afternoon. He split and hauled wood not for exercise but out of necessity. The two fireplaces and one stove in the old house were hungry for wood in the January bitterness, and O'Neil was kept busy feeding them in temperatures hovering near zero much of the time. In writing to Meek about the bustle of activity he was engaged in, he said: 'The volume of repair work is increasing, and hopefully I can keep up with the demands on my time, while at the same time not neglecting our other activities and research. Busy, busy, busy, and I love every minute of it!'

But in the face of his optimism and jubilance, there were serious problems shaping up that would remove the lustre from his expectations rather abruptly. In the middle of January he was informed that his employer was going out of business. Because of the scant attention O'Neil paid to practical matters, a considerable number of debts had piled up which were about to threaten not only his work but the little property he had: an odd mixture of unsaleable electronic equipment, two cars that were alternately inoperable, and the house that required half a cord of wood a day cut from O'Neil's own efforts. O'Neil was going to have to lean heavily on his prayers, and they would be sorely put to the test.

* * *

As 1977 began, Meek was seeking a delicate balance in the face of O'Neil's unwieldy dreams that spun around his sporadically brilliant genius. He urged and cajoled O'Neil to re-establish his day-to-day electronic repair work, and carefully budget his spare time to continue the research to which they were both dedicated.

The same impractical side of O'Neil was evident in regard to the magnetized iron oxide exploration that Doc Nick had presented for the treatment of cancer. Although Meek believed that this sort of suggestion from a 'spirit guide' should be explored, he did not feel that it should be accepted uncritically, as O'Neil had a tendency to do. In fact, O'Neil proposed testing the chemical on himself, which brought a sharp reprimand from Meek:

> I feel very strongly that you should not take material of this type into your body. There is absolutely no way of telling the extent to which there will be a gradual retention of the particles at some

> critical spot . . . You are up to the point where the next phase must be carried on in laboratories with suitable animals for detailed testing . . .

Meek, however, was steering a middle course. He was disenchanted with the painfully slow pace of the medical establishment in cancer research, but at the same time wary of charlatans and frauds. What he was hoping to do was to bridge the gap between the conventional and the exotic – as long as the latter was disciplined and controlled in the process.

Modern medical research is often afraid to reach out into unexplored territory. It often has disdain for re-examining many of the medical traditions that appear irrational, yet have produced confirmed results. The primitive witch doctor or medicine man, for all his wild gyrations and mysterious herbs, exercised some highly effective techniques that were discarded by conventional science only because they were surrounded by such a large envelope of superstition and unsavory black magic rituals. Yet the great modern tranquilizers such as reserpine (sold under many trade names) long lay dormant in modern pharmacology. The Indian snakeroot plant from which reserpine derives, known as *Rauwolfia serpentina*, has been used in India and Nigeria for centuries. Curare, one of the most effective adjuncts in modern anesthesia, is a resinous poison derived from several varieties of tropical plants. This had been used by Brazilian Indians as poison on the tips of their arrows. Scientists at the University of Ibadan in Nigeria have recently crystallized a herb concoction that seems to have an amazing capacity to bring about remission in malignant tumors in test animals. Initial tests have shown it to bring 100 per cent remission of such tumors in laboratory mice. Only recently has acupuncture been taken seriously by science.

The Brazilian doctors at the Hospital das Clinicas in São Paulo – some of them trained at the best medical schools in the United States – who meet regularly to consult mediums, believe fully that the mediums draw on the skills and knowledge of doctors no longer living to bring them diagnostic and treatment information they could get nowhere else.

Meek's complete knowledge of all this made it possible for him to believe in the potential value of O'Neil's persistent advisor, Doc Nick – as long as what he suggested could be thoroughly checked out. Meanwhile, he was continuing his explorations in the labs of Fort

Myers and Philadelphia, hoping to get the help he needed from the *soi-disant* voice of Professor Swann, still coming through the medium Sarah Gran in regular sessions. The tapes of each session were carefully transcribed and studied meticulously for technical clues that would point toward a breakthrough.

O'Neil, however, was unable to record the voice of Doc Nick, and could only pass along the information he received clairaudiently. Meek now realized that a tape recorder would be useful in this case, and encouraged O'Neil to use one at the time Doc Nick came through, repeating aloud the information he heard clairaudiently, and also recording his own questions. O'Neil willingly complied. He transcribed reconstructions of some of his sessions that appeared to be the rambling sort of conversations of his ham radio days. Much of the discussion was discursive, much of it on the technical electronic side, and some of it an attempt on O'Neil's part to find out what the dimension Doc Nick experienced was like.

On one chilly night in February, 1977, the solid image of Doc Nick appeared in one of his frequent visits. By this time, O'Neil was almost blasé about these occurrences. He turned on his tape recorder to send a report to Meek, with his own questions on the tape. In turn he reconstructed on the tape what he heard Doc Nick saying.

'Hold it a minute,' O'Neil said as the session started. 'This is something that I have been wanting to ask you. Somehow or other we get off on an electronic kick when you are here and I forget to ask about this. What's it like over there? Are there trees and mountains, and music and animals, and vehicles and all the things we have here, on what you call "there"? I'd feel a lot better about this whole thing if you would tell me about the place there.'

After a pause, O'Neil's voice began repeating what he heard. He spoke slowly, as if he were repeating what he heard on the other side of a telephone conversation.

'George,' O'Neil said, addressing Meek on the tape. 'He's saying: "For now, Bill, let's just say it's pretty much the same as where you are. But much, much more, too. But since you can't believe completely what's happening, even at this very moment, with me here and you there – you know what I'm talking about. I'm just afraid you'd – no, not pass out, that's not what I mean – lose your mind, or something like that."'

O'Neil interrupted his translation to tell Meek that he could see

Doc Nick plainly, as well as hear him through clairaudience. 'I see him looking over his shoulder,' O'Neil described the scene. 'He's apparently speaking to someone I can't see. Now he seems to be speaking to this unseen person. He's saying, "Yes, you're right." Now he's turning back to me.'

O'Neil continued to repeat on the tape what he was apparently hearing from Doc Nick. 'I'll try to catch it exactly how he says it: "He's right, Bill. Let's say you wouldn't lose your mind. But your mentality is not ready to handle it yet. Let's just take it easy in that direction, okay?"'

O'Neil posed another question. 'What do you mean by "he", Doc?'

'Oh, I forgot,' Bill reported Doc Nick as saying. 'You can't see my friend here. Let's get back to what we were talking about. Oh, yes. I agreed with my friend here, that I don't see how they can make any headway down there unless . . .'

O'Neil broke off his paraphrasing at this point.

'George,' he said to the tape. 'Doc Nick seems to have suddenly disappeared. He does this every once in a while. I'll take a break and get a cup of coffee and see if he comes back.'

About an hour later, O'Neil reopened the tape. 'He's back now, George. I'll try to find out where he went.' Now addressing Doc Nick, O'Neil said, 'Can you tell me where you went, Doc?'

'Oh, that,' O'Neil said as he continued to paraphrase what he was hearing. 'I don't remember. But as I said, I don't see how they are going to make any headway down there unless . . . unless . . . Oh, yes. Professor Swann. Unless he can give your friend more specific information. Or perhaps you can fill me in on exactly, I mean specifically, Bill, on what they are building down there . . .'

O'Neil reported on the tape that the conversation went on about the iron oxide project and the progress the Philadelphia group was making. Then O'Neil summed up his comments to Meek on the tape:

'Everything Doc said, George, is not verbatim. However, I recorded it to the best of my recollection. I'm surprised at how much I remembered, especially when he was talking to his friend whom I couldn't see. I can't understand how I can see and hear Doc, and not see the person beside him. Can you explain this?'

The only way Meek could explain it was to refer to the many case histories of other mediums who reported the same sort of experience. Meek summarized his rationale and conclusions in his book *After We Die, What Then?*

> The material world and our physical bodies are not the solid matter we think we see and touch. All matter, the chair you sit on, the building in which you find yourself at this moment, the 'solid' foundation on which the building rests, consist almost entirely of empty space. That is why your vision can pass through 'solid' glass several inches thick. That is why hundreds of radio and TV signals carrying speech, music and pictures are at this moment traveling right through the 'solid' walls of your room and your 'solid' body.
>
> Only if you can comprehend the above concept can you begin to realize that it is possible to have two or more things occupying the same space at the same time.
>
> Your physical body is being experienced in our common everyday three-dimensional world of space and time. Your mind and soul are living in another space-time system which interpenetrates your physical body and occupies substantially the same space as your physical body.
>
> Hence, the 'next world' is the one in which your mind and soul *already* live and in which your mind and soul will *continue to live*.
>
> When you shed your worn-out physical body you will be aware of the surroundings in which your mind and soul are living – the astral planes.

As usual Meek was applying his penchant for cold logic. He could not have accepted even the premise for O'Neil's strange encounters unless he could form a clear rationale as to how such events could take place. To him, the inability to imagine or picture the possibility of life after death or communication with those who had died, was the main cause why the modern scientific materialistic world had turned away from the concept that had been accepted down through time and across tribal borders since the beginning of history. The same was true of mediums, whether they were called shamans, voodoo, ju ju, witch doctors, medicine men, seers, prophets, psychics or sensitives. There were good and bad levels of all of these, but the basic element was the same: the capacity to sense and interpret the world beyond the senses. The fusion of these elements in a technical and scientific ambiance was the focus of the frustrating challenge Meek was continuing to face.

* * *

Although the healing that O'Neil felt compelled to follow was diversionary from the main purpose of a direct, two-way electronic breakthrough, he continued to receive referrals from both doctors and those whom he had treated. Some cases were successful and some were not. This troubled O'Neil. One cancer victim from Cincinnati, who seemed to be improving, died unexpectedly. But another woman named Boo Wood from Connecticut, had confirmed cancer of the liver, spleen and uterus and several small tumors throughout her body. He was deeply concerned about her condition.

O'Neil had met Mrs Wood and her husband when he had visited Maryland back in the autumn of 1976. Shortly afterwards, they visited O'Neil at his farm, having learned of his healing activity. O'Neil treated her just as he had treated little Tracy Stover: with a prayer and laying on of hands. Then he heard no more news about her.

Then one day in March, 1977, he went to his post office box to find a letter from Mr and Mrs Wood with incredible news. The lymphosarcoma that she had been suffering from for three years had miraculously gone into remission after her visit with O'Neil. But what surprised O'Neil when he opened the letter was the enclosure. It was from W. Richard Glendon, MD, on the letterhead of the Fairhaven Community Clinic in New Haven, Connecticut. It read:

> *To whom it may concern:*
> This is simply to state that in the fall of 1974, Boo Wood, 31 years of age, of Mansfield Center, Connecticut, was diagnosed as having Stage IV lymphosarcoma.
>
> In the fall of 1976, she requested the help of William J. O'Neil for a psychic healing.
>
> In the spring of 1977, she was examined by a physician and, after a complete physical and liver function test, found to be free of any and all symptons of the former disease, and to be in none other than excellent health.

It was signed by the doctor.

O'Neil was proud and pleased. But his reaction to any confirmation like this was strangely laconic. He took no personal credit. Instead, he gave the credit to God, and claimed that he was only a channel. In fact, his concern continued to grow under the responsibility. Although he was not prescribing medicine other than the homespun dietary recommendations of Indian or folk-medicine lore, he continued to worry about the possibility of censure from the medical establishment. He pondered over Meek's suggestions that his successes could be the result of a placebo effect. When he sent the affidavit on to Meek, O'Neil noted that he had received 11 new patients as a result of Mrs Wood's healing, all referred by medical doctors. He added that 90 per cent of the past and present patients had been diagnosed as terminal. Then he concluded, 'I am sure you will understand that the growing responsibility is becoming more and more frightening. Your understanding and encouragement, George, has always given me the strength to go on . . .'

* * *

When I came across this part of the Meek/O'Neil file, I had to pause and reflect on my own experience in researching the book I had written on the Brazilian healer, Arigo. I had been filled with doubts as I gathered the startling, palpable evidence of what this psychic surgeon had accomplished over two decades and thousands of patients. After interviewing nearly two dozen responsible doctors and reviewing their medical reports, I had to concede, almost reluctantly, that something was going on beyond conventional medical science. How and why such events were taking place, I had no way of knowing. Nor did the doctors. All they could certify was that they happened.

Arigo himself couldn't explain what he did. Usually, he was in a trance when he worked on his patients. When a team of doctors showed him surgical films of his treatments, he fainted. As a journalist, all I could do was to report in low-key understatement what happened.

But I had come to two conclusions that I emphasized in the book. One was that the subject needed intensive scientific study to try to incorporate the phenomenon as an adjunct to the marvelous advances of modern medicine. The other was that all these advances should be tried first, before considering going to a healer. I was asked by an aggressive critic in a television interview, 'You don't mean to tell me you would go to Arigo if you had cancer, would you?'

'Of course not,' I told him. 'I'd exhaust every medical channel first. But if everything else failed, and only then, I wouldn't hesitate.'

I was glad to note that both Meek and O'Neil felt the same way. Holistic healing, like medical treatment, did not always work. This was a fact that had to be emphasized.

* * *

It was not surprising that O'Neil was troubled by his successes as well as his failures. As requests for healing increased, he finally decided to seek the advice of a local minister. He explained what he was doing, and wanted to know how his work fitted in with the concept of divine healing.

The minister listened politely, then suggested that they both kneel down. 'Let us take it to the Lord in prayer,' he said.

They both kneeled, and the minister continued, 'We pray thee, O Lord, that this servant of thine will at all times make sure that he is doing God's work, and that he not be blinded by what might appear as miraculous healing, but might in fact be the Devil's work.'

O'Neil believed completely in God and had faith in Jesus. But he was non-theological in his approach, and bitterly disappointed in the minister's failure to have any understanding of his dilemma. The brief session made O'Neil feel like a leper. His letter to Meek following the incident revealed his anxieties:

> I have never been what one might term a religious man, George, in keeping with the orthodox definition of religious. I have never claimed that I am a good man. Accordingly, I have laid awake at night, praying and asking 'Why me?' Why not a minister, a priest, a rabbi who could handle such a burden and gift?
>
> I have tried to back off, George, but just can't bring myself to ignore the people who are sent to me, without any consideration of my own problems of earning a living or whatever. Try as I may, I especially can't bring myself to disregard the suffering of a little child, such as Tracy Stover, Susan John, the little deaf Taylor boy or the many others. And after a healing, being unable to explain *what I did*, when you know as well as I, that I had nothing to do with whatever happened.

I know that Mary Alice is quite concerned, and has been my sole mainstay of love and understanding. But honestly, George, something has got to give.

What emerged from the pages of the letter was an overwhelming sense of poignancy and sadness mixed with a sense of floating anxiety and guilt. In spite of his tendency to over-write, O'Neil reflected the picture of a man who recognized that few would believe his experiences. Like Meek, he needed sharp, palpable evidence or he faced being shut out from the society he was groping to help.

O'Neil continued recording on tape his questions to his friend Doc Nick, and paraphrasing the answers. He was convinced he was hearing Doc Nick at length clairaudiently. The problem was that nothing said by Doc Nick was coming through electronically. What he desperately wanted was to capture Doc Nick's actual voice on tape, so that he could show Meek and the world that what he was hearing was not fantasy, but hard evidence of life after death. He designed special equipment. He tried building a special crystal microphone based on the old fashioned spider-web design once used in broadcasting. Nothing seemed to work. There was nothing to present to the outside world that would even provisionally confirm that actual contact had been made with Doc Nick, or anyone else. To O'Neil it began to seem like a pipe dream in a vacuum chamber, and a strange one at that. His wide swings of mood were continuing, a result of the pressures he was putting on himself.

His mood was more than glowering on one evening in July, 1977. He was looking over some experimental photographs he had taken. As a diversion, he had shot them in an attempt to corroborate Meek's efforts to get some psychic evidence in the ultraviolet range. All O'Neil's pictures were failures, and he was furious at the results. The incident triggered his growing mood of frustration, and he let loose with a string of profanity.

Mary Alice heard him, and came upstairs to his lab.

'To hell with it,' O'Neil told her. 'I'm through with the whole damn business.'

'You can't do that, Bill,' she said. 'You've got too many people looking to you for help.'

'It's all coincidence,' Bill said. 'It's my own overworked imagination.'

Mary Alice was calm. 'What about those affidavits?'

'They don't mean a damn thing.'

'You know they mean a lot,' Mary Alice said.

'I think you better just go to bed,' Bill said.

'If that's what you really want me to do, I will.'

'I do. I'm in no mood to talk.'

Mary Alice hesitated, then she went back to the bedroom. After she left, Bill started to light a fire in the fireplace to burn the pictures. He picked up the first picture and got ready to throw it in the fire.

At that moment, he felt a hand on his shoulder. Thinking Mary Alice had come back, he turned round to tell her to leave.

But it wasn't Mary Alice. It was a man, someone he had never seen before. He was tall and distinguished, dressed in a business suit, and clearly audible. O'Neil knew now he was facing another materialized apparition, and was again struck with fear.

'Who are you?' he demanded.

'I'll tell you that when you calm down,' the figure said.

'What are you doing here? What do you want?'

'Are you calmed down?' the visitor asked.

'I'll calm down if you tell me what you want here?'

'It's very simple,' said the figure. 'I need your help to carry out research in several areas.'

'What kind of research?' Bill asked.

'Research in just the kind of thing you are doing right now, and not succeeding. I can help you.'

'Nobody will believe any of this anyway,' O'Neil told him.

'Would you like some facts so you can prove you're not just seeing things?'

'What kind of facts?' O'Neil asked.

'Name, former address, background – all the details you need to know to confirm what I was when I lived on your plane.'

Hearing Bill in the extended conversation, Mary Alice got out of bed and came to the lab. At first O'Neil didn't see her and he spoke to the image of the visitor. 'Even if your facts do check out,' Bill said. 'Who will believe me?'

From the doorway, Mary Alice said, 'I'll believe you, honey. I know you're not crazy. I can see him, too.'

Bill turned towards her. 'You can?'

'I can see him standing right there beside you,' she said.

'I don't believe you,' Bill said. 'You're just saying that to humor me.'

But the visitor interceded. 'Of course she sees me. Why shouldn't she? You can, can't you?'

'Mary Alice,' Bill said. 'Tell me the truth. You can see him?'

'I swear to God I can, Bill,' she said.

'Ask her if she can hear me,' the visitor instructed.

'Can you hear him, Mary Alice?'

'I can see his lips move, but I can't hear him,' she replied.

There could have been no place more fit for a ghost appearance. A lonely farmhouse on a windswept hill on a dark summer night – all the cliché ingredients. But O'Neil was becoming used to the sudden appearance of voluble and articulate apparitions, and purportedly useful ones. What was of interest on this occasion was that here was another literate and technical figure who wanted to work with O'Neil along the same lines of his own research.

O'Neil gradually regained his composure. He elicited the full details of the background of the night visitor, repeating them out loud on the tape recorder as the details were given:

> Name: Dr George J. Mueller. Former Social Security number: 142-20-4640. Ancestry: English, Irish, German. B.S. in Electrical Engineering, University of Wisconsin. Top fifth of his class in 1928. M.S. in Physics, Cornell, 1930. Ph.D. in experimental physics at Cornell, 1933. Additional training, New York University and UCLA. Meritorious Civilian Award from the Secretary of the Army. Physics Instructor and Research Fellow while at Cornell.

Urging O'Neil to check all these details to verify his former existence, Mueller added that at Wisconsin he had been a member of the Haresfoot Club and the Triangle fraternity.

'That should be enough information to remove your doubts,' Mueller told O'Neil. 'But if you still don't believe this, I'll give you a complete rundown on every detail of my accomplishments and experience.'

To O'Neil, Mueller seemed rather testy and irascible. He responded with the same attitude. 'Of course I want a complete rundown,' O'Neil said, 'if I'm to have any hope of getting anybody to believe this.'

'You'll get it,' the voice of Mueller snapped. 'And you might be interested in knowing that I once worked for the Government and the United States Signal Corps. In design and development. A lot of miscellaneous electronic equipment, and a lot of specialized medical electronics for hospital use.'

'I still need every scrap of proof I can find,' O'Neil warned him.

'Look – I rather resent your questioning me so much. I think you're being rather childish. But if you want something further, here's the name and address of my daughter. You can verify my death records through her.' He gave them to O'Neil, who added them to the tape he was running.

'I've run into this problem of trying to establish proof of existence with a discarnate who calls himself Doc Nick. Have you encountered him?'

'I don't know anything about him,' Mueller answered.

'He has some pretty good ideas,' O'Neil said.

Mueller replied stiffly, 'I simply want to help you if you'll listen. If you don't feel you want or need my help, just say so and I won't bother you any more. I won't be offended, and I'll understand.'

O'Neil assured him that he wanted all the help he could get. Before he could say anything more, however, the same thing happened as with his other strange visitors: Mueller simply disappeared.

Even though Mueller's voice could not be heard on the tape, O'Neil now had something tangible to work with. He sent off a duplicate copy of the tape he had dictated of Mueller's background to Meek, and prepared to check every item down to the last. But what he still feared was that this might be just another chapter in mythology that would lead nowhere.

# *CHAPTER 9*

## *Search – 1977*

When Meek received O'Neil's tape and letter, he was elated. Even though Mueller's voice was not recorded on the tape, here was material that could be verified by fact-checking all the details thoroughly. The new turn of events created the fabric that Meek's engineering mind liked to work with. It was tangible, traceable, solid. It could be nailed down or discarded. Verification would be a giant step forward. He wrote to O'Neil that it was critical to follow up on every fact, and that he would do the same from his end.

Meek immediately got off a letter to his friend Tom Bearden, a nuclear engineer who had just retired from a military career, including five years with Air Force Intelligence in Germany. He had helped Meek interpret one of his ultraviolet pictures that had shown strong evidence of psychic activity. Bearden would be helpful in checking out Dr Mueller's military awards and activity. Meek also sent off a letter to Dr Walter Uphoff, a former professor at the Universities of Minnesota and Colorado, and a leading researcher in parapsychology. Living in Madison, Wisconsin, Uphoff would be in a good position to check the records at the University campus there.

With Tom Bearden tracing everything from Mueller's alleged 'Meritorious Civilian Award' to his 'Top Secret Clearance', and Walter Uphoff doing the same on his academic records at Wisconsin and Cornell, Meek turned his attention to other confirmatory details. There was a different situation here compared with that of Doc Nick. The identity of Doc Nick was vague. O'Neil felt that he might have been a former ham radio contact, but was not sure. With the case of Mueller, there was no chance for ambiguity. The key here was verification, and both Meek and O'Neil were determined to get it. If so, the search would take on a new impetus.

*　*　*

While Meek was sending out his probes, O'Neil lost no time in following other leads. He confessed to being still somewhat skeptical, more so in a sense. He swore to himself that if the Mueller information did not check out, he would disregard any further appearances of those entities he had already encountered, and charge them off to pure hallucinations. As he wrote to Meek, 'I know something is going on here, but I cannot continue to function as a lucid, normal human being unless I have irrefutable proof of the reality of these entities. My whole future healing and electronic activities will depend on the authenticity of the Mueller incident. Especially in the light of what has been happening to me. Please, George!'

The first thing O'Neil did was to sit down and write to the Bureau of Vital Statistics in Sacramento to find if there were a record of Mueller's death. Then he wrote a letter to the daughter whose address Mueller had given him. Both probes seemed to have failed. The letter to the daughter was returned undelivered. He did finally receive a note requesting a $2.00 fee for a search by the Bureau of Vital Statistics. He sent the money on, and waited.

* * *

In Florida, Meek was waiting too. He was beginning to feel that another blind alley had developed. The most important items that would provide veridical information were the minutiae, the small scattered facts of Mueller's life, like the fraternity and activities while he was at college. Trivial as these were, they could provide substantial evidence of the man's existence.

In Madison, Wisconsin, however, Walter Uphoff was having some success. Uphoff was as stubborn and relentless a digger as Meek. He found that Mueller was enrolled at the University of Wisconsin when he said he was, in the class of 1928. He was also listed as a member of the Triangle Club. Uphoff traced this through a group picture of the club in *The Badger*, the university yearbook. But he was not listed as a member of the Haresfoot Club, a small detail but an important one.

Finally, Uphoff dug up some old pictures of the club. It was an informal drama group at the University. Uphoff studied several of the group pictures. He finally located Mueller's name and picture in one of them, fourth from the left in the third row. His picture in that group matched that of the Triangle Club picture.

Since Uphoff's son, Norman, was a professor of Government at Cornell, Uphoff wrote asking him to check the records to see if Mueller had received his Master's in Physics there. While he waited for the results, he called Meek to pass the news along.

Meek was again elated. He in turn passed the information on to O'Neil, who wrote back with further recollections of his encounter with Mueller. Mueller did not particularly appeal to him. He found him brusque and domineering in his attitude. 'He is tall, like you, George, but heavier in appearance and with broader shoulders,' O'Neil wrote in his letter to Meek. 'He said he was six feet, one inch tall, and weighed 185 pounds prior to his passing. Thinning brown hair, and greying around the temples, with blue eyes, and he looks as stern as he acts.'

O'Neil included a long tape that described in further detail his session with Mueller. The data included not only the corporations Mueller had worked for, but the large number of employees who had worked under him, and the multi-million dollar operational budgets involved.

According to the purported Dr Mueller, he had cut quite a figure in the industrial world, including the design and development of automatic test equipment for the polar IRBM program, and the design and construction of the launch facilities at Cape Canaveral. The information even described his Government Civil Service pay classifications, which he stated moved from P2 up to GF15.

O'Neil claimed that Mueller sounded like quite a braggart. 'I don't think Dr Einstein had a background like this,' O'Neil wrote Meek. 'In fact, it's awfully hard for me to believe, George.'

Meek was enthusiastic because he was now confident that nearly all the material supplied would check out. O'Neil, however, remained shaken by the experience. On August 8, 1977, he wrote to Meek:

> I'm sorry, George, but I am still frightened, and I just can't believe my eyes and ears until you and I get a verification of a death certificate from Sacramento. I'm sorry. I didn't ask all this, and I can't take any more until I have absolute proof. I want to believe all you have told me, and have to believe that Dr Mueller did attend those colleges, etc. I told him this, and he said proof would be forthcoming. I said – good, I'll wait. And that upset him. I just don't know George. I hope you understand. I believe that anyone 'over there' could get that kind of information if

they wanted it. I haven't forgotten my experience when I lived in that trailer 'x' years ago. It could happen again.

Further confirmation came in from Walter Uphoff's son, who telephoned Meek from Cornell to say that Mueller's record was exactly as reported. In addition, Meek's inquiry through the Social Security Office not only confirmed the correct number, but provided a former address where Mueller's surviving family could be reached.

Meek lost no time in following this up. The fact that the Social Security number was correct was of substantial evidential value. It would not have appeared in any public data about Mueller. A letter to Mueller's widow, who was now living in California, brought a confirmation that Mueller had died on May 31, 1967, and that she would be glad to be of any assistance for other information. Meek followed up with a long letter explaining the purpose of the research of his Metascience organization, and describing the strange encounter in which O'Neil had received the lengthy information about Dr Mueller's background. Meek included a transcript of this, with a request for Mueller's widow to confirm it. She did so, pointing out that it was correct in all details. Immediately after this Meek received the official death certificate from the California Department of Health.

But one important piece of information that O'Neil had reported had not yet been confirmed. It was the booklet Mueller claimed he had written as an introduction to electronics for the US Army. To Meek this was critical. It would not only be an important piece of evidence to confirm O'Neil's contact with Mueller. It would also be a clue to Mueller's thinking about the potential of electronics and communication devices.

This would bear directly on what Meek's research group was trying to do. Perhaps Mueller's writing in the past might bring some rich insights into the devices the Metascience group was attempting to design and build. Since Mueller had apparently appeared so vividly to O'Neil, perhaps he would fill a role similar to that of Professor Swann, who was advising the Philadelphia group in rich but still unproductive detail.

Meek checked several libraries, including the Library of Congress, the military, and science libraries. He got nowhere, found nothing under either Mueller's name or the title. He refused to give up, but had to shelve his search until he could try other sources. It was a major disappointment in the verification process.

Meanwhile, O'Neil was reporting more contact with Doc Nick, who seemed to know nothing about the Mueller visit, and was apparently continuing to press for further research on his iron oxide cancer treatment theory. He was also urging the completion of the electronic equipment he was directing O'Neil to devise for direct conversational exchange. He kept insisting, O'Neil stated, that such inter-plane communication in both the audio and video departments was bound to come through. O'Neil, however, was concerned about the new intrusion in the form of Dr Mueller and hoped that it would not interfere. 'If Dr Mueller is who he says he is,' O'Neil wrote to Meek in August, 'perhaps he might be willing to supplement Doc Nick's information with some of his own. Be that as it may, I will hopefully be able to work with each of them, independently. I don't know what I am getting into at this point, and I keep praying that my sanity won't be eroded by my uneducated ability to keep up with their "urgent" attitude.'

* * *

In August, Meek made one of his infrequent visits to O'Neil in Pennsylvania. He was concerned about O'Neil losing confidence in himself, and his worries about the strange encounters he was experiencing.

He arrived at the isolated farmhouse to find O'Neil in a dour mood.

'George,' O'Neil told him, 'I'm just not making enough income to stay afloat. I've got to make a radical change in my routine. I can't even think straight with all the money problems I've got.'

'We can try to do something about that,' Meek said. 'Sometimes you're too proud to let anybody help you.'

'I like to make my own way,' O'Neil said. 'I don't like handouts. I've been doing a lot of thinking about what to do.'

'What have you been thinking?' Meek asked.

'I think I've got to cut back on all my healing work on an individual basis,' O'Neil replied. 'And then, for a while at least, I have to give up the research I'm doing with both Doc Nick and Dr Mueller. At least until I get economically self-supporting again.'

'Bill, I understand that completely,' Meek said. 'I think there's a way to handle both problems – the work on Dr Mueller, and the finances too. Do you figure you could put in just a few hours a week on the electronic problem?'

'A few hours, yes, I guess,' O'Neil said.

'That's all we'd really need to keep going. And what I can do is this. I can supplement your income from other work with a regular weekly fee of $60. It would only take a small portion of your time.'

'I said I didn't like handouts, George,' O'Neil said.

'This isn't a handout,' Meek insisted. 'It's a regular fee for working in your spare time. You can devote a full working week to making a living. Does that seem fair?'

O'Neil admitted that it did.

'But I've got another option,' Meek added. 'You see, you're one of the few people around who is both a medium and an electronics specialist. If we can only get the voices of Doc Nick or Dr Mueller on tape, it will be a major breakthrough. I think you've got a real chance of doing that.'

'I get the voices, but I don't get them on tape,' O'Neil said. 'What good is that?'

'If we make the electronic breakthrough, it could influence the whole world. We'll be able to show people that life is continuous, that death is just a transition. Isn't that what you want, too?'

'It's a big "if",' O'Neil said.

'The other thought I had, Bill, is that I would be willing to move you down to Florida. I'd sponsor you financially until you got on your feet. The extra fee would still apply.'

'I'm sorry, George,' O'Neil said. 'But this is where my roots are. I love this old house, shabby as it is. I love the quiet, the solitude. I just can't think of leaving it for any amount of money.'

Meek stayed with his first offer, and added another. He would try to set up a major testing program through regular medical research channels for the magnetized iron oxide idea.

In addition, Dr Mueller had come through separately with another idea. It was an electronic device for the treatment of arthritis that Dr Mueller was apparently urging O'Neil to create under his instructions. As with the magnetized iron oxide project, Meek would see that proper research testing would be carried out by qualified scientists. In other words, although the source of the seminal idea was bizarre, the confirmation of its value would not be.

O'Neil thought that the plan Meek proposed was too generous, but he welcomed it. 'Where else could I ever hope to find,' he wrote to Meek later, 'anyone foolish or trusting enough to allow me to rip them off for $60 per week, purportedly conducting research somewhere off in the wilderness of Pennsylvania, hundreds of miles removed from the hand that holds the whip . . . So if you wish to continue your own private brand of madness by contributing to the welfare of a no-account dreamer of dreams, fire away! I will make no promises to do other than my very best at all times. God's Love, Bill.'

* * *

My own bafflement continued as the story unfolded in the Meek/O'Neil file. Was O'Neil a no-account dreamer of dreams? It would be a simple matter to brush off such preposterous activities and ideas into the scrap pile. But all through these chaotic times, there seemed to be an elusive undercurrent of believability that could not altogether be dismissed. There was a ring of truth to his letters and reports. There was a consistency to his purpose, if not his moods. If it had been a case of massive delusion, some wide crack might have shown up by this time. If it was a case of losing his sanity, O'Neil was already ahead of the game by constantly challenging his own status. In fact O'Neil decided to face this fact completely when he and Mary Alice went to visit his old hunting and fishing buddy – who was now an MD, a psychiatrist in active practice.

The psychiatrist, who does not want his name to be used for professional reasons, invited Bill and Mary Alice to have dinner with him at the local Holiday Inn. It was a congenial reunion, with many reminiscences of their old fishing and hunting days. With their old relationship renewed, Bill finally got up the courage to bring up the shocking series of events he and Mary Alice had encountered.

'Doc,' he said to his doctor friend, 'I don't know how to bring this up to you, even though you're a psychiatrist.'

'I'm also your friend,' the doctor said. 'That's better than being a psychiatrist.'

'This will be tough to explain,' Bill said. 'And if you feel I'm losing my sanity, you'd better damn well tell me.'

'I'll be the judge of that, Bill,' the doctor said.

'Well, first I'd better tell you the good part,' Bill said. He had brought some of the medical healing affidavits with him, and took them out to show the doctor.

'I've had this compulsion to become a healer,' Bill told him. 'You'd be able to figure that out better than I can. But for some God-unknown reason it's been working. Here are some of the affidavits. Mary Alice helps me with the healings.'

'*Tries* to help, you mean,' Mary Alice said.

The doctor looked through the affidavits. 'Interesting,' he said. His tone was casual. 'How do you go about it?'

Bill explained his simple method – the short prayer, the laying on of hands. The doctor nodded. Bill felt embarrassed about his lack of response. He was reluctant to go on to the really disturbing things that had happened. But he forced himself to do so.

'You don't think I'm insane yet?' Bill asked.

'Did I suggest anything like that?'

'No,' Bill replied. 'But wait till you hear what I've got to say now.'

'Relax, Bill,' his friend said. 'You're getting all tensed up.'

'You'll understand why when I tell you,' Bill replied.

Then he went on to recount the scenes of possession, when 'Lorna' and 'Philip' took over both him and Mary Alice. The doctor was listening attentively, without comment. Bill kept on going, however, describing the scenes of the inexplicable appearances of Doc Nick and Dr Mueller. Suddenly, Bill felt that he had spilled out too much, that the doctor would make some serious suggestions about immediate intensive treatment for possible psychosis. He suddenly regretted that he gone so far, that he had permitted the doctor's professional skill to draw him out so completely. He even considered asking him to institutionalize him. Finally his friend spoke.

'Let me tell you something, Bill,' he said. 'And you've got to keep it in confidence.'

'You can trust me,' Bill said, surprised that the doctor wasn't shocked at what he had been describing.

'All through my practice, I've been coming across patients with histories suggesting possession, clairvoyance, ESP, and other paranormal things. Constantly. A small but constant section of my patients. They got me interested, and for the past couple of years I've been doing a lot of reading on the paranormal. Right now I'm reading a book called *Psychokinesis*. Are you familiar with it?'

Bill was immeasurably relieved to hear the doctor talk this way. He almost forgot to answer the question. Then he said, 'I don't know that title, but I've been reading a lot about the whole subject myself. I still haven't found the answer to what I've been running into. In fact I've stopped reading about the subject altogether, after these last contacts with Doc Nick and Dr Mueller.'

'You should probably keep on studying in the light of that. You might find you're in pretty good company,' the doctor said. 'And let me assure you of one thing. After this talk with you, I can assure you that you haven't gone round the bend. The chances are, these encounters of yours will probably continue. The literature is filled with perfectly normal people who are either cursed or blessed with being mediums. So you'll just have to ride with it, and let me know if you really get upset about the situation.'

The evening ended with both the O'Neils feeling an overwhelming sense of relief. They returned home in good spirits. The doctor's appraisal of Bill's sanity gave him a lift, and he continued his Spiricom and Vidicom projects with a renewed sense of dedication. Even when Dr Mueller appeared several times again, O'Neil was able to keep calm. The confirmation of the death certificate gave him confidence that at least he was in touch with a discarnate personality who was confirmed to have once existed, with a record of considerable scientific achievement.

Late one night in mid-September, the figure of Dr Mueller appeared again in O'Neil's darkened laboratory. He was puzzled, because in two appearances that night, the image only appeared in part. At first, the lower half of his body was not visible, and later, Mueller's left leg and left side of his face were not visible. When O'Neil mentioned this to him, Mueller merely replied, 'Yes, I understand.'

Mueller seemed to be a rambler. He rambled on about music, then electronics, then botany, then government and world conditions. He was perfectly audible to O'Neil all through his discursive lecture, and went on at such length that O'Neil actually found him boring. When he mentioned Doc Nick to Mueller, O'Neil was sure there was a distinct trace of jealousy. O'Neil was curious about this. He had thought that in further development in the next life, this negative quality would be lost. He asked Meek about what looked like a fair measure of competitiveness, envy, even jealousy 'over there'.

Meek wrote back that the answer was probably yes, at the level of Doc Nick and Mueller. He pointed out that mediums in every region and every age have reported that at some post-living levels, some may be convinced that they are still alive and mystified that no one pays any attention to them. 'If a man has been a heavy drinker, he may hang out in the bars and try to take over a personality. Both Dr Mueller and Doc Nick appear to have proceeded directly to a higher level, but keep reminding yourself that they do not suddenly get all-wise. The name of the game is evolution, progression – and I am talking about spiritual evolution. Only gradually do the personality characteristics get polished.'

He reminded O'Neil that they were still in the age of the crystal radio set – full of static, unreliable, but still possible for communication. Most encouraging to Meek was that he received from Dr Mueller's widow a description of her former husband that matched O'Neil's current description almost identically: about six feet in height. Between 180 and 200 pounds. Large frame. Brown eyes. Moderately stern. A perfectionist and a little impatient in regard to time schedules. But a very kind person, well liked and with many friends.

Meek was now almost convinced that the whole story might go down in the history books. He was most anxious that O'Neil should learn to focus on just two developments: the Spiricom project and Mueller's apparent desire to create what was now referred to as the Integrated Frequency Response Treatment for arthritis. He pointed out that by concentrating on just these two projects at this time, solid progress could be made, instead of scattering energy over too many projects.

There was no question that O'Neil was having trouble concentrating on a simple, immediate goal. One problem seemed to be that Doc Nick and Dr Mueller not only appeared not to have any connection with each other, but they were at odds about their suggestions for O'Neil. Mueller favored the development of the arthritis device, and had very few suggestions, according to O'Neil, for the Spiricom communication process. Yet this was essential. To Meek, this was the primary target. Healing was important, but was limited to the physical body. Communication via Spiricom went beyond the physical to show that the spiritual world was the true reality, and that death was a myth. Doc Nick seemed to be more helpful than Mueller in developing the Spiricom ideas. According to O'Neil, Doc Nick was developing a theory about how much communication could be possible. The theory could supposedly result in recordable evidence that a layman could hear, understand, and even believe. When O'Neil told Meek about Doc Nick's ideas, Meek urged him to drop everything else to track them down.

There were thousands of frequencies, Doc Nick told O'Neil, which could and would be made audible on the earth plane when the Spiricom was able to be brought into full operation. The frequencies consisted of thousands of individual channels that could be tuned in to individually, since they were independent of each other. 'It will be incumbent on you,' Doc Nick purportedly told O'Neil in one of his appearances, 'to screen, log and avoid those frequencies that we call "universal frequencies". By that I mean those that are more broad-banded in nature, allowing multiple entities to take advantage of the contact at one time, thereby making the audio unintelligible. In other words, hundreds of voices scrambled together – like several radio stations trying to broadcast on the same frequency.'

This explanation appealed to O'Neil more than Meek's esoteric explanations of various levels of astral planes. It sounded more scientific and less spooky. It also seemed to make the goal more attainable in technical terms. It made O'Neil think that he might be able to find an established frequency that Doc Nick might appear on, and permit him to record so that others might hear what O'Neil was hearing. '. . . Thereafter repeated contact with him will be more immediate and direct when tuning the Spiricom to that frequency,' O'Neil reported to Meek, 'as opposed to the hit-and-miss tuning through the entire frequency spectrum.'

* * *

The deeper I got into the Meek/O'Neil papers, the more exotic they seemed. Two discarnate entities proposing theories and mechanical instructions from the next world was not exactly a routine menu for the day. I had to agree with O'Neil's opinion that different radio frequencies seemed to be easier to grasp than Meek's theory of astral planes.

Of course the whole concept they were working on, from beginning to end, was hard for any type of mind to grasp or even consider. Going through the papers, I was constantly wavering between belief and disbelief about life after death. I had always been doing that since my earliest days in Sunday School. But the intensity of both O'Neil's and Meek's probings kept me going. The sheer importance of the subject of life after death deserved attention from anyone with cosmic curiosity.

I recalled one incident that probably accelerated my interest. I was having a drink with a delightfully skeptical friend many years before at the bar of The Players, a venerable club for the theater, publishing and broadcasting fraternity. He was the late Irving Gitlin, the outstanding originator and producer of many of NBC Television's documentary series. Gitlin was brilliant, erudite and tough-minded. For some reason, we wandered on to the subject of life after death, a most unlikely subject to come up over a dry martini in the atmosphere of The Players, in the chaotic pace of the network television scene.

'You know,' Gitlin said to me, 'I find myself thinking a lot about this. And I often ask myself the question, "What if they're *right*?" '

'What if who's right?' I said.

'You know who I mean,' he said. 'Back to the old Biblical stuff. They were always sounding off on that.'

'I never really thought about that too much,' I said.

'Did you ever stop to think that maybe – just maybe – they knew more than we do?'

'What was your conclusion?' I asked.

'I'm sure I don't believe them,' he said. '*Almost* don't believe them.'

Several years after that, Irving Gitlin died of leukemia. Several years after that, I interviewed the famous medium Douglas Johnson. He knew nothing about me or Irving Gitlin. But during the interview, Johnson suddenly interrupted his conversation and said, 'You have recently lost a friend. He was a brilliant man, an outstanding figure in the television business. He died of a thrombosis.'

Then Johnson went on to describe many details of Gitlin's life that I knew nothing about. I did know, however, that he died of leukemia, not a thrombosis. My interest was so great that I finally checked a long list of the facts Johnson had given me with his widow. Not only did she confirm all of them, but told me that he had died from a thrombosis resulting from the leukemia.

I was shocked at what I learned. For the first time I began to take seriously the idea that mediums were not to be taken lightly, that there seemed to be genuine palpable evidence that our consciousness did continue after death. From then on I gathered other evidence that built up to substantial persuasion. Yet I always tried to keep at arm's length from an ultimate conclusion.

I was still doing this as I continued through the Meek/O'Neil papers. The story went so far beyond anything I had encountered before, I had trouble reconciling it with what I had learned in the past. What would make a dent in my armor plate would be a series of repeatable demonstrations of any electronic voices Meek and O'Neil might be able to produce. So far, this was not showing up.

* * *

This of course was Meek's final objective: a clear, two-way conversation recorded on tape – and later video – and he continued driving toward it relentlessly. He was pleased that O'Neil was better stabilized than in the previous months, and glad to learn that Mary Alice was working several days a week as an auxiliary volunteer in the local hospital. It fulfilled her clear desire to help others, but relieved her from the job of assisting Bill in the atmosphere that had created the possession problem in the past.

Not all was going smoothy, however. As October of 1977 began and the O'Neils were visiting Mary Alice's parents in town, vandals threw bricks through three windows in their house. There were no witnesses, and without them the police could do nothing. Nor could O'Neil. He improvised two burglar alarm systems, and went on with his work. The new circuits and frequencies he was working with on Doc Nick's theories seemed to be showing promise. He felt he was now getting so close to the point where an actual voice would come through the speakers and on tape that he was determined that he would let nothing interfere.

# CHAPTER 10

## *Breakthrough . . . and Tragedy – 1977-79*

The fragmentary voices in the earlier experiments of the Electronic Voice Phenomenon in the United States and Europe and elsewhere had appeared on tape. But they could not be heard until after the tape was replayed. There was little doubt that Jürgenson and Raudive had come up with unexplained voices. Raudive, in fact, had recorded some 70,000 voices, scratchy and short as they were. Most often they were smothered by the 'white noise' of the radio frequencies they were played on. Although they could not be heard at the time of the recording, the fact that they were heard at all when they were played back was enough to stimulate several thousand experimenters to continue in their attempts to improve the process.

With no two-way conversation possible for an immediate dialogue, however, it was hard to get meaning out of the procedure. The Meek-O'Neil procedure was innovative. First, there was the soliciting of technical information through a medium, and collecting that information as to how to proceed. Then there was the building of the electronic device according to those instructions. Finally, there were the long hours of attempting to hear a response directly through the radio speakers, a response that had still not come along.

According to the purported Dr Mueller, the 'white noise' used by the EVP researchers was not a good energy source to act as a carrier wave for the discarnate voices. To accomplish the job, Mueller prescribed everything from a frequency counter and generator to a stable DC power supply and oscillators. By following instructions to set up a sustained background of 13 varied tones, O'Neil remained convinced that the voice of either Doc Nick or Mueller could come through on tape. But the background tone against which the hoped-for voice of Doc Nick could speak was harsh and penetrating. Mary

Alice found it nerve-shattering even outside the laboratory door. O'Neil found it difficult but necessary to put up with. High volume was necessary in order to hear the weaker background audio where O'Neil hoped to register the voice, if and when it came through.

There was one moment when O'Neil felt the breakthrough was beginning to happen. Behind the loud and rasping sound of the carrier wave, O'Neil heard the faint sound of a voice. There were a few scattered words, but they were not plain, and there was no sign of intelligible dialogue. But words were there. He felt a chill creep up the back of his neck. But he tried to check his excitement. There was work to be done on the pitch of the background noise, and also on 'compatible beat frequencies' that needed to be smoothed out to clear up the erratic reception.

* * *

During the second week in October, 1977, the image of Doc Nick made another appearance. As usual, it was sudden and startling. According to O'Neil's notes, he spoke in serious and somber tones.

'I feel you are getting near to the point, Bill, where Spiricom will become a reality. I don't want to alarm you, but if it becomes known to the public, there will be problems.'

'What kind of problems?' Bill asked.

'There may be personal danger if you are identified as a researcher and developer, both to you and the others working on the project.'

'We're working for the good,' Bill said.

'I know that. But maybe others won't consider it that way.'

'What should I do?' Bill asked.

'One thing is to treat it with the same reverence as you have your other activities. Wrongfully used, Bill, it might very well destroy you, you must surely realize that. Try to realize that those who in the beginning disbelieve you will be the first to take advantage of you when the truth of Spiricom is acknowledged as fact, and not fiction.'

Bill told him that he would carefully follow the advice. But he resolved that it would not deter him as he went on with his work. Mary Alice managed to put up with the high volume screeches of the background noise as the testing went on.

Late at night on October 21, O'Neil adjusted the dials and frequencies of his labyrinthine equipment on his work bench. In between the hissing and howls that came from the speaker, he was sure he heard a voice. He flipped on the tape recorder, hoping it would repeat itself again. It did, more clearly now. It sounded like the ludicrous voice of a robot, but it was still a voice. O'Neil asked it again to repeat itself. It did. There was no mistake about it.

O'Neil had been frightened before. But never so much as at the present moment. He was convinced that he was receiving audible communication from another plane of existence, and the thought of it overwhelmed him. Although he had been reaching for this goal over many months, the realization of it shocked him even more than the first uninvited appearance of Doc Nick and Dr Mueller. Mary Alice came into the lab. She was also shocked. O'Neil finally pulled himself together enough to try to pursue the conversation. What followed was the first sequence Meek was to use later to announce what he was convinced was the first major breakthrough, a recorded two-way conversation with another plane of existence:

'Try it again,' Bill said.

*'All right. Do you hear me now, Bill? Can you hear me, Bill?'*

'Yeah,' Bill responded. 'But you make it sound just like – oh, boy – a robot on television.'

Doc Nick's answer was muffled, but understandable. *'Yes, we always will . . . when we . . . we will . . . the one thing . . . you hear, Bill. You hear?'*

On the tape, O'Neil's voice is trembling. He seems to be trying to control himself. 'Yeah. Okay. Uh – you have to forgive me but – uh – I know this is . . . you have to admit this is kind of scary.'

The response was unintelligible. O'Neil broke in. 'It's all garbled. I can't understand you.'

This time, he could hear the answer: *'I said, why are you . . .'* Then, as O'Neil's hand reached for the dials, the voice continued. *'Leave it alone. Leave it alone. Did you hear me, Bill? Do you hear what I say?'*

The conversation went on in this way for another minute or so. It was hardly a literary masterpiece. There was talk of the frequencies changing, of which frequencies Doc Nick found more comfortable, and the importance of O'Neil marking the frequency changes. Then as quickly as it had started up, the conversation ceased. O'Neil was left with nothing but the background sound of the carrier wave.

O'Neil turned to Mary Alice, who was listening in disbelief. 'I've never been so scared in my life,' he said.

'But you've made the breakthrough,' she said.

'It was very sketchy.'

'Doc Nick warned you that it would be.'

'Some of it was unintelligible.'

'Why don't you play it back?'

O'Neil did so. In spite of the harsh sounds of the carrier waves, the conversation could be understood – most of it. 'I've got to reduce the sound of that carrier wave,' O'Neil said. 'And make the audio more clear.'

'You can still understand it. Both voices,' Mary Alice said.

'Those frequencies. They're nerve-racking. I know I can get rid of them.'

The he headed for his typewriter to write a full report for Meek. He sent it off the next morning, along with a copy of the tape.

* * *

Meek opened the package the minute it arrived. He put the cassette on his tape recorder, and listened. He could hardly believe what he heard. In spite of the uncertain quality of the voices and the screeching carrier wave, the results were there. There were identifiable and articulate responses to O'Neil's questions that were unmistakable. Meek felt like Thomas Edison when he heard 'Mary Had a Little Lamb' as it came off the tinfoil of his early talking machine. But euphoric as he was, he realized that the big problem would be credibility. When Edison had first demonstrated his talking machine to a group of both laymen and scientists, they listened in disbelief. A member of the French Academy of Sciences investigated the machine, and reported with confidence to his colleagues, 'I have examined Mr Edison's phonograph and can assure you that the effect is accomplished by ventriloquism.'

If that had happened with Edison, Meek knew that he would be facing the same kind of charges. In other words, who could possibly believe that this breakthrough was real, in spite of the evidence clearly on the tape?

Overcoming incredulity would be a major problem. Not only would the process have to be refined, but some way would have to be worked out to announce it to a skeptical public. Further, Meek was hoping that the parallel research by the Metascience group, and those he was working with in Europe, might provide confirmatory evidence. So important was this in his mind, that he planned to take

Will Cerney and Hans Heckmann to Germany at his own expense to confer with two scientists there who were working with a liquid laser form of communication.

Driving Meek now, as in the past, was his concern for the state of the world. Not only did the daily news reports make this shabby condition obvious, but gloomy forecasts were ostensibly being repeated by both Doc Nick and Dr Mueller, along with other psychics who were sensing that a radical turnabout was necessary if the planet were to survive. To Meek, a Spiricom breakthrough that could convince a skeptical public could contribute more to world peace than any other program on the current scene. What had come through on the first scratchy tape was of course trivial. Meek's aim was to establish the first electronic bridge, and then move on to higher levels where he felt the accumulated wisdom of history could be tapped. Doc and Mueller were just junior executives in the areas he wanted to reach. 'We have ultimately to escape all of the minutiae Doc is so worried about,' he told O'Neil, 'and go to far higher vibrational levels. We have to modulate – ultimately – the high ultraviolet range.' In the meantime, the fragmentary evidence that man actually lived on as an individual conscious being might possibly make him reassess his anti-social and aggressive actions while he was here on earth, Meek reasoned.

Meanwhile, O'Neil was going ahead to try to subdue the bothersome background frequencies that made the words and sentences so difficult to hear. That he was taking his responsibilities seriously regarding the breakthrough was evident when he wrote to Meek, 'I ask God every waking moment to guide me away from selfish motivation, and accordingly I ask that you add the strength of your own prayers to mine.' He admitted frankly that the excitement of actually capturing a voice from 'the other side' was not enough to overcome the fact that he was still frightened by what, to him, was the enormity of the event.

Waxing more effusive in the hyperbole he found hard to resist, O'Neil added, 'I have dedicated the balance of my sojourn on this plane toward making myself available to be used as an instrument of healing, and have pledged to be additionally used in whatever labors are required of me, and to be used as a physical instrument to advance both spiritual and scientific proof of man's immortality, and to communicate with former residents of this plane with contemporary scientific research and development, spiritually motivated.' He went on to say that he pledged himself to foresake all material gain or public recognition.

The words were heavy-laden, but his sincerity was evident. Whatever challenge he received, O'Neil was now utterly convinced of the reality of an after-life, and heaven-bent to proclaim his belief. But he continued to remain anxious and frightened by the experience of actually hearing and recording Doc Nick's voice. He said as much to Meek in a phone conversation at the beginning of December. Meek tried to reassure him.

'You've got to realize, Bill,' Meek told him, 'this is the only thing that you and I can do that might be of some small hope to mankind.'

'It's still scary as hell,' Bill said.

'But it's our big chance to show the spirit levels of being, Bill. Demonstrate it. Clearly.'

'There're other things happening here in the lab. Objects moving across the room. Like poltergeist activity.'

'Does it happen often?'

'Not too often. Just enough to make me worry about it. But forget that. I'm going to stick at it.'

'What we're doing, Bill, is trying to rig up a temporary telephone line so people can actually listen in to what is going on in the higher planes of living. To show the reality of spirit levels beyond us.'

'I guess I'm worried about what my peers might think,' Bill said.

'I can understand that,' Meek said. 'I ought to have a lot more to worry about on that point than you do. But what we're trying to do is so important that peer pressure is really meaningless.'

'Well,' O'Neil said, 'I'll keep going anyway.'

'We'll both be glad we did, Bill.'

Meanwhile, the quixotic appearances and reappearances of Doc Nick and Dr Mueller continued. They seem never to have appeared simultaneously. O'Neil reported that he tried to acquaint each of them with the other's work, which seemed to bring about an attitude of indifference on both sides. Mueller, however, seemed a little more interested in the Spiricom communication effort. 'They are evidently not familiar with the existence of each other,' O'Neil wrote, 'except by way of my mentioning them one to the other. Weird! I pray that one day they will show up here at the same time. Very mysterious. With both of them acting as a team, what wondrous developments might be envisioned.'

* * *

The year 1978 began on a tide of optimism for both O'Neil and Meek. Spurred by fresh new equipment supplied by Meek, O'Neil enlarged his laboratory work space and prepared himself for what he called the Big Push. In Florida, Meek and Will Cerney were putting the finishing touches to their Mark IV assembly, much of it based on the advice O'Neil was passing along to them from Pennsylvania. To put it simply, it consisted of an audio tone generator and a radio frequency signal generator linked to a transmitting antenna. A few feet away was a Hammarland SuperPro 600 AM receiver and receiving antenna connected to a five-inch speaker, with the sounds picked up by a tape recorder and microphone. The operator worked the controls and was able to hear any sounds coming from the speaker, and later to analyze them on the reel-to-reel tape.

Through the winter months, O'Neil worked in his chilly lab, as Meek continued other experiments, several of them involving ultraviolet photography with a lens that screened out most of the visible spectrum except in the UV range. But by May, 1978, Meek began to be concerned. In spite of several letters and memos to O'Neil, he had received no reply over a six-week period. Wary of the volatile shifts of O'Neil's moods, Meek urged him at least to tape record whatever sessions he had with his scientific visitors, even if he didn't have time to write. At a time when the real breakthrough in communication seemed to be within grasp, the project suddenly appeared to be on the verge of falling apart.

One of the reasons soon became apparent. O'Neil revealed that he had just developed what he thought was a major advancement in a television antenna that could be marketed successfully. The design did seem to have good possibilities, Meek thought, and he was glad Bill was working on something that might bring in some additional income. It was a multi-directional antenna in the form of a hoop that O'Neil claimed could double the range of an ordinary antenna in some circumstances. But this was the impractical side of O'Neil coming to the fore again. The same story of the long and expensive patent process came up again, the months and years of waiting for anything to happen – if it ever would. Meek would help – but before he could he would have to have complete reports and diagrams and results of all the experiments O'Neil had conducted. They were not forthcoming.

But it was obvious to Meek that something else was gnawing at O'Neil. In spite of the two-way contact that had come through on the Spiricom equipment on that one memorable occasion, nothing further had developed. In July, Meek decided to make another trip to Pennsylvania, where he found O'Neil measurably depressed.

'To tell you the truth, George,' he said, 'I feel like throwing the whole thing over.'

'We all feel that way at times, Bill,' Meek said. 'What's bothering you the most?'

'It's serious,' O'Neil said. 'I haven't mentioned it to you, because I keep hoping that it won't keep up. But Doc Nick hasn't shown up for weeks on end. There hasn't been any communication. Not even clairaudiently or clairvoyantly. To say nothing of electronically. I'm working blind in the lab, with no guidance at all. So I'm back where we started. I'm back to the same old question. Was this Doc Nick only a figment of a sick imagination? Was he a pretender taking advantage of how stupid I am?'

'What about Mueller?' Meek asked. 'Does he still show up?'

'He does. Yes. But he's not much help.'

'How do you mean?'

'All he says is that I'm the only one who can answer why Doc Nick has stopped appearing.'

'Look,' Meek said. 'I can understand the pressures you're under. And I think it's a good idea to knock off the work in the lab for a while. Will Cerney and I will try to keep the experiments going down in Florida. You can decide later if you want to rejoin us. Also we'll help test your antenna idea, and help launch it if it seems possible.'

'Maybe that's just a fluke, too.'

'We can find out if it is,' Meek said. 'Now, another thing I wish you could think about. Jeannette and I are getting ready to move our home and part of the lab to Franklin, North Carolina. It's in a beautiful part of the Smoky Mountains, and we'd be glad to have you and Mary Alice come down and visit. If you like it, we'll stake you out to move down there, and help you find a job. All we'd ask is that you contribute ideas, and only work in the lab when you felt like it.'

'I couldn't ask for a better offer, George,' O'Neil answered. 'But you know how I feel about this old place here. I don't think I could face moving out.'

'Think about it, anyway,' Meek said. 'Relax, and give yourself time. Meanwhile, don't force yourself in the lab here.'

O'Neil did force himself to relax a little. He visited his psychiatrist friend again, who reassured him about his sanity and who understood about the pressures that psychic sensitives faced. The talk with the doctor made him feel much better. He went ahead with the design and construction of his omnidirectional antenna, preparing to send it to Will Cerney and his marine electronic company to have it tested on several of the boats in the marina there. O'Neil was still hoping the antenna might get him out of his economic pinch. The O'Neils were invited, with all expenses paid, to come to the wedding of his old patient, the always-grateful Boo Wood, in Storrs, Connecticut. It was a festive affair, and it seemed to boost O'Neil's spirits. What had happened about the disappearance of Doc Nick remained a mystery, although Dr Mueller was still apparently showing up regularly, several times with rather gloomy forecasts on world conditions. O'Neil seemed to have the feeling that there was a strong element of jealousy involved between Doc Nick and Mueller, and that, perhaps, was the reason for the disappearance.

In his renewed work in the lab, O'Neil went back to analyzing the tape of the first breakthrough with the recording of Doc Nick's voice. He found that Doc Nick's frequency range began at 1,202 cycles per second, and dropped to 1,029. O'Neil's voice was in a much lower range, ranging below 1,000 cycles per second. Although he continued to analyze the breakthrough tape from many different angles, he still made no progress in replicating the experiment.

* * *

Meanwhile, Will Cerney was installing the experimental antenna on a shrimp boat, and Meek's move to his new location in Franklin, North Carolina was in process. Meek was bothered by the fact that the identity of Doc Nick had never been established before he disappeared. This was in sharp contrast to the exact data on Dr Mueller which could be checked and verified. He also sent a book along to O'Neil called *The Mediumship of the Tape Recorder*, which O'Neil was glad to have. On receiving it, O'Neil wrote back, 'I'm interested from the standpoint that perhaps after all, I am not the only nut on this planet.'

In referring to the continued visits of Dr Mueller, O'Neil complained to Meek that Mueller was acting too much like a boss instead of a teacher. He felt distinctly inferior in his presence. But O'Neil was interested in some of the predictions Mueller was suggesting.

One of them, in early October, 1978, was that by a year from that date, a new archeological find would be made in Africa that 'will surpass all others to date'. O'Neil reminded himself to check the news on that forecast as an interesting index to Mueller's ability. He was, however, somewhat disturbed that neither of the two communicants had ever referred to God.

Eventually, Mueller did bring the subject up. When he did, he indicated that religious dogma was often harmful: that God or Intelligence boiled down to love as the essential basic, which was not a particularly new observation. In the meantime he apparently lectured O'Neil extensively on many subjects that the latter found difficult to understand.

One subject Mueller was apparently absorbed in was music and harmonics, both of which were indirectly related to the work of the Spiricom instruments. O'Neil found that some of his suggestions pointed towards ideas he could use in the audio range that might improve reception. O'Neil was back working full force in his lab now, and Mueller appeared to be getting more and more interested in the Spiricom work. The problem was that O'Neil was swinging to another obsessional extreme again. Once in his lab, he would work through the night until Mary Alice called him to bed at dawn.

But now more than a year had gone by since the first Doc Nick breakthrough tape, and there was still no further progress on getting any voice through on the equipment that had been so laboriously designed and built. The clairaudient, non-electronic encounters with Mueller, however, remained lengthy and frequent. Toward the end of 1978, on December 5, Mueller came out with another prediction that O'Neil noted because it could be verified or discounted relatively soon. Mueller stated that, within three months, the Shah of Iran would be deposed, and would leave his country. The fact that the Shah and his family did leave Iran some five weeks later, on January 16, 1979, impressed O'Neil, although conditions in Iran at the time of the prediction pointed in that direction. It was hard to tell whether or not it was a veridical clue to post-mortem capacities.

* * *

In February, 1979, Meek tried to analyze why the Spiricom project was not making progress. The analysis centered on O'Neil, whose paranormal capacities held the key. There were strong positive and negative sides, but it was hard to tell which held the upper hand. Listing the negatives with his usual engineer's proclivity for organization, Meek found O'Neil rather lazy, undisciplined, disorganized, unable to work as part of a team, with no sense of money management, opinionated, and too content to live almost as a recluse in the shabby condition of his house. On the plus side, Meek listed O'Neil's love for Mary Alice, his high native intelligence, his technical ability, his healing ability (although it now seemed to have declined with the departure of Doc Nick), his capacities for clairaudience and clairvoyance, his love of children, his sense of reverence, and his dedication to the inter-plane communications project. In all his long professional career, however, Meek had never encountered a more complex associate.

The frustration was exacerbated by the fact that Meek was sure that only O'Neil held the key to success in the Spiricom project. He held on to this hope tenaciously, regardless of the apparent loss of the elusive Doc Nick. There was still Mueller, and Mueller had provided verifiable data about his life that Doc Nick had never done. Something was bound to break, Meek felt, even with O'Neil's frequent doubts and uncertainties. The signs that O'Neil was back working with new confidence led Meek to believe that there was hope on the horizon.

In spite of the bitter Pennsylvania winter, O'Neil was continuing with his all-night laboratory work, oblivious of the cold and feeble heat the fireplace provided. He stubbornly refused to follow Meek's suggestion to add another coal stove or space heater. But in his improving mood, inspired by Mueller's continued appearances and advice, O'Neil was eliciting further electronic suggestions that were specific and promising. In fact, late one night, Mueller startled O'Neil with an unambiguous statement: 'If you follow these suggestions on the circuitry, William,' O'Neil heard him say clairaudiently, 'I am almost certain that my voice will break through directly on both your speakers and tape.' This was a stunning statement coming from the usually laconic Dr Mueller. It spurred O'Neil on with renewed energy.

By the time the Thanksgiving season approached, O'Neil's confidence was burgeoning. The intricate puzzles that Mueller was suggesting to him in the way of circuitry, frequencies and data seemed to be coming together. He found it hard to keep down his enthusiasm. 'Full speed ahead on Spiricom,' he wrote to Meek, outlining the latest developments he had just incorporated in the instruments. The carrier wave tone was greatly improved, the equipment far more sophisticated, and all that was missing, O'Neil was convinced, was to hear and record Mueller's voice. If this could be done, he would be released even from his own doubts about the long encounters with his visitors that only he could see and hear.

* * *

The fire struck the O'Neils' farmhouse at 4.25 a.m. on November 13, 1979. The flames ripped through the flimsy wooden frame house in minutes, bursting out through the roof and windows. The local fire company arrived in time to save the outer shell of the house. The inside was mostly gutted. In the lab, much of the equipment had melted down, but some remained. One room downstairs was relatively untouched. The rest of the house was scorched and charred. The O'Neils were physically unhurt. Emotionally, they felt almost destroyed. The cause was unknown. Later, however, a local volunteer fireman was apprehended after similar fires struck six other houses in the area. The fireman was charged with arson.

There was no insurance. For anyone except O'Neil, the house would have been completely abandoned. He swore not to give in, that he would somehow restore it with his own hands. He sat down to write to Meek about it, trying to cover his bitterness. He was not too successful in doing so:

> I have the unpleasant task to advise you that disaster has struck and that at 4.25 a.m. on November 13, our home caught fire. It and all the contents are a total loss. Living on a back road in a rural area as we do, the services of the two fire departments which responded succeeded in saving only the external shell of the house.
>
> Because of this being an old frame house in this location we had been unable to purchase any insurance coverage.
>
> The room on the second floor which I used as my research laboratory was partly intact, but the intense heat, flames and smoke from the adjacent areas destroyed most of the electronic apparatus you had loaned me as well as my own test equipment, tape recorders and tools.
>
> As you know I have tried without success to find employment in my area to supplement the part time work I have been doing

> for you on your research. In view of this, and my age, I have to tell you that we see no possibility whatever of paying anything toward either the principal or accumulated interest on the house loan.
>
> I regret this more than words can express, but I feel that I owe it to you to let you know that these are the facts.

The letter was signed by both Mary Alice and Bill O'Neil. It did not close with Bill's usual 'God's Love' phrasing. But it did reflect his resolve with a brief PS: 'Once again, George I will *never* vacate these premises, except to move to the "Other Side".'

Meek responded quickly. He sent a check for immediate aid. O'Neil used it to replace broken windows and doors in the room directly below the lab, about the only room in the house without the satin-black charred walls. Meek flatly cancelled the mortgage loan he had made on the house, and arranged for a modest monthly check as Bill tried to recover. Mary Alice went to live with her father, but brought Bill food and hot coffee daily as he struggled to make minimum repairs, and to keep warm with a potbellied stove.

What the shock would do to the work on the Spiricom project was bound to be disastrous. But worse than that, the shock to both Bill and Mary Alice could be inestimable. Whatever was going to unfold over the next months, Meek thought, could only be bleak and desperate. The loss of some six years of painful, faltering effort towards an almost impossible goal was agonizing. The loss to both the O'Neils could only be thought of as tragic and devastating. It would be hard to find any resiliency left on the part of any of the cast of characters in this unwelcome drama.

# CHAPTER 11

# *A Clue Found . . . and a Voice Lost – 1979-81*

But a strange thing happened. The mercurial Bill O'Neil had an unpredictable shift in mood, and a sudden infusion of confidence. In spite of the wreckage of his home and equipment, of the bitterness of the winter, of Mary Alice being forced to live apart from him, he felt a strong resolve to get on with it and to try to overcome an almost hopeless situation. When Meek received his letter of December 15, 1979, only a month after the tragic fire, he found it hard to believe:

Dear George,

I am now presently warm and comfy enough in the room below the lab and have managed to bounce back to relative normalcy (whatever that is).

I am now working to repair the lab, so I can get on with Spiricom. When finished it will serve as a combination bedroom and lab with a panel partition separating the two. I finished rebuilding the stairs today.

Tomorrow I plan to rewire the lab and this room only in order to have the electricity turned on again.

Mueller says he will help me repair the signal generator and frequency counter. According to him that will be all that is necessary except for a tape recorder to record proof of same. I pray that he is correct!

Sitting here now reminds me of doing my homework by lamplight when I was a little boy back on the farm. Wonderful nostalgic memories. Something comforting about lamplight.

God's Love,
Bill

Meek was markedly impressed by O'Neil's resiliency. 'A lesser soul would have folded up or hit the bottle,' he replied to him. 'The best part of your letter is what I read between the lines. Yes, you really have survived this cruel twist of fate and are a far stronger and more stable man in consequence. You have taken a giant stride towards maturity.'

But bad luck continued to plague the O'Neils. Mary Alice's mother died after a long illness. Bill O'Neil had come to think of her as his own mother, and shared Mary Alice's great sadness. The death did, however, spur his determination to get on with the Spiricom project in the hope that they could possibly contact her.

As part of his reports to Meek, O'Neil attempted recording on tape some of his clairaudient sessions with Mueller. Some would go on for a half hour or more. But all that could be heard on the tape were O'Neil's responses to the presumed comments by Mueller. Thus the tapes O'Neil sent off to Meek were disjointed and wandering. They did however suggest in more concrete form what was happening at the times Mueller apparently chose to visit. Clairaudient encounters were a strange form of communication even to those familiar with paranormal study. To an outsider who observed such a session as O'Neil was recording, all he would see would be O'Neil sitting in a chair with a tape recorder, and responding the way that he would if he were on the telephone. In other words, only his side of the conversation could be heard.

* * *

When I reached this point in the Meek/O'Neil files, I grew more puzzled than ever. It was so difficult to picture this scene, a man sitting alone with a tape recorder carrying on a conversation with someone whom only he could see and hear. I picked out a tape dated January 30, 1980, several weeks after the disastrous fire, to try to analyze how O'Neil carried on these strange conversations.

O'Neil's voice was on the tape, loud and clear. But what was mystifying were those long gaps in between his questions and the silent answers that were purportedly coming from Mueller.

Mueller was apparently directing some kind of experiment that involved beating different frequencies against each other – the same sort of thing, I guess, that had brought about the aquarium incident, although now I assumed that O'Neil had the situation under better control. O'Neil, continuing in the style of the other end of a telephone conversation, was engaged in some heavy technical jargon that made little sense to me.

'Yes, Dr Mueller?' he was saying. 'Yes sir . . . yes sir . . . I see. No, what I am talking about is this. This oscillator you had me build . . . the beat frequency oscillator . . . yes sir, the BFO . . . beating against this frequency . . . well, that's strange . . . Well, perhaps Will Cerney will understand it better than I can.'

Then there was a pause. 'Hullo?' Bill said, as if he had lost the connection. 'Hullo – are you there, Dr Mueller? Are you there?'

There seemed to be no answer from Mueller. It sounded just like a disconnected phone call, and O'Neil addressed Meek on the tape.

'Hello, George,' O'Neil continued. 'I just lost him. Maybe he'll come back again. I'll wait a few more minutes. He does this periodically – comes and goes two or three times. So I'll shut this off and have another cup of coffee. If nothing more happens tonight, I'll send the tape off to you anyway.'

Since there was a lot more technical information on the tape, all presented in this same one-way manner, I assumed that Meek would get something out of it. The fact was that I was looking over 200 pages of transcripts of the taped material, all of a similar nature, and all of it based on these fleeting encounters with an apparition.

Most of the material was technical, some philosophical, some political, as O'Neil groped for the right combination of frequencies and carrier waves that might possibly bring through a recordable two-way conversation with Mueller.

My question to myself was, where did O'Neil get the patience to do all this, whether this was self-delusion or not? Two hundred single-space pages' worth of technical detail that had taken hours to tape and record. In fact, O'Neil continued to keep up this steady stream throughout 1980. All through the sessions O'Neil was constantly challenging his own experiences, but this didn't deter him from continuing.

I put on another tape of a later date, as O'Neil addressed the inaudible Dr Mueller.

'Dr Mueller?' O'Neil said. His tone was plaintive, as if he were almost begging for an explanation. 'You say that, even though you are here; I can see you, I can talk to you and I can even touch you like I can touch this table or that tobacco can, and you are solid. And I know that it is not in my mind, because you have proven it to me by picking up things while I watch you do it. But you have to understand, Dr Mueller, that sometimes, for instance, I turn around and there you are standing there. It frightens me. And yet I know I am not making a fantasy or hallucinating.'

It appeared to me that O'Neil's new surge to bring through a two-way conversation on Spiricom was because he hoped he could remove himself from the category of subjective delusion and hallucination. Beyond that would be the removal of doubt that the voices recorded were genuinely from discarnate entities, and not contrived.

The original Doc Nick tape was a breakthrough, but the quality of the voice was substandard, the background noise almost unbearable, and the conversation brief and frustrating. This was not enough to satisfy either O'Neil or Meek.

I picked out another tape. It was dated March 23, 1980. In this one, Mueller seemed to be coming up with some more predictions. From O'Neil's responses to the unregistered voice, Mueller seemed to be a tough task master, rather dour and pessimistic, and very demanding. His forecast on this date was gloomy: all American oil personnel were going to be banished from Libya in the near future. The prediction was to be proved accurate when, in November, 1981, a year and a half later, Libya took over the American-run oil fields and most of the American oil company personnel withdrew to the United States. I figured that such signs were in the air at the time of the O'Neil/Mueller prediction, which took some of the edge off judging this as a predictive triumph.

In the same tape, Mueller brought up a point that did intrigue me considerably as a potential check on the reality of Dr Mueller. He reminded O'Neil of the unlisted telephone numbers he had given him earlier. These, he told O'Neil, would provide confirming evidence that what he was saying was valid and real, and not merely figments of O'Neil's imagination. I was interested to hear O'Neil say on the tape that he had already forwarded the unlisted numbers of 'a Rear Admiral Stillman and a Dr Libby' to Meek.

Mueller must have spoken in a commanding tone to O'Neil, because O'Neil responded: 'Sir, I think George Meek should be the one to check these out. He's much more experienced at this sort of thing than I am . . . Dr Mueller, I would really be hesitant to try that . . . Well, the point is they will want to know who is calling, and I won't know how to explain it.'

To me these unlisted numbers were a critical point. I dug through the Meek/O'Neil papers to find out what had happened. I discovered that Meek did go on to check the unlisted numbers. One was for Rear Admiral Carl Stillman, and the other for Dr Willard Libby at UCLA. I was amazed to find that both numbers were correct for the parties Mueller had identified. But there was something of a let down when I learned that neither of these gentlemen could recall anything at all about Dr Mueller. Just what Mueller may have had in mind in urging the contact remained a mystery.

Wading through the tapes and transcripts was mysterious enough for me. Mueller was pushing for a refinement of the 13 different tones blended for use as the background sound to carry what voices could come through, replacing the harsh tones used in the original Doc Nick reception. The tones were not melodious. They sounded in fact like a bad Scottish bagpipe stuck on a single note. Instead of getting enlightment from the endless technical minutiae revealed on the tapes, all I was gaining was increasing puzzlement. If I had been going through all this at the time when Meek and O'Neil were doing so, I know I would have tossed in the sponge. However, the files were beginning to hint that something was about to happen, and I found myself turning the pages more quickly in anticipation.

* * *

On the night of September 22, 1980, O'Neil began his usual vigil in his lab. He started by monitoring the varied frequencies on the Mark IV equipment. If nothing else happened, he figured, Mueller would probably make one of his clairvoyant and clairaudient visits that had now become almost routine. If the visit were anything like the 'normal' occasions, they would talk about the circuitry and frequencies, and perhaps about the state of the world. O'Neil no longer questioned the reality of these visits as far as he was concerned. Even though the image occasionally faded in and out, he could clearly see and hear Mueller's image, ghostly as it was. At other times, he could see Mueller's lips moving, but could not hear him. Mueller was three-dimensional to O'Neil's eyes, just as a laser hologram appears to the eye, where the viewer perceives the three-dimensional form as if it were actually in front of him. The hologram was a scientific equivalent of an apparition. Perhaps there was a clue here.

On this night, however, Mueller had not appeared. O'Neil was working alone, logging varied frequencies and checking the results.

Mueller's suggestions to use the multi-frequency audio tone instead of incidental random and uncontrollable white noise convinced O'Neil that he could capture tonal inflections of the incoming voice – if it came through. Further, Mueller's knowledge of music theory had helped select a mixture of audio tones that might make the tonal inflections more articulate. His instructions for the tonal mixture were specific: a mixture ranging from 131 to 701 cycles per second. Beyond that, the use of a carrier range frequency between 29 and 31 MHz was hoped to provide the best results.

Suddenly, in the middle of his dial-turning and adjusting, O'Neil was startled. Over the generator tone, he distinctly heard a voice. It was faint and harsh. But it was definitely there. O'Neil snapped on the tape recorder. He began fine-tuning the instruments. The voice grew louder, plainer. It emerged over the background noise. It was still rasping and robot-like. O'Neil felt a chill down his back, but he shook it off. Abruptly, the first understandable sentence came through:

'*Can you hear me, Williammmmm?*' The last part of his name reverberated through the channel.

He pressed his ear closer to the speaker. His voice began to tremble. 'Yes,' he said. 'Yes. Who is this?'

The voice came through again. '*You must be joking, William.*'

'But I don't know who you are. You sound like a robot.'

The voice grew clearer. '*All right then, William. May I introduce myself? I'm a friend of yours, William. Don't you remember? "Robot" Mueller.*'

O'Neil was stunned into momentary silence. He tried tuning the dial. Then the voice of Mueller came through again.

'*William, I think that's much better. Right there, William. Now . . . William, did you understand? Williammmm?*'

O'Neil still had trouble in speaking. But he finally said, 'Yes, I understand, Doctor.'

What puzzled him most was that, now that he could hear Mueller's voice clearly through the speaker, and registering on the tapes, he was no longer visible in the studio.

'*Very well,*' Mueller's voice continued through the speaker, '*I will give you a count from one to ten. One . . . two . . . three, four, five, six, seven, eight, nine, ten. One moment, William.*'

'Okay,' O'Neil answered, still astounded and not a little frightened.

After a pause, Mueller spoke again. '*Very well then,*' he said as he prepared to make another audio test. *'Mary had a little lamb, its fleece was white as snow. And everywhere that Mary went the lamb would go-o-o-o-h. G-o-o-o-oh.'* He seemed to be deliberately holding the last syllable. Then he added: *'Play that back for me, William. William?'*

'All right, Doctor, I'm sorry,' O'Neil said. 'I was lighting a cigarette.'

*'Those cigarettes again!'* Mueller was actually scolding.

Mueller, revealing himself as a perfectionist, went on with more tests. He seemed satisfied with them. Then Mueller's voice disappeared as abruptly as it had come through the speaker.

Still numb, O'Neil played the tapes back. The words were distinctly audible, both O'Neil's and Mueller's. The conversation was clearly two-way. The quality was measurably above the original breakthrough with Doc Nick, and longer – long enough to make an extensive analysis of it later. Right at the moment, O'Neil felt like yelling 'Eureka!', and getting a copy of the tape off to Meek. He hoped that Meek would feel as he did: this was proof positive of the reality of life after death.

He did not have to wait long to get a reaction. Meek received the tape, and listened to it in awe. With his engineering instincts, he got out a stop watch and clocked the two-way conversation at 13 minutes, three times the length of the earlier tape of Doc Nick. He listened again, and a third time. There was no question in his mind now. He agreed with O'Neil. This was clear evidence that two planes of existence had made direct contact, verbal contact, the result of eight years of struggle. He urged O'Neil to keep going, certain that he would be able to record further conversations with Mueller. He also showed O'Neil his appreciation in a very practical way. He sent him a $3,000 bonus with no strings attached.

* * *

I found myself replaying a copy of this first Mueller breakthrough tape late one night. I had to admit it gave me a chill. The material in it was laborious, faltering, mundane and boring. But if the conversation was what it purported to be, the implications were staggering. Mueller's words were clearly understandable. O'Neil's trembling inquiries were equally so. It was a strange and eerie mixture to listen to, a fragmented picture of possible life beyond the earth, combined with the chatter and testing routine of audio engineers. The tape created a sense of reality and non-reality. Since the greatest mystery of life is death, I found myself being inexorably drawn into this confused vortex of metaphysical mechanics. I again felt the urge either to prove or disprove this absurd claim. It was too important a theme to accept glibly or reject categorically.

Meek had provided me with several hours of the O'Neil/Mueller two-way conversations that followed in the wake of the initial breakthrough. Like a ham radio buff, I sat up until the late hours of the morning to listen to them.

The contrast to the brief Doc Nick tape was marked. Dr Mueller continued to come through, clearly heard on the tapes that followed sporadically over the ensuing weeks. In casual, everyday terms, Mueller and O'Neil would discuss the progress on Vidicom, the next hoped-for breakthrough. The discussions remained pedestrian and dull, certainly providing no evidence of an exalted existence in the immediate life after death. If they were making this up, I was thinking, they would certainly have painted a more exotic picture. Mueller's character continued to emerge as a stern professor of electrical engineering, coaxing, prodding, and sometimes encouraging. I listened to one tape with Mueller pushing ahead on the Vidicom idea:

'*The television set with the metal screen*,' Mueller's voice said. '*I didn't put that in the magnetic input from the signal generator in conjunction with the input . . . from the camera to the television system.*'

'Yeah,' O'Neil answered. 'I think that's it.' His voice was no longer shaky. He was apparently used to this by now.

'*By the way*,' Mueller asked him, '*did you get that multi-faceted crystal?*'

'No, I didn't, Doctor,' O'Neil said, always with a respectful tone. 'I got that five-faceted one from Edmund's.'

'*Edmund's?*' Mueller asked. '*Who is Edmund's?*'

'Edmund's is a company. Edmund's Scientific . . .'

'*Oh, I understand*,' Mueller said. '*What were the results?*'

'Well,' O'Neil replied, 'I inserted it into the lens of the camera, but all I got was a lot of crazy colors of light. I didn't get any imagery.'

'*Oh, I see. Well, very good. I think if we follow this other procedure, William, and I am not absolutely sure, but I have a feeling that this will help clarify the image so we can discern features on the subject . . .*'

Listening to the tapes, I tried to pick out false notes, ones that might rule out this ridiculous thought that the deceased could actually converse electronically with our own plane of existence. Was, for instance, O'Neil carrying on a conversation with himself? There was no evidence of this, because the voice quality of Mueller's voice was of an entirely different fabric than O'Neil's. In some cases, the sounds of the two voices overlapped. In others, the response came immediately on top of the questions or answers. Was this another ham radio operator engaged in elaborate hoax? If so, wouldn't there be a much more colorful fabrication involved? The tone of the conversation was natural, off-hand, unforced, and undecorated. Later, I wanted to get full expert opinion on this. If I decided to go ahead with a book, that is. Even though I was being drawn more and more into this mystery, I still hadn't made up my mind.

I picked out another tape, and slid it into my cassette recorder. Apparently, O'Neil would leave his electronic equipment turned on when he was away from the lab, in case Mueller should want to come through. I was a little startled, when I heard Mueller calling out through the equipment, a sudden appearance that apparently caught O'Neil off guard:

'*Williiaamm . . . William . . . Wiiillliaamm? Are you there, William?*' Mueller's eerie voice suddenly burst on the tape. There was a pause, then, fading in from the background, O'Neil called out.

'I'm coming, Doctor. I'm coming.' O'Neil sounded out of breath. 'Oh, boy. I am sorry, Doctor. I am sorry.' He sighed, and then went on. 'I went downstairs for a cup of coffee. I'm sorry.'

The brief dialogue was convincing enough. It added to the credibility, but of course didn't prove anything. Interesting, however, was the conversation that followed. It got into Mueller's own experience just after he had died from his heart attack. He suggested that O'Neil pay attention to his own health.

'Yes, I understand, Doctor,' O'Neil's voice said on the tape. 'But do you understand, Doctor. I know I am not getting any younger.'

Mueller answered paternally, '*I know. I understand, William. Well, in my case – well, I was fortunate. It was sudden. However,* you *know in advance. The important thing . . . the one benefit that you will find as a result of our contacts* – you are aware! *I was not aware of this side. I didn't know the potential over here before. So when I got over here, it was like waking up in the morning, and not knowing where you are at. Like having a bad dream . . .*'

This situation matched many reports that came through mediums, especially from those who died suddenly. But Mueller didn't dwell long on the point. Still speaking like a professor to a student in a lab, he moved on to the subject-matter that Meek was concentrating on: that inventions and design developments often arrive through psychic channels to inventors. Meek believed this about his own work, especially the astounding rush of inventions that had poured into his mind that enabled him to amass the immense funds to carry out his current search.

Mueller gave some technical instructions to O'Neil on the tape, and said, '*Not very well but . . . now William.*'

'I think I've got it now, Doctor.'

'*Try adjusting that frequency,*' Mueller added. '*I'll give you a count of five. One, two, three, four, fiiiivve. I think that's the best frequency, William. Now the next project, William. William?*'

'Yes sir. I'm listening.'

'*Very well. The next project, William, is the elimination – as you call it – of the zombie-like sound of my voice. You know we have more . . . at this moment . . . is that about right, William?*' Mueller raised his voice on the last phrase. Apparently, O'Neil was dozing off.

'Yes, that's right, Doctor.' His tone continued to be deferential. 'I'm sorry, sir. Please forgive me.'

'*That's all right, William. That's all right.*'

'All right, sir.'

'*You know in order to figure that,*' Mueller continued, '*we are going to have to have a more stable frequency. By more stable I mean we have to do away with the AC frequencies in the background. We are going to have to find a way to eliminate it, the – uh – fractional frequencies.*' He spelled out the word fractional. '*You understand me, William?*'

'I understand you, Doctor,' O'Neil said.

The more I listened to the two-way, direct conversation tapes, the more I vacillated between belief and disbelief. Because of the background sound and the scratchy but understandable voice of Mueller, the dialogue was strained and clumsy much of the time, with frequent repetitions necessary. But this only added to the verisimilitude.

But were Meek and O'Neil right in being convinced they were talking directly to someone whose mind, memory banks and personality had survived the death of the physical body, and whose consciousness was articulate and aware of two different planes of existence at the same time? The thought was awesome and overpowering. I had to admit that I had trouble coping with it. And yet my late friend Irving Gitlin's question kept popping back in my mind. 'What if they're *right*?' he had said, referring to the ancient prophets. I found myself asking the same thing about Meek, O'Neil, and Mueller.

The apparent voice of Dr Mueller was clearly audible and in lively exchange with O'Neil through the electronic instrumentation. It was therefore an unassailable fact that someone at least purporting to be Mueller was coming through the speaker. Meek and O'Neil had now spent several years of painfully slow and laborious energy to reach this point. They believed the breakthrough was there. They also knew that it would be hard to get anyone else to believe it. As a result, Meek kept searching for every scrap of evidential material that would support the facts.

There were the background data on Mueller, in full detail, and nearly all confirmed except for the book Mueller had mentioned that he had written back in 1947, *Introduction to Electronics*. Meek had still not been able to track it down. He felt that it might support the fact that the information they were getting was correct, and that there might be clues to Mueller's philosophy that might have motivated him to seek communication through this strange Spiricom channel.

Oddly enough, a sudden reminder of this tantalizing clue source came up in one of O'Neil's two-way sessions with the recorded discarnate voice of Dr Mueller.

In a sudden shift in the conversation, Mueller asked O'Neil: '*Did you obtain that book of mine yet?*'

'Oh, that book of yours,' O'Neil said. 'No, sir. By the way, our friend Mr Meek is really going all out to find that because I want to read those pages you mentioned.'

'*Very well,*' Mueller replied. '*I want you to read that, William. There must be copies available somewhere.*'

'Well I think George – that's Mr Meek, our friend . . .'

'*Your friend,*' Mueller interrupted brusquely.

'Yes,' O'Neil continued. 'Even if he has to go to the Library of Congress. He'll probably do that.'

'*I see,*' Mueller said. '*All right.*' And the discussion ended.

Meek had already been to the Library of Congress, but when he received the tape, he set out on a renewed search, determined to track it down.

* * *

The articulate breakthrough of the two-way electronic conversation with Dr Mueller had come on September 22, 1980. From that time on, over the next months, Mueller's apparent voice was recorded and logged as he responded to O'Neil's questions in more than 30 hours of sessions. O'Neil shipped the tapes regularly to Meek who had them transcribed. Then he analyzed them carefully. He continued to be concerned about eventual listeners to the tapes who would have extreme trouble in believing they were really conversations with a scientist whose funeral had taken place nearly a decade and a half before. He recognized the great importance of going beyond this single series of contacts, and was looking for ways to replicate the project with other personnel at other locations. What Meek sought now was reinforcement and replication.

He was troubled about where the priorities lay. To him, the message was of such importance that the sooner the world learned about it, the better. At the same time, the breakthrough was still crude, and in the infancy stages. But the articulate evidence that he did have, if presented properly, would have a chance of letting tens of millions of people know that there was no such thing as death, that life goes on as a natural transition, and that consciousness could exist without a physical or material base. To Meek, nothing exceeded the importance of this message. Beyond that, he wanted to stimulate other researchers to follow up with their own experiments.

* * *

All through 1981, the sporadic contact between O'Neil and Dr Mueller continued on tape. The sound and voice inflection improved, as O'Neil tinkered with the circuitry under Mueller's instructions. Meanwhile, Meek was focusing on the development of a detailed technical manual that would be made available at cost to electronic technicians everywhere, who, he hoped, would be interested in carrying out their own research. All the material in the manual would be *freely* available to people of 'all races, all over the world.'

For Meek, this was a critical step. If it could be shown that the reality of life after death had been established in a tangible, concrete, and technical way, the modern mind could accept it much more easily than on faith alone. In this way, it could be a complement to established religions without being in conflict with them. It would add a component that matched the skeptical mind of the scientific age, and reach towards the goal he had long sought – the fusion of religion and science.

Just how to make such an announcement troubled him. As early as 1974, he and Heckmann and Paul Jones of the Philadelphia experimental group had asked themselves the question: how would we handle this situation in the way of a public announcement if and when tangible evidence came through – when voice communication with the deceased could be shown to be a reality? What if it were shown in technological terms that death were just a rebirth into a new dimension? Wouldn't the implications of a two-way connection have a tremendous impact on practically every level of civilized life in the world?

At that time, in the mid-70s, he decided to ask the advice of what he considered to be the wisest men he had met on his world-wide travels. He and Jeannette had gone to Great Britain specifically for this purpose.

One of the men was D. M. A. Leggett, retired first Vice Chancellor of Surrey University, a fellow of Trinity College, Cambridge, and a former Professor of Mathematics at the University of London. Another was Sir Kelvin Spencer, former Chief Scientist at the then Ministry of Power, in London. Both were highly respected in their professions, spiritually orientated, and good friends of the Meeks.

They listened attentively, as Meek outlined the possibilities he was sure would eventually come through. Both said that the only thing they could do was ponder the question carefully, and get back to him with an answer. It took several weeks before the answer came. In substance, it said: First, Meek, we doubt if you or anyone else can pull it off. And, second, if you do, the ramifications would be so great we wouldn't know how to go about such an announcement.

The instructions were hardly helpful then, nor were they in the middle of August, 1981, when Meek felt that the time was right for a full public announcement. The recorded tapes of the two-way O'Neil/Mueller conversation were fully demonstrable. He was sure they would be controversial and contested. He felt they could, however, have a beneficent impact on a heavily troubled, materialistic world.

A major problem was O'Neil's intense desire for anonymity. He reiterated this desire many times, and could be as stubborn as Meek in his opinions. But in an irritating sort of way, Meek could be remarkably persuasive, even though he could be remarkably annoying in the process.

Meek was convinced that O'Neil genuinely felt that the demonstrable evidence that life was continuous was important. He was also sure that O'Neil felt the news about Spiricom would have an extreme influence on a world that had slipped away from the belief in life after death since science had brushed it aside. If the hard evidence of the Mueller tapes could be presented right, Meek believed, a skeptical public might be persuaded to reassess behavior patterns on a personal, local and international level.

Meek made a special trip to Pennsylvania, convinced that it was essential for O'Neil to be a key figure in a major announcement. It would be useless to make it without his co-operation. O'Neil remained stubborn, as Meek pleaded that he, O'Neil, owed it to himself to take credit for making an historic contribution to man's understanding.

Not making much headway in his arguments, Meek reluctantly decided to take an admittedly crass approach. O'Neil's car had recently broken down, and was beyond repair. Meek told him that his future work with the Spiricom project was so critical that he had earned an increase in his monthly fees that would be enough to cover monthly payments on a different second-hand car which was essential to him.

O'Neil was still stubborn, but with Mary Alice's urging, he finally agreed to drop his anonymous status. With this obstacle cleared, Meek was now sure he had enough ammunition to formalize his plans for a public announcement through a press conference under the most prestigious possible circumstances.

Through all his years as an executive and engineering specialist, Meek never enjoyed half-measures in anything he did. Whatever steps he took, were taken in quiet but firm style, always with dignity and decorum. The announcement of the success – partial as it was – would be no exception. He began making arrangements for a press conference to take place at the prestigious National Press Club in Washington, to be held some eight months away in April, 1982. This would give him time to draw up a complete presentation of the whole history and development of Spiricom.

What precipitated his haste in planning for the press conference was that he began to notice that the communications with Mueller were starting to fall off in length and frequency. Meek was worried about this. He felt there was much more to learn and develop if the project could actually reveal what he called the 'foreverness of life'. In fact, Meek received a recorded session from O'Neil that foreshadowed an inevitable end to their two-way contact.

'*William?*' Mueller's voice opened the brief session.

'Yes, sir?' O'Neil answered with his usual deference.

Mueller brought up a reference to a new unlisted phone number he had provided O'Neil. '*Did you make that telephone call yet?*'

'No, sir,' Bill answered.

'*May I suggest you do, William,*' Mueller said. '*Now you must understand one thing, William.*'

'Yes, sir.'

'*I cannot be here forever. I cannot guarantee how long I'll be visiting here. However, I will do my best. Do you understand, William?*'

'Yes, sir,' O'Neil replied.

'*There is a time and place for everything,*' Mueller said. '*So, as I have mentioned before, this is something I think you should be aware of.*'

As Meek listened to the tape, he sensed in the tone of Mueller's voice that he might not be continuing his electronic contacts much longer. The plans for the press conference became all the more urgent, before the news should become stale. He began to plan not only for a Washington press conference, but for a preliminary series of conferences with his contacts around the world, so that they might make an announcement simultaneously with Washington, with the express purpose of stimulating parallel research. His trip would take him to Japan, the Philippines, India, France, Germany, Norway, Sweden, Britain and Switzerland, where he would personally present the O'Neil/Mueller tapes and background material. In addition, he would forward the same material to associates in Australia, New Zealand, Hawaii, Brazil, and South Africa, all of whom were highly regarded and distinguished in their professions.

* * *

As he made the elaborate preparations for the press announcements, Meek was still bothered by the fact that he could not track down the elusive book that Mueller insisted had valuable confirmatory evidence of the reasons for his work on the Spiricom project.

The search had now gone on for a year and a half. There were many blind alleys. He believed Mueller completely that the book existed. His painstaking checks of every detail of Mueller's life had convinced Meek that Mueller was not a spinner of tales. Yet still the search was fruitless.

Meek's Holmesian bloodhound instincts kept him pressing. He called on the archivists of the Olin Library at Cornell to see if they could track down the elusive *Introduction to Electronics*, and waited.

A letter came back, and he opened it in great anticipation. But the news was insufficient. The library had been able to find a record of Mueller's Ph.D. thesis, *The Distribution of Initial Velocity of Positive Ions from Tungsten*. This was interesting enough in itself, but not what Meek was after. He went back to the Library of Congress National Union Catalog, with no luck. He went to the British Library General Catalogue. It showed no entry for George J. Mueller's book.

Still Meek wouldn't give up. He asked his son, George, Jr, a journalist with the Voice of America, to go again to the Library of Congress, and also the Pentagon. He made seven contacts in all, but was unable to come up with a single trace of the publication.

Remaining convinced that the book contained a clue to Mueller's motivation for his interest in Spiricom, Meek made a special trip to the library at West Point. Here was another blind alley. Then Meek made his own follow-up mission to the Pentagon. He called on over half a dozen offices. There was still no result.

But he did learn one important clue on his last call there. Mueller's book might – just might – be part of a series of training manuals published by the military back in the 1940s. But they were all out of print. As Meek was leaving the last Pentagon office, the officer called him back. He recalled that there was an Army archive collection at the State Historical Society of Wisconsin.

Meek wrote there, and waited again. About two weeks later, he opened a letter from the Society. It stated that they had a full set of army manuals from the '40s, and that Mueller's publication was among them. Meek was overjoyed that the long search had come to an end. He lost no time in ordering a photocopy which arrived within a few days. Quickly, he went to the pages that Mueller had designated as important. They included a summary of the progress of electronics since 1895. Mueller's words pointed out that back in that era, the popular belief was that everything of importance had already been discovered, and that the eighteenth and nineteenth centuries were considered the ultimate in all that could possibly be discovered in the universe.

Meek read on, sensing that the words would reveal insights that were even more directly in line with his own research. The opinion of scientists, Mueller's words were stating, was that future generations would have to be content with making 'minor refinements and rearrangements of the established order of science'.

But finally, Meek's eye struck a paragraph on the final page of the book that he felt made the long search for the missing document worthwhile. As Mueller had phrased it in 1947: 'Men are reaching even into the spectrum heights of those fabulous cosmic rays. Out of the work, new techniques and instruments of electronic wizardry will emerge, but only after seemingly impossible problems have been solved.

'These solutions will require the careful thought and patient work of many people, whose findings will be correlated with other efforts, verified by experiments, and aided now and then by sparks of genius to *reconcile the irrational and so accomplish the impossible*.'

That was it for Meek. The last phrase of the book. To reconcile the *irrational*, and so accomplish the impossible. What better description could he find for the Spiricom efforts that he and O'Neil and the others had been pursuing for such a long time?

He underlined those last words carefully, and re-read them. No wonder, he thought, that Mueller had insisted throughout the long sessions with O'Neil that the book be found, and that those exact words be read. But what they would mean in the face of a skeptical press corps in Washington remained to be seen.

# *PART 3*

# CHAPTER 12

## *Breaking the News*

From the time that I had first met Meek in November of 1981, up to the time he was preparing his full-scale press conference at the beginning of 1982, I had not had the chance to learn the details of the bewildering sequences experienced by O'Neil in his Pennsylvania farmhouse and Meek in his laboratories in Philadelphia, Florida and North Carolina. I did, however, succeed in sorting out some thoughts about the fragmentary information I had learned about Spiricom on Meek's first visit to Connecticut, plus my own reflections and studies on physics, metaphysics, and obstacles in probing the paranormal.

There was little question that, in the climate of modern materialism, the story would be hard to believe. On the other hand, there was a gradual rise in the feeling that modern science was not quite the all-seeing and all-knowing sovereign it was once thought to be. The fruits of the technological age came in two classifications. One consisted of those that brought comfort, enlightenment, ease, pleasure, and knowledge of the universe never known before. The other consisted of those that brought toxic contamination, atmospheric poisons, environmental destruction and the imminent threat of the pulverization of the planet. Because of the overhanging threat of the latter, many were willing to seek and look beyond the tangible and into other unexplored dimensions.

I had long prided myself on being a realist, until I gradually discovered that realism embraced a lot more than was obvious on the surface. This expanded view came about very slowly over the years. The result was an undeniable urge to explore in the frontier areas of science, but with caution and vigilance. Even with the little knowledge I had of it at the time, the Meek story was so alien and anomalous that I hesitated in even exploring it further.

I was more or less jolted into considering the story in more depth when Meek called me from North Carolina in early 1982, and asked if I would talk to a journalist he was working with to set up the Washington press conference. His name was Bruce Swain, and he would be in the New York area toward the end of March, and could come out to Connecticut to give me more background on the progress of both Spiricom and the forthcoming press conference.

I agreed, and Swain came out to visit me on March 26. Casually dressed, he looked as if he had just stepped off the campus, which in fact he had. In his 30s, he looked younger, a well-designed handsome face that went well with a wry sense of humor combined with an intense seriousness that soon revealed that he was intelligent, analytical and forthright. He was an assistant professor of journalism at the University of Georgia, having been a stringer for the *New York Times* in Kentucky, and a copy editor and reporter for the Louisville *Courier-Journal*. He had got his Master's degree at Harvard and his doctorate at Columbia. I was interested in how he became associated with Meek, and he told me.

Before he joined the faculty at the University of Georgia, Swain was doing freelance work for a variety of publications including the *New York Post*, the *Village Voice* and others. A mutual friend of his and Meek's asked him if he would like to do some public relations work for Meek, and perhaps some other general editorial work. He said he was not interested in PR work, but he'd be glad to talk with Meek about the editorial side. After helping out on two of Meek's books, Swain was considerably impressed. The upshot was that in October, 1981, Meek and his wife Jeannette stopped off in Athens, Georgia, where Swain lived with his wife and two children.

Meek took the Swains to the Hunan Chinese restaurant on Baxter Street, and before the won ton soup and the egg rolls arrived, Meek, as he always did, went straight to the point.

'Bruce,' Meek said, 'you did an excellent editorial job on two of my books. Do you think you'd be interested in another job?'

Swain chuckled. 'All depends on what it is.'

'This is something that might just blow your mind,' Meek said. 'But since you've been exposed a little to my crazy projects in the past, it might also interest you.'

Swain had been lightly interested in the paranormal for some time, having had some slight psychic experiences in his childhood, none particularly astonishing. The books he had read on the subject had piqued his curiosity, and had brought him to the conclusion that something, at least, was going on, even though he was uncertain as to what it was.

'I think I've already mentioned to you, George,' Swain said, 'that the one thing that concerns me about the psychic area is that people are sometimes capable of misleading themselves.'

'I agree with you completely,' Meek said. 'I run across this all the time in my research. It's something you have to watch out for.'

'You know what I mean,' Swain said. 'They *want* to find something, and sometimes it's not there.'

'Well,' Meek said, 'I promise you that what I want to tell you about is backed up by solid evidence. Evidence that you can almost feel and touch.'

'I'm willing to listen,' Swain said.

Then Meek began spilling out all the details on the Spiricom project. He told of O'Neil and Mueller and the long patient hours, weeks and years until the recent breakthrough. Swain listened, somewhat stunned. The possibility of electronic contact, of course, had enormous implications.

'But George,' he said finally, 'you've got to ask yourself the question, who would believe this?'

'I think when you listen to the tapes, you'll be able to believe it yourself.'

Swain laughed. 'If anyone could do this, George, it would have to be an electrical engineer like yourself. The nuts-and-bolts approach you have is an advantage. But what is it you'd want me to do?'

'We need to lay out a full public relations program, and I need someone with your experience to do it. I want to keep the whole thing away from either science or theology. In other words, go straight to the media and the public, without the red tape that official sanction requires.'

'But George,' Swain said, 'this is a tremendous thing to ask the press and the public to believe.'

'I don't expect to persuade the world with a press announcement,' Meek said. 'But what I do think we can accomplish is a first step. To get as many technically-qualified experiments as possible to try to replicate the results. To get them intrigued by a public announcement. Then we will provide all the schematics and instructions at cost.'

Swain listened carefully. He was intrigued. But he was also worried. He couldn't help thinking: what are the chances that this thing is fraudulent? At the end of dinner, he told Meek that he would like to think things over, and he would get back to him. Like Meek, Swain had a precise and analytical mind. In his short experience in working editorially with Meek, he had found him to be direct and above board. Meek never haggled, paid promptly, and was cautious and direct in his writing and correspondence. He had a no-nonsense approach in his daily routine and his dealings with others. His professional accomplishments were obvious, and his sense of dedication to the project seemed selfless and clearly apparent.

But Swain needed time to think. Since he would be laying his own reputation on the line, he wanted to look at all the aspects. First, he had to examine carefully the possibility that it could all be a hoax. If it was, what was in it for George Meek? Meek was a very reputable, internationally-known engineer and executive. His work with the Carrier Corporation was known throughout the engineering world, and highly respected. His patents were of such value that he had been able to retire at the age of 60, and also to invest over half a million dollars in his non-commercial venture that would bring him no income. As technical advisor to Averell Harriman during World War Two, he had held an important position of trust. With Spiricom, he was placing 50 years of professional reputation on the line. If Spiricom should happen to turn out to be a hoax, the impact on Meek's reputation would be devastating, and certainly not worth the risk.

Another thought was, could Meek simply be out to gain fame? This could be possible, Swain speculated, but such fame would be much more likely to be on the down side. Whether Spiricom were true or not, Meek would be subjected to ridicule and suspicion, as all pioneers in the paranormal field were. In addition, Meek's personality simply didn't lend itself to someone who sought to be a celebrity. There was no evidence at all of his hustling for such a goal. On the contrary, there was ample evidence of integrity, modesty, and hard work.

Another question Swain asked himself – was Meek out to make money out of the project? He found this an easy question to answer. If Meek were seeking a fortune, he was going about it in an exactly opposite way. If he wanted it, the first thing he would do would be to take out a patent. This was one field where Meek was an expert. It would be a simple matter for him to do so. Meek was doing just the opposite. He was releasing everything he knew to the world at large, no strings attached. Meek would be making a small charge for the technical manual and tape materials to cover the cost of a private printing, but in no conceivable way could it be profitable. This aspect would, Swain felt, be troublesome for reporters in general to accept. The half-million dollar outpouring of Meek's own funds was in total negation of the profit motive. Still, it would be hard to get this across to a skeptical press.

After Swain went through his analysis of the motives of Meek, he turned his attention to those of O'Neil. O'Neil was the only person who had apparently been able to get these strange communications on tape in a two-way conversation. For that reason alone, his part in the process would bear close scrutiny.

Meek offered Swain the chance to go through all the voluminous correspondence with O'Neil, from 1973 up to the present. Swain waded through it. The minuscule sums that Meek helped O'Neil out with were below poverty level. O'Neil was only required to put in a few hours a week on Meek's experiments, and there was no profit or gain remotely possible even if he worked full time. There were so many other things he could have done with his electronic knowledge, that Spiricom was the lowest money making potential on the scale.

But Swain had run into people in his newsbeat who wanted to tell their story just for the notoriety of being on the front page – or even an inside page. Swain naturally wondered about that aspect in terms of O'Neil. He was relieved to find, however, that O'Neil had been dead set against having his name involved, and had insisted on anonymity. It would only be Meek's fierce arguments and modest financial boost just before the press conference that persuaded O'Neil reluctantly to change his mind.

Another factor Swain thought about was that intangible urge to *want* something to be true, and to want it so hard that self-deception creeps in. Some psychologists claim that people discover what they want to discover. Both Meek and O'Neil were involved in a belief in the spiritual, even if not in a conventional way. But as Meek told Swain several times, it would be one of the most cruel hoaxes in the world if someone were intentionally to falsify such an attempt – especially when there was no motive for gain on the part of either of them. Further, Meek's desire to get the procedure out for others to share all across the world was additional evidence that he held no proprietory interest.

In putting himself in the position of the reporter he was trained to be, Swain tried to assess the percentages of probability that the story could be true or false. After going through all the peregrinations above, he came to the conclusion that he was well over 90 – if not 99 – per cent certain that the story was what it looked like. And with that kind of probability, it could be one of the most critically important stories of the age.

He finally told Meek he would take on the PR job of setting up the press conference, which was strange to him because he would be on the other side of the fence from the position he held when he acted as a reporter. He could recall many instances when he battled with PR people, trying to figure out if they were telling the truth or not. Now he would be in that position himself, and found the idea somewhat amusing – especially in a story as strange as this one.

* * *

After Swain's visit, I found myself in agreement with his approach and his analysis. I did not yet have the information about Meek and O'Neil that he did, but I was impressed with Swain's high-calibre background and his no-nonsense attitude, to say nothing of his courage in taking on the assignment which was bound to be difficult. But I did not envy him. The press corps – especially in Washington – was a tough house. I too had been on the other side of the fence, both when I had been with the networks and as a columnist for the *Saturday Review*. This was before I had done any exploring at all in the paranormal, and I knew how unfriendly a skeptical reporter could be, especially with a subject as bizarre as this. I found myself continuing to worry about how Meek and O'Neil would be able to survive a barrage of hard-hitting questions. Intelligent as Meek was, I wasn't sure how much experience he had had in standing up against a series of hostile interrogators, which most of them were bound to be. Here was an electrical engineer and businessman claiming to make an historical breakthrough that would, if it could be established, literally startle the world and perhaps usher in an entirely new era.

Meek, however, was going ahead blithely with an abundance of confidence. He kept pressing me hard to attend the Washington conference, and was convinced that I would find it interesting. The date was set for April 6, 1982, and the large ballroom at the prestigious National Press Club was booked for ten o'clock that morning. Meek would not be content with anything less.

I could not exactly share Meek's enthusiasm, but I was beginning to admire his persistence and confidence. I hated to see him led like a lamb to the slaughterhouse, however. In a sense, I felt the same concern about Bruce Swain, although his experience would act as some sort of armor plate for him. Whether Spiricom was a reality or not made little difference in this situation. The very fact that Meek had the audacity to bring the project out into the open was enough to leave him vulnerable.

Some protection would be afforded him by the fact that several of his associates indicated their willingness to share the podium with him at the conference. Meek sent me the list just before he took off on his around-the-world tour to set up the announcement for simultaneous international release. The list included the colleagues who had been working closely with him on both design and theory – Will Cerney, Hans Heckmann, and Walter Uphoff – plus several others, such as Professor Ernst Senkowski, who would make the trip from Germany to be there, Bruce Dapkey, the electronics engineer who was working as a consultant to the Metascience group, and Professor William Tiller, the internationally-known professor of Stanford University.

As Chairman of the Department of Materials Science and Engineering at Stanford, and consultant to the US Government in the fields of metallurgy and solid state physics, Tiller was an important figure. He was also a director of the California Academy of Parapsychology and Medicine, and active in the development of reliable instrumentation for the detection and study of psychoenergetic fields. Although he had not been working directly with the Metascience group in this project, he had a great deal of respect for Meek, and had contributed to Meek's book *Healers and the Healing Process*. One of his theories was that human consciousness was undergoing an unfolding evolution. 'We may liken conventional scientific understanding of the universe to the visible tip of an iceberg,' he wrote in Meek's book. 'We have come to know that exposed tip very well; however, like the iceberg, most of Nature is still hidden from us.' Professor Tiller's stature would be helpful, along with that of several of the others.

On March 9, 1982, slightly less than a month from the scheduled Washington conference, I received a letter from Meek from Manila, one of the first stops on his journey. He was pleased with the reception he was getting from those he had contacted prior to the trip. They had agreed to set up press announcements abroad. With O'Neil's willingness to discard his anonymity and to appear in Washington, he was sure the program would be a success. Meek looked forward to my attending a pre-conference meeting in Washington, and was sure that I would find the reaction interesting.

I was again impressed by Meek's confidence, but I still had not made up my mind to go to the conference, let alone write a book on the subject. That decision was a long way off. In fact I had been ready to drop the idea until the meeting with Bruce Swain. His reserved interest and analysis from the point of view of a journalist impressed me. Other commitments prevented him from writing a book, although I was wishing he would because I would have found it interesting to read about the story at arm's length.

When Meek phoned me at the beginning of April, a few days before the conference, I finally decided to come down to Washington, still rather worried about what could happen when Meek faced the onslaught of the press corps.

I arrived there on April 5, the day before the conference. It was in time for an afternoon meeting scheduled by Meek for his associates. It was held at a mid-town motor inn, and Meek's associates were already gathered in a conference room there when I arrived, including Bill and Mary Alice O'Neil. This was long before I had had a chance to research the story in any depth at all, and I didn't quite know what to expect.

O'Neil was dressed in a dark suit and tie, and, except for his gnarled features, looked very much like a businessman. He looked somewhat uncomfortable in the suit, and I later learned that Meek had insisted on making him a gift of it. Mary Alice looked pleasant and cheerful in tan corduroy slacks and plaid shirt. She was smiling and gracious when she introduced herself to me. Bill O'Neil was quiet and reserved. He smoked incessantly. He was a little nervous, as if he wasn't at all comfortable in correctly anticipating that he would be the focal point of the press conference, regardless of how the story was received.

Meek called the preliminary meeting to order. He sat at the head of the table, serene, unperturbed, a picture of sobriety. Like nearly all the others at the table, he was wearing an impeccably groomed dark blue suit, a plain dull red foulard tie and a white shirt. When he spoke, he was serious, meticulous, sometimes boring, and a few times humorous.

I found it hard to relate this gathering to the subject matter. Hans Heckmann sat next to Meek on the other side of the table from me.

He had a broad forehead, well-chiseled features, close-cropped hair and shell glasses. He was pleasant and seemed ready to break into a smile at any time. Sitting next to him was Professor William Tiller, with a sensitive and alert face framed by a neat white beard. He was wearing a blue worsted suit with a waistcoat and a striped blue-gray tie. Professor Walter Uphoff kept the meeting on a lively keel, cheerful and communicative, with white cropped hair surrounding a bald top. Both he and Hans Heckmann spoke with mild German accents. Professor Senkowski, freshly arrived from Mainz, had a thick but understandable German accent. With a friendly open face he listened intently and spoke little. The same was true of Bruce Dapkey, younger than the others and more casual. With a faded blue denim shirt and blue jeans, he could pass for a featured player in a daytime soap opera.

Next to me was Bill O'Neil, at the opposite end of the table from Meek. He was flipping over a pack of cigarettes, alternating with a sip from a cup of coffee, never more than a hand span away. He said very little at the meeting, content to let the others discuss the phenomenon he was experiencing.

'Most of you are familiar with the work our little group has been doing since the early '70s,' Meek began the meeting. 'That's when we began the Philadelphia experiments where we feel we got direct advice from deceased scientists like Professor Swann and others. We continued on two lines of research, one in Philadelphia, and the other with Bill O'Neil in western Pennsylvania. And of course you know what we were after – to demonstrate *instrumentally* that death was not the end, but only the beginning of life.'

Then he went on to say that in his 12 years of travel and research, he had not encountered anyone with O'Neil's psychic sensitivities. He spoke of how he had faced a critical decision in 1981. The breakthrough then with the recorded voice of Mueller was far beyond anything that had been reached with the fragmentary voices of the EVP phenomenon – which was astonishing enough in itself. The difficult problem was to decide whether the research should go on for another five or ten years to get the full answer, or whether to share the incomplete discovery with the world now, so that others could make a widespread effort to replicate the accomplishment.

It was the chaotic state of the world, Meek told the meeting, that prompted him to decide that the time was now. The event was of such importance that he felt a tremendous sense of responsibility to announce it widely. He knew that conventional science was not ready to consider the phenomenon, and that the moral majority and established religions would balk at the prospect. Because of this, he felt the need to bypass both and go direct to the public. Even if he failed to convince the press or the public, the stimulus for others to research was what was most important.

The others at the table listened attentively as Meek spoke. He pointed out that the studies of Raymond Moody and Elisabeth Kübler-Ross showed medical evidence of what happened at the point of death, but that the Metascience and Spiricom research went beyond that to suggest what took place after death, and how a more constructive life here would bring further advancement in the next world.

There was profound interest in the room as Meek played the tapes of the O'Neil/Mueller two-way conversations. These of course were the focal point of the entire project. Even though I had listened to them before, the effect was chilling, whether they could be believed or not. Mueller's voice echoed and reverberated in the room with an other-world quality, and yet dealing with such mundane matters as schematics and circuitry. The mere possibility that this could be real had an impact.

After the last tape had been played, there was silence in the room as the group seemed to reflect on what it had just heard. Except for general laughter when O'Neil's voice said on the tape that he had run downstairs for a cup of coffee, the group remained silent, intent and serious, absorbed in the other-worldly sound of Mueller's somber voice.

Walter Uphoff spoke up first after the tapes were completed. 'What impressed me,' he told the gathering, 'is that when I checked out the background information on Dr Mueller at the University of Wisconsin and Cornell, it was absolutely accurate. I think this is important from an evidential point of view.'

'Mueller's words in the training manual he wrote were also startling, didn't you think, Walter?' Meek said.

'I did.'

Heckmann spoke up with his German accent. 'How did you feel, Bill,' he asked O'Neil, 'when Mueller's voice came through?'

O'Neil shook his head. 'It is impossible to imagine how frightened I was. I don't mind admitting it.'

'What I'm interested in,' Professor Tiller spoke up, 'is how big a part Bill O'Neil, as a medium, played in energizing the electronic equipment to bring the voice through. It seems apparent that a direct equipment response without the presence of a medium is not yet possible.'

Meek agreed. 'That would be the ultimate goal. To prevent "coloration" by the medium's consciousness. We still haven't reached that point.'

'What I've been interested in,' Will Cerney spoke up, 'is trying to duplicate a voice like Mueller's artificially. Just to rule out mechanical parallels. But I've had no luck.'

'What method did you try?' Uphoff asked.

'I tried an artificial larynx, various filters and all kinds of devices. No luck. Also I found it interesting that the pitch of Mueller's voice rose up and down with minor frequency changes. It shows that the voice was not superimposed on the tape.'

The meeting eventually broke down into several simultaneous discussions that embraced such theories as the difference between absolute time – if there was such a thing – and serial time; how there may not be such a thing as the speed of light – that it might just *be* there; how at other levels of consciousness there may be such high frequencies that the brain can't conceive it; and on to the possibility of using pure light as a transducer. I had a hard time following any of the discussions because they became so technical and mathematical that I was lost in the maze. I was most fascinated by the discussions between Tiller and Senkowski, because there were two highly qualified physicists who were delving into paraphysics with great enthusiasm, and not shackled by the conventions of their profession.

I was thinking that there couldn't be a more alien or extraordinary subject to bring such a group together, anywhere in the world. It seemed to be almost a fantasy, an articulate group of extremely intelligent people gathered to discuss the possibility that man had spoken directly with the deceased by electronic means. The more I listened and thought about it, the more incredible it seemed. This group was unquestionably learned, scholarly, rational and stable. They were qualified not only in paranormal studies, they were highly qualified in other fields of practical, academic and theoretical importance. As a journalistic observer, I felt rather out of place.

* * *

While the preliminary meeting delved into the puzzling and complex potentials of bringing physics and paraphysics together, an entirely different sort of drama was going on behind the scenes. It involved the everyday world of journalism and public relations. It also involved Bruce Swain, who was facing the gargantuan job of arranging the details for all the major media to cover the conference at the National Press Club on April 6.

The problem began just about a week before Meek had gathered his group in the motel conference room, and was continuing as the meeting went on. Meek had selected one of the most prestigious and powerful public relations agencies in the country to set up the press conference, the Gray Agency. This was Meek's choice regardless of the beefy fee required. As usual, Meek was going for excellence. In a preliminary meeting, the agency executives had indicated that they would take on the assignment, and the National Press Club was booked. They asked Meek to fill them in on the details just before they notified the press of the impending conference. An invitation from the Gray Agency was equivalent to a command performance for the major media.

When Meek and Swain played the tapes for the top executives of the Gray Agency, and explained the background of the story, there was a stunned silence in the room. It was hard for Meek to figure out their reaction. They asked to study the material over the weekend, and get back to Meek on Monday morning. One executive said, 'I can't imagine any other news I would rather see in these days.' But on leaving the meeting, Meek told Swain he was sure they would turn down the assignment, and they were going to be faced with the conference coming up in a week with no experienced agency to handle the job of notifying the press services, newspapers, magazines and broadcast media about the event.

Meek was right in his forecast. Gray turned down the job on the basis that they felt they 'could not provide the result that the client wanted'.

Meek was now in a jam. The large ballroom of the National Press Club was booked, and there was little time to try to obtain another PR agency, especially one of Gray's stature. It was such a complicated and unique project that it took hours just to explain the details. Fortunately, Meek had prepared and assembled a comprehensive press kit, and Swain had prepared the press release. After a couple of futile attempts to find a capable PR outfit, Swain and Meek decided to contact the key media people directly. Just to prepare and get out the invitations was a complex job, especially without the organizational contacts an agency already had. Further, there was the problem of getting back RSVPs so that there would be an indication as to how many would show up. The ballroom of the National Press Club was a grand and elegant room that could easily sit dozens of reporters. A handful of them would look ridiculous.

The big question in Bruce Swain's mind was: would news reporters turn out for such a 'far out' announcement? Other questions were: would they stay to hear it through? And would they give it serious coverage? On the basis of the late notice, he figured they would be lucky if five or six showed up.

On Friday, April 2, four days before the scheduled conference, Swain had the press kits and invitations delivered to all the major key media sources in Washington, hopefully in time enough to get back replies that would indicate how many would show up. Through his reporting experience, Swain knew of other sources to which he could get the information out for a reasonable fee, such as Washington Broadcast News, Associated Broadcast News, PR Aids, and others. The preliminary news release was brief and to the point:

NEWS CONFERENCE
A Startling Breakthrough in Electronics Communication

10 a.m., Tuesday, April 6, 1982

National Press Club Ballroom

After 10 years of research, a group of engineers and scientists will announce that they have electronic proof that the mind, memory banks and personality survive death of the physical body.

George W. Meek, an American engineer and inventor who is President of Metascience Foundation, will be joined by well-known American and European researchers in announcing the breakthrough.

The system devised by Meek and his associates combines electronic communication with the operator's psychic energies.

Meek will release, without patent, full details of the equipment – including wiring diagrams. His goal is to encourage other researchers to replicate his efforts and expand on them.

Phone contact Bruce Swain (202) 842-1020 ext. 605

By the evening before the conference, only two acceptances from the invitation list had come in, and one of those was shaky. Swain was worried, but Meek maintained his confidence. He went through a practice run of his presentation with Swain, and asked him to fire as many hostile questions as possible. Meek's son from the Voice of America joined in with the tough questioning, and Meek fired back the answers. And they were tough:

– What's in this for you, Mr Meek?
– How much money do you expect to make?
– Why should anyone believe this?
– Are you trying to start a new religion?
– How do we know it's not a straight radio connection?
– If it's so important, how come someone else hasn't invented it?
– Are you under psychiatric care, Mr Meek?
– How do you know O'Neil isn't conning you?

Meek fielded the questions respectably well, responding in his slow gravelly voice, which could have been livelier. On the other hand, his appearance and demeanor were not unlike those of a career diplomat of long standing, and Swain figured this was an asset. The main question on everybody's mind was: would Meek be speaking to an empty house?

# CHAPTER 13

# *Meeting the Press*

The next morning, on the day of the conference, Swain still did not give up. He got on the phone early, but the response was still minuscule. About the only thing he could tell Meek was that he had two definite and two possible, which was hardly an adequate media pool to spread the news of Spiricom. There were, however, some 50 reporters who said maybe. I left the hotel around quarter to ten to walk to the National Press Club, and I felt terribly embarrassed for George Meek, with all the effort he had put into what he sincerely believed in. I envied his certainty, because I constantly had a belief struggle within myself when it came to investigating the paranormal.

What was confusing was the enormity of the subject of life after death itself. On the chance that Spiricom was verified, there couldn't be a more newsworthy story. Yet the media in general either avoided the subject or treated it as a spook-and-kook item. In one way, the daily press was almost forced to do this. A two-hour deadline could never permit digging into the deep background of paranormal studies, to say nothing of investigating a single project in depth.

The reluctance of the press to treat a radically new subject seriously was not a new phenomenon. On December 17, 1903, the time of the Wright brothers' first flight, a Coast Guard radio officer tapped out a radio message to the *New York Times*: JUST WITNESSED MAN'S FIRST POWERED FLIGHT. WOULD YOU LIKE EXCLUSIVE STORY? The *Times* radioed back immediately: NO THANK YOU. About a month before that day, the *Times* had run an editorial saying that there were people idiotic enough to want to put Government funds into aviation research. 'In our opinion, it has taken birds thousands of years of evolution to learn to fly. It will take man 7 to 10 million years to reach that point in evolution.' The *Times*, incidentally, had declined the invitation to the Meek conference.

I reached the National Press Club shortly before ten and rode up in the elevator to the thirteenth floor with two reporters. They were carrying the Spiricom press kits with them, so at least there would be two reporters present. One of them said, 'I'm not a believer in this sort of stuff. Are you, John?' The other replied, 'I guess you could call me open-minded.' That at least was a refreshing sign.

There was a sign on a stanchion in the paneled hallway saying: PRESS CONFERENCE – METASCIENCE – BALLROOM. I walked towards it with a sense of trepidation. There is nothing more discouraging than a giant room with only a scattering of people to fill it up. The ballroom at the Press Club was graced with the elegant style of the '20s, with an enormously high ceiling and tall windows with impressive draperies.

On the dais were long tables stretching on each side of the podium, where Meek and his colleagues had already gathered. In front of the podium were some 50 chairs arranged in rows and facing it. Only about six of the seats were filled. I couldn't help feeling more sorry than ever for Meek. It was now five minutes after ten, and hardly seemed worthwhile for the meeting to begin.

There was some trouble with the audio equipment, and about ten minutes went by while it was being fixed. In that time, the room suddenly began to fill up, until more than half of the seats were taken. I felt a great sense of relief. There was also a TV crew from the Washington ABC-TV affiliate, and several radio stations. With the newly-gathered momentum, representatives were there from the AP, UPI, Reuters, *Business Week*, *Harper's*, National Public Radio, Scripps, Chicago *Sun-Times*, Baltimore *Sun*, and others. It had suddenly turned into quite a respectable turnout. I was considerably surprised.

The big question now was: how many would stay to hear the story out? This was an imponderable, as Meek rose to begin the conference. At the long table at each side of the podium were all those who had been at the informal meeting the day before: Tiller, Uphoff, Heckmann, Senkowski, and Cerney. O'Neil was there, too, still looking somewhat uncomfortable in his business suit and necktie, but surprisingly calm.

As Meek began to talk, he looked distinguished and impressive, announcing the conference was about to begin with some preliminary comments by Professor Tiller. Meek's voice was a little shaky and thin, but it was obvious that he took command of the audience because the chatter stopped, and the reporters listened attentively.

He introduced the panel first; then Professor Tiller came to the podium.

Because of his stature, Tiller held the attention of the reporters. Although he had not worked directly with the Spiricom project, he pointed out that he had had 12 years of experience with Meek, and knew him to have extremely high integrity and commitment to the truth. He told about Meek's track record as an engineer and executive, and his giving up his professional career to devote his full time to research into the important question of survival after life.

When Meek came back to the podium, he thanked the audience for coming out, and emphasized that the press conference was not about science fiction, even though it would seem that way to many of those here. He pointed out that the Spiricom equipment was only an elementary start toward an electronic communication with persons very much alive in higher levels of consciousness, and that the reason for the announcement at this point was to encourage other researchers around the world to duplicate the results, and carry the project beyond its present state. The fact that the communications with Mueller had now ceased made this an important priority.

He then went on to play excerpts from the 18 months of two-way conversations between O'Neil and Mueller, as the audience followed the words on the transcripts that had been furnished them. Before he started up the tapes, Meek stated that he realized that, in themselves, the tapes would not be sufficient proof, and that he expected skepticism and doubt from scientists. 'As a methodical and skeptical engineer,' he said, 'I have subjected our findings to every conceivable test, and I am convinced they are valid and will withstand the closest possible scrutiny by the scientific community.' He also added, 'After almost half a century of building a reputation internationally for integrity in research and engineering, I am not about to perpetrate any hoax. In this instance it would be a cruel and senseless hoax indeed.'

At the playing of the tapes, the audience followed the transcripts carefully. I was half expecting a large handful of reporters to walk out of the meeting at this point. But none did. I began to feel a little less nervous for Meek, although I wondered about the barrage of questions that were bound to follow.

They did follow, in rapid succession. They were along the lines that Swain had anticipated. A key question to Meek was, as expected, 'What's in it for you?' He replied that he was unquestionably a visionary, and was confident that within 50 years, others would complete the job he had started. 'I'll be satisfied,' Meek answered, 'if it gets across two important things. One is that death is just a door. The other is that the quality of life lived here will determine how it is lived on the next level of existence. The result, I'm sure, will be a revolutionary leap for mankind. For one thing, people are not likely to murder or commit suicide if they feel sure of this. That is the legacy I want to leave my children and grandchildren.' Then he smiled and said to the audience, 'And yours. It's also why my wife and I have put hundreds and thousands of dollars into this we could otherwise leave to our offspring.'

Asked what the offspring thought about this, Meek admitted frankly that they thought he was nuts to throw over a successful career for such an ephemeral goal. But they had finally come to accept the decision, much of it on the basis of what they had learned about the importance of holistic healing, an adjunct of his research.

Other questions followed in rapid succession. I was surprised at the interest shown, and nearly all the reporters stayed on for over an hour of questioning. One interesting exchange came when a reporter asked, 'Let's get away from any sort of confrontation questions. This is not going to prove anything to those who don't want to be convinced. But just tell us this – what do you think, on the basis of your research, is going to happen to you when you die?'

Meek thought a moment, and answered, 'The answer to what is going to happen to you –'

The reporter interrupted. 'I'm not interested in what's going to happen to me. What do you think is going to happen to *you*?'

Meek held up a booklet from the press kit, and said, 'The detailed answer is in this booklet that you have in your press kit.'

'Okay,' the reporter said. 'But what I want is a response out of your mouth.'

Meek chuckled at the reporter's persistence, and said, 'Well, there is, if the evidence is right, a short period of adjustment. In a normal death, it is not particularly traumatic. There's purportedly a simple adjustment to make, but I expect to be free of pain and discomfort, and perhaps on the middle level of consciousness.'

'Why there?' the reporter asked. 'Don't some people come in on a lower level?'

'Well,' Meek replied. 'Some have had in their lives difficult situations they're not very proud of. It may take some time to get perspective. Some are completely unprepared for the possibility of a new life after death, and it takes them longer to adjust. The research has at least shown me to expect a continued existence.'

'Go on from there,' the reporter said. 'After your arrival, what happens?'

'I can't get into too much detail at this meeting,' Meek replied. 'But I promise that if any of you really study and understand the material in your press kit, you will probably know more about the details of life after death than has been known by scientists, clergymen and philosophers over the years.'

'All right,' said the reporter. 'What about the opinions of religious leaders?'

'Just as we have not sought the opinion of scientists, we have not sought those of religious leaders,' Meek answered. 'When I wrote my book *After We Die, What Then?* I felt I could say that it transcended, but was a complement to, other religions. It has been of interest to many religions, and has been translated for publication in Japanese, Portuguese, and several languages of India.'

'All right,' the questioning continued. 'Where are the spirits?'

'We have explained how it is easy to visualize these levels of spirit more or less stacked up,' Meek replied. 'We are living in both the physical body and the etheric body at the same time. But this concept is for visualization only. Actually, all the levels of consciousness interpenetrate. The consciousness is an energy that is not off in space. As Professor Tiller has said, "We must think in terms of life energies, not space." The concept of interpenetration is critical. It can't be thought of as space. You have to think of a radio being able to be tuned up and down the dial – to higher rates of vibration. There are radio and television signals in this room right now. We can't see them or hear them, but they are here. They're of different wavelengths, and we have to have the equipment to tune them in. Our object with the Spiricom equipment is to try to find out how we on this plane or level of existence, can tune in on other frequencies.'

Another complex question came from another part of the room. 'You mention that apparently Dr Mueller has progressed in his consciousness and his learning since leaving this life. Do you conclude from that and other research that the progression is eternal? Is there a point where that has stopped because of things we have done in this life?'

Meek had dealt with the question in his research that had indicated that spiritual development continues after death, but it requires continued work on the part of the individual consciousness. In other words, no pink clouds. He answered, 'There is no practical limit. The sky is the limit. We have to get into the theological area here. Apparently the growth and progression is unlimited for mental, emotional and spiritual growth. We can evolve to the point of Nirvana, according to the Eastern philosophy. But we have discerned no limit except that. Apparently, the very high levels are beyond the comprehension of those now living on earth.' Meek did not have the time to get into the theory of reincarnation, a whole complex subject beyond the scope of the meeting.

Then a question turned to more practical aspects. 'How can you be sure that these communications are not just radio interference – or some ham operator picked up on your signal?'

Meek pointed out that the material was so specifically related to the details of the current operation, with names, facts, and technical suggestions over a year and a half that stray signals were next to impossible. For a ham radio operator to conduct 18 months and hundreds of hours with intimate knowledge of what was going on with O'Neil in his lab, or with the EVP experimenters across the world, would be so unlikely that it could be ruled out.

A reporter from a local radio station asked whether Meek or O'Neil had been approached by the military or any of the Intelligence agencies. The answer was no, although there had been some indirect queries. There was an apt question in view of the later report in the *New York Times* that the Pentagon and other agencies were allocating considerable sums of money to investigate extrasensory perception for practical use. Several of Dr Mueller's forecasts had come true, and the one about a new major paleontology discovery would shortly do so, several months after the time of the press conference. Richard Leakey and his associate Hidemi Ishida, of the National Museums of Kenya, announced in August, 1982, the discovery in that country of a jawbone possibly eight million years old, that would, according to Leakey, be 'of tremendous importance in tracing human lineage'. It might, he added, fill a 'critical fossil gap'. Mueller had forecast such a discovery in 1978, but his timing was out by two years.

When another reporter asked, 'Why should we accept this?' Meek replied, 'We can't expect you to accept this. All we are hoping is that you will report it to your readers or listeners. Then we are hoping that large research laboratories will become interested, along with the EVP researchers, organizations like ITT, ATT, Bell, IBM, and the like. Scientists at Telefunken in Germany are already working on EVP. We hope they'll do the same with Spiricom.' Meek added that physics had come almost to a dead end in its progress, and was undergoing profound changes. It was almost like having a sign on the door, *Closed For Repairs*.

Meek closed the formal meeting on a whimsical note. 'I want to thank you all for coming,' he said. 'I just want to remind you that for all of us, including your readers, there is a funeral at the end of the road. Maybe you'll think back to this meeting in 1982, and say "My funeral is not going to be such a big deal, after all."'

The meeting had ended, but still practically no one had left. Instead, the reporters crowded around the dais, and continued putting questions not only to Meek, but to the others on the panel – especially Bill O'Neil who, in spite of his natural reticence, took the questions in his stride. They asked the question that I had continually wondered about: how could O'Neil see a materialized image? O'Neil explained that the image was similar to an artist's portrait that wasn't quite finished; there was very rarely a full figure. Other questions were for technical information about the equipment. Heckmann and Cerney joined in to provide many details. Senkowski and Tiller fielded several tough questions on the relationship of physics to the paranormal, and all the questioning continued for another half hour.

I found myself considerably surprised at the interest taken by the reporters. I had expected an attitude of indifference or raw skepticism, but regardless of what was to be written, the question were fair and intelligent; severe at times, but fair. One reason was that Meek made a clear and unambiguous presentation. He held nothing back, and was unruffled throughout. Overheard in the elevator going down after the conference was a colloquy between two reporters.

'Well, what do you think of all this?' one of them asked.

'Well,' said the other, 'I believe it. I believe these guys are for real.'

'How will you report it?'

'That's another story,' was the answer. 'I'll never get it past my editors.'

* * *

I talked with Swain after the conference. He said that some reporters never did get their story past their editors. The Associated Press, for instance, never put a word about Spiricom on the wires. But the competing United Press International put out a long, straightforward account by one of its senior science writers. The story began, 'It is now possible to communicate with the dead through electronic instrumentation and psychic energies, and man may some day be able to have television-like conversations with the deceased, the President of Metascience said on Tuesday.'

'You could hardly ask for a more objective coverage than that,' Swain said. He added that of course such coverage was offset by the expected ridicule the story met with in some other places. The Chicago *Sun-Times* wrote that the taped voices played for the press sounded 'like Igor responding to Dr Frankenstein through a closed door on a windy night in Transylvania'. The same reporter also referred to George Meek as a 'self-confessed idealist'.

'Columnists in Boston and Bangor,' Swain added, 'could not resist writing about fanciful interviews with Edison or George Washington on the subject of Washington's wooden teeth, via Spiricom. And some headlines were just as bad: NEW COMMUNICATIONS SYSTEM A GRAVE MATTER, and REACH OUT, REACH OUT AND HAUNT SOMEONE, or DIAL D FOR DEAD.

A welcome variation, Swain said, was the massive radio coverage the story received. National Public Radio ran a segment about the press conference in its popular 'All Things Considered' program, and Canadian stations went all out in picking up the story. In the two weeks after the press conference, Meek did telephone interviews with 22 different radio stations across the US and Canada. Some of the top 50 American TV stations carried short clips of the video recording of the announcement.

A sampling of the opinions of the listeners who called in to a Hamilton, Ontario, station produced results more favorable than expected. About 27 per cent said they believed the Mueller tapes are what they are claimed to be. Another 27 per cent said they thought the concept and claims are possible. And 46 per cent said they do not believe such communication is possible at all.

While the Spiricom announcement did not exactly create front page news, Meek felt he had accomplished his initial purpose. 'In retrospect,' Meek said, 'my basic strategy worked as planned. This was to totally ignore and avoid confrontation with the scientific establishment and the religious hierarchy, and carry the story to the general public.'

* * *

I took the Metroliner on the way back from the conference, and had plenty of time to think over the decision as to whether or not to take on the writing of the book about Spiricom and its implications. There was no question that I was intensely interested in the subject as a whole. I was inclined to agree with Meek that *if* the bulk of the population were convinced that there was hard, sound, unimpeachable evidence of life after death which would support the articles of faith that religion presented, the world might not be in the mess that it already was. My feeling was that religion was not necessarily failing; it was simply faltering in the face of the materialistic philosophy that had eaten away like a moth the outdated outer garments it was wearing. With such a thing as a validated Spiricom or EVP, science could possibly shift from the position of an attacker to that of a supporter, a welcome shift in the face of the forest of nuclear warheads being planted in such profusion.

By the time the Metroliner had reached Pennsylvania Station, I was almost certain that the book should be written – but whether I should take on the job myself, I wasn't sure. There were a lot of questions that had to be answered, and a lot more probing to do. There was the important question of whether Meek's experiments could be replicated. This was, of course, what Meek was after, the main reason he had opened up his material to anyone else who would follow it up. There was still the question of whether the material could have been staged, unlikely as that seemed to be. Also, what were the thoughts of his associates? And what about O'Neil himself?

What I would have to do, I decided, was to put everything possible to a test, to challenge directly the Spiricom results, the EVP researchers, and the general theories on which they were basing their contentions. Starting with Meek and O'Neil, I decided to follow through on this before making a final decision about the book.

* * *

With many interruptions, and several deadlines, my own search extended over several months. It involved following Meek's footsteps both abroad and in the US. The difficult job was to try to get to the essence of what had propelled all those working with Meek, or who shared these same interests. The assessments that Swain had made about Meek and O'Neil could apply to all those exploring the strange circumstances of an electronic breakthrough to another dimension: there was clearly no profit in it. In fact, it required a heavy financial burden and a ponderous investment of time. There was really no fame attached to the pursuit; in fact skeptics were ready to try to tear down any effort.

Nearly all who were involved shared Meek's conviction that the marriage of religion and science was of critical importance, and the only way to bring skeptical positivists and a world steeped in mechanical materialism into the fold. They also knew there was a long way to go in attempting to establish this. In other words, they were realists. But what I wanted to find out was why a group of rational realists should want to spend so much money and time and energy trying to reach such an ephemeral goal. And had the Spiricom project actually reached that goal?

In spite of the fact that I had confidence in the basic integrity of Meek and O'Neil, the primary question above all others that had to be answered was: could the communication between O'Neil and Mueller have been staged? This would be the central focus of my follow-up and challenge. Staging, of course, would be manifestly easy to do. The motives for doing such a thing were manifestly weak, however, lacking the conventional drives of fame and fortune. Before planning to go down to North Carolina to see Meek, several weeks after the Washington press conference, I wrote to him that, as a first step, it was critically important to establish that at least the apparent voice of Mueller was not that of O'Neil carrying on a conversation with himself, or of Meek taking on the part of Mueller, even though the tapes distinctly revealed two different voices of entirely different character.

Meek, I found, was already ahead of me. He was in the process of having several speech and electronics experts analyze the voices. The preliminary reports showed that voice prints indicated clearly that there were two separate voices. He had sent some of the Mueller tapes to his colleague, Dr Hiroshi Motoyama, founder and director of the Institute for Religious Psychology in Tokyo, and author of 30 books on the subject. Motoyama had submitted the Spiricom tapes to a voice synthesis expert at the University of Tokyo, who analyzed them carefully. The conclusion was that the voice of Dr Mueller was clearly not that of either O'Neil or Meek. The expert added that the voice prints offered only one alternative suggestion: it might possibly have been computer-generated. The problem with that theory is that it would have required a million-dollar computer set-up, and many hours of complex rehearsal and adjustment, far beyond the reach of O'Neil's remote farmhouse and Meek's funds.

There was also a report Meek had just received from a British scientist named Alexander MacRae. He was considered a top expert on voice production and synthesis. As a consultant to NASA, he had helped solve the perplexing problem of 'helium speech', the major distortion that made voices sound like scrambled eggs when astronauts and divers had to converse in an atmosphere of a helium-oxygen mixture.

When MacRae first learned of the O'Neil/Mueller tapes and Spiricom, he reacted strongly against them. He felt the entire project was riddled with discrepancies. He had been doing major research himself in EVP, and simply could not embrace the idea of full two-way conversations, in spite of the fact that he acknowledged EVP voices as unquestionably true.

After a conference with Meek, when he learned about the project in full, MacRae changed his outlook. 'Much of what earlier seemed to be discrepancies,' he wrote to Meek, 'was due in fact to having only partial information in the UK. That I have completely reversed my previous position on this, I do not apologize for. I have no interest in "proving" myself right or defending a particular position if the truth as I see it dictates otherwise.'

He went on to say that there were a number of points he would still query on technical grounds but they were outweighed by cases where technical solutions paralleled his own.

Since I knew nothing about technical solutions, I would have to depend on the quality of expertise that others could bring to this enigma that was gaining in importance to me the more I learned about it. MacRae was working along different channels to reach for the same goal as Meek, but the expertise he brought to the subject reinforced the possibility of its validity, whether it was EVP or Spiricom.

Still reluctant to be drawn into this story and get bogged down in its complexities, I planned a trip to North Carolina to visit Meek in his lair, to see just how he was going about his relentless pursuit. I guess I had always undergone this sort of reluctance in the other stories of the paranormal I had written. It was so much easier to work on hard-fact, straightforward stories which at times could be physically difficult but were simple to write, once the factual detail was straightened out. In the paranormal areas, I found myself almost apologizing for getting mixed up with material that often went beyond the reach of ordinary perception. Then there was usually a reversal of mood, when I resolved to say the hell with everything else, I would do the story with the same cautious journalistic approach I would use on any story, keeping a heavy foot on the ground.

Another reason that kept me on the story was Meek. He was an interesting enigma, a cross between Executive Suite and a Buddhist monk with everything but a begging bowl and a claret-colored robe. He was the picture of sobriety – dogged, stubborn, patient, and often dull. Yet he could be relaxed at times, with daylight cracks of humor and cheer. When it came to O'Neil, here was a turbulent vortex of mixed energies that ranged through a spectrum from bright genius to cussed irascibility. Regardless of Spiricom or anything else, his story was one of the most perplexing a writer could encounter, and probably one of the most inexplicable. In either case, I was determined to challenge the incredible results they were getting, if only to convince myself of their reality.

* * *

To reach Franklin, North Carolina, the most convenient way is to fly to Atlanta and make the four-hour drive through northern Georgia to the town. It lies in the surpassingly beautiful landscape of the Great Smoky Mountains, a favorite resort area and one where many have moved in retirement. Since Bruce Swain was planning to visit Meek at about the same time, he offered to meet me at the Atlanta airport and drive me to Meek's home.

On the way up through northern Georgia, through the country where the film *Deliverance* was filmed, Swain reflected on his experience with the press conference.

'Frankly,' he said, 'I didn't expect to get the turnout we did. And I was surprised at the radio follow-up. I got back home about midnight, and the phone began ringing at 3 a.m. It was a reporter from Salt Lake City. He said he was sorry to call at this time, but he had a deadline to meet.'

Swain of course got a lot of ribbing from his faculty colleagues at the University of Georgia. 'One of them called,' Swain said, 'and said, "Hey, Bruce, this is John Belushi, and I've got George Washington waiting on the line." Another faculty member asked if he could have a press kit. "Just in case," he said. "Just in case this turns out *not* to be a fraud, I'd like to be able to tell people I knew the guy who handled the PR on the story."'

As expected, Swain said, everywhere the reaction was mixed.

We crossed the North Carolina border, with parts of the roadside scarred by an overdose of tourist signs and cabins. It was interesting country. Nearby was the Cherokee Indian reservation. They had been marched all the way out to Oklahoma by Andrew Jackson's armies to get rid of them. Thousands had died. But a few had drifted back. It was a sad story for a tribe that had an advanced culture, developing its own printing press and alphabet of 28 characters.

This was also ruby country. Signs were everywhere offering to rent equipment to tourists to go and dig for rubies. Sometimes they found them. But some suspected that some of the ruby areas were salted to keep business brisk.

News of the Spiricom press releases had reached Franklin, the first time that Meek's neighbors were fully aware of Meek's research. The local paper ran a story on it, and the reaction was mild. The minister of the Methodist Church merely commented, 'There's a lot of stuff in this story I've been preaching for about 20 years.'

Meek's home was modest, trim, and set on a promontory that overlooked the Great Smokies on the horizon. Next to it was a near-duplicate that served as a guest house, with one of Meek's two laboratories in the basement. In the basement of his own house was his office and the laboratory where he was conducting his experiments with ultraviolet and infrared photography. Like Meek, the lab was methodical. It was almost swallowed up by cameras and electronic equipment, but it was so neatly and meticulously stacked that it gave an illusion of space. There was a work bench with carefully stowed precision tools, all in mint condition. The $70,000 special TV camera and gear sat near it, furnished by Jim McDonnell of McDonnell-Douglas, whose interest in the paranormal had been equal to Meek's before he died. Through the special quartz lenses Meek was hoping to probe into what the eye could not see on the monitor.

On the wall of the office section, I noticed two framed documents. One was the flyleaf of an old annual report of the Carrier Corporation.

On it was scrawled a note from the president and chairman back in the time when Meek was his technical assistant:

> To George Meek, whose perseverance, thoroughness,
> and practical ingenuity made this notable achievement possible.
> – Willis H. Carrier

In the other frame was a letter from the president of the Munters Corporation of Sweden regarding one of the giant cooling systems Meek had designed. It read:

> The equipment you designed ran 24 hours a day for 11 years.

I couldn't help noticing the juxtaposition of these two testimonies to the mastery of part of the technical world with the exotic, fantasy-like equipment which surrounded them. I think this is what intrigued me the most, and why, in spite of Meek's occasional irritating stubbornness, his work intrigued me so much.

I talked with Meek for a day and a half. Basically, I reviewed with him the three main things he was driving towards. First was the elimination of the human medium as a go-between, and the attempt to bring the communication through completely by electronic means. What had developed so far depended considerably on O'Neil acting as a psychic channel as well as building the equipment. Meek had still not been able to separate the two. There was the same problem with O'Neil's healing abilities. Like all holistic healing it was hard to document, yet the testimonial evidence was there. But as far as the instrument for arthritis was concerned, it was hard to tell whether the results came from O'Neil's charisma or the instrument itself. Further, the instrument would have to be tested by standard procedure, and Meek had not yet found the proper organization to do this.

The second goal Meek was now driving towards was replication. The large number of EVP researchers were a natural target for this, and Meek would continue his travels to consult with them both at home and abroad. They still had not reached the point where sustained two-way communication had been held, although the reality of the voices coming from a different level of consciousness was now conceded by many who had been reluctant to do so.

The third goal Meek felt was the most important. He was determined to persuade some of the large electronics research laboratories to set up full-scale research programs to utilize their pools of top scientists and facilities to work independently on the Spiricom process. Meek felt that this type of support could boost Spiricom in the development of the finer tuning needed to reach upper astral levels where the accumulated wisdom of the highest minds should reside.

'This is where we hope to reach with our new Mark VI, VII, and VIII systems,' Meek said. 'What we're trying to do is to fly at higher altitudes than we have before.'

Sitting on the terrace of Meek's house, with the Great Smoky range looking like a cyclorama of a distant stage set, I couldn't help feeling a sense of wonderment at the far horizons Meek and his colleagues were reaching towards. The interesting thing was that their spiritual aims were matched by their pragmatic and technical perspective. Meek had a favorite quotation that seemed very apt for the occasion. It more or less summed up his outlook and efforts.

It was written by a man named R. W. Raymond:

> Life is eternal;
> And love is immortal;
> And death is only a horizon;
> And a horizon is nothing save the limit of our sight.

Visiting Meek had a profound effect on me. To see the elaborate technical lengths he was going to and the precise, organized time and effort he was applying to his objectives brought a new sense of reality. His was a hob-nailed approach combined with lofty aspirations. The problem was that I had no technical expertise to challenge his findings as a devil's advocate. I had to go by his track record (which was excellent), my own journalistic judgment (which I always protected carefully), and my appraisal of the material he had provided me. If this had been an ordinary story, I would have had little trouble in accepting its reality.

But it wasn't an ordinary story. As a devil's advocate, I would have to do considerably more probing to reach some kind of rational conclusion in the face of an irrational but critically important subject for the world.

One question in my mind was whether the world was ready for something as awesome as this, a clearly substantiated bridge between two totally different planes of existence. This was why Meek's third aspiration intrigued me. Why weren't the large electronics research laboratories setting up major programs to probe such an important question? They had huge laboratories, large research funding, unparalleled staffs of scientists, and all the equipment they needed to dwarf Meek's intense but limited methods. There were no signs anywhere that this was being done. Even if such research were merely being attempted in this exalted milieu, it would add credibility to the Spiricom efforts. I knew at least that it would have a measurable effect on my own thinking.

* * *

Some intervening projects made it difficult to me immediately to make a sustained effort to follow up on the Meek story. I was planning, however, to visit O'Neil personally as soon as possible, as well as talking directly to Meek's other associates both here and abroad as soon as time was available.

In the meantime, Meek was still continuing his dogged pursuit without a let-down. Several months after my visit to him, he received a letter. It was from one of the largest electronics research laboratories in the world. It also had, as Meek had projected, one of the largest pools of electronics scientists and facilities available anywhere. The letter was from a staff scientist there. It requested a copy of the Spiricom manual and the Mueller tape recordings, as well as any other information regarding the system. An official corporation check for $24.95 was included, the amount Metascience charged for the material to cover the expense. Meek shipped off the material, without comment, and decided to wait before following up for a possible reaction.

He waited almost six months. Then he finally called the scientist who had written. Although the scientist requested that his name and the name of the corporation remain anonymous, the reaction of both the individual and the organization was extremely interesting in the light of the high stature of both. Meek took copious notes of the phone conversation.

'This is very interesting,' the scientist said when Meek called him. 'I was going to phone you some time ago. Matter of fact, I told my associates only yesterday I was going to contact you.'

'Well,' Meek said, 'I wanted primarily to learn if you have any continuing interest in our research. Whether you want me to keep you up to date on any further developments we might make.'

'We certainly are interested,' was the reply. 'I've been involved in these matters since 1946. In Vienna. My scientific colleagues and I formed an organization called the Psychic Science Institute. One of the reasons I wanted to contact you was to tell you we plan to get some equipment together and begin experimenting with what you call the Mark IV. Would you have any up-to-date suggestions?'

Meek explained that his research had gone on to concentrate on the later models, especially a flame transducer using the plasma in the flame to move higher up in frequency.

'That certainly would make an outstanding speaker for the higher frequencies . . . and let me say that we feel that you are basically correct in trying to develop a transducer.' He was referring to the device that converts one form of energy into another, such as a microphone or a speaker. 'That is the crucial problem. We are up against the situation where we just do not know what kind of energies we are trying to connect with. Theoretically, if we learn enough about psychic matters, it should be possible to locate or develop such a transducer. Over the years, my associates and I have explored many facets of the psychic field. Personally I am quite comfortable with the idea of trying to prove there is something out there.'

Meek found the next comment interesting in view of the fact that it came from a laboratory that is one of the most scientifically advanced in the world. 'Let me tell you,' the scientist continued, 'that from our experiences we *know* that telepathy exists. We have proved it. Repeatedly. We have proved it in front of groups, many of whom are hostile to the idea. But we have to state that we do not know anything about the energies that are involved yet in this particular field of telepathy.'

'I've been wondering,' Meek said, 'if you or some of your associates have tried to make a voice print analysis or otherwise study the conversation between O'Neil and Dr Mueller?'

'Yes,' the scientist replied. 'Some rather extensive tests were made. The opinion was divided. There were some who were quite convinced that it was a valid exchange between the two parties. Yet there were the others who took the position that it would be a very easy matter to stage or create these conversations.'

Meek was aware of this, as a result of his own attempts with voice prints. 'Where do you stand?' Meek asked.

'Well,' the scientist replied, 'because of my years of research, I feel inclined to believe that they are what you think they are. However, as a hard-headed scientist, I have to say that they do not constitute proof. Not until we get such an activity to the point that we have with telepathy will there be a basis for saying we have proof.'

Meek agreed. 'That is the exact position that any qualified scientist must take at this stage of the research. If I suspend my position as a pure scientist, I can say that I've convinced myself that there is no fakery involved. But of course that's not enough. There is, though, a long list of confirmatory date we've pulled together about Dr Mueller that is very convincing. But we're still working to plug the loopholes.'

'This brings me to the reason for wanting to telephone you,' the scientist said. 'Is there anything we could do to help you with your research?'

'Well,' said Meek. 'You've caught me completely unawares with that question. I'll have to give the matter some thought.'

'Let me emphasize this,' the scientist added. 'We want to co-operate with you fully. Please tell us what we can do. Let me point out that we have available the combined knowledge of a great group of scientists. We have the expertise in almost any field that you might need information in, and men with 30 to 40 years' experience.'

'That certainly is a remarkable offer,' Meek said. 'Most generous of you.'

'All of this is only a phone call away from my desk,' the scientist continued. 'And let me state that this is not a personal matter for me or my employer. This must not be considered a means for making a profit. Few people realize what we are working with here. What is involved here is something which will someday change the course of man's evolution . . .'

Meek thanked him profusely. He found it hard to keep down his enthusiasm. It was a well-known fact that this institution had one of the world's greatest accumulations of scientists. He regretted that he had to keep the identity of the laboratories confidential. The prestige involved would add considerable impetus to the goals he was determined to reach.

When I reviewed the record of the conversation, it had a heavy impact on my thinking – and on my own vacillation. Meek told me in confidence the name of the laboratories involved. I knew them well. If scientists of this stature were seriously interested in the subject, and actively exploring it, it was a strong impetus to continue my quest.

# CHAPTER 14

## *The Challenge*

I think it is probable that anyone who digs into the anatomy of a phenomenon like the paranormal has to face a belief struggle within himself. At least that continued to be the case with me. At one point the evidence would appear clear and unassailable. At another, the transmission of a voice from another dimension seemed ridiculous and impossible, in spite of the evidence. Yet the voices were there and fully audible, whether in the case of Meek's Spiricom project or in the thousands of experiments of the Electronic Voice Phenomenon. Neither could be easily or even rationally explained away.

When I looked at the scene in one way, Meek was making absolutely ridiculous claims. They had to be challenged, even if they couldn't be explained away. I reflected on the scene when Meek had first arrived at our house, and presented his story. I thought then that such ideas would have to be subjected to the most meticulous scrutiny. Many months later, I was still feeling the same way. What I would have to do was consult with the most responsible and reputable people in the field, Meek's associates and others, while Meek went on to try to reach his goal of finding replication elsewhere.

There was Walter Uphoff, for instance. In his 60s, he was now turning his exclusive interest to the study of the paranormal. That was not necessarily a good sign, because it put him in a biased position. However, he was working from a broad base, having had a long and successful career in economics and labor relations at the Universities of Minnesota and Colorado.

I visited him on his farm just outside Madison, Wisconsin, where his basement office was smothered with a clutter of documents, books, periodicals and tape cassettes, all of them on the subject of psychic research. They were all part of the non-profit organization he and his wife Mary Jo had formed, called the New Frontiers Center. Uphoff and his wife had recently brought out a revised edition of the book *New Psychic Frontiers.* It covered the many years of research they had carried out since Uphoff had taught a special honors course in parapsychology at the University of Colorado.

Uphoff had a blunt, direct congeniality about him. I told him of my reservations about the Meek project and the entire EVP scene.

'The evidence is impressive,' I said. 'But do you feel it is well substantiated?'

Uphoff thought a moment, then said, 'Well, I pitched in to help George in tracking down the facts on Mueller's life at the University of Wisconsin here. The results were quite impressive. The small details, especially.'

'What particular ones?' I asked.

'There were a lot of facts about Mueller that were easy to come by,' he said. 'His general records and that sort of thing. But let me give you one example. He brought out the fact that he was a member of the Haresfoot Club. This was a very obscure organization here, and you would have to have been very conversant with campus life in the late '20s to know it even existed. In fact, it was not recorded in his college year book. The record was found in a remote theatrical program that the archivist just stumbled on by accident. To me, this lent a lot of credibility.'

'What about the EVP voices?' I asked. 'There seems to be a lot of controversy about them. Do they bolster George's cause?'

'They appeal to me,' Uphoff said, 'because they are a lot more difficult for skeptics to dismiss than many psychic phenomena.'

'In what way?' I asked.

'They are admittedly very brief. Just a few short phrases at a time. But in spite of their brevity, it's impossible to explain how specific names and identifying detail can repeatably be received on the tapes. They rule out the wandering radio signal theory that seems to be the only objection to their validity.'

'And you feel Meek's project goes beyond that?'

'It goes far beyond that. The voice communication responds directly over a long sequence of questions and answers. It responds directly through speakers without waiting for the tape to be re-run.'

'Is there any way you can picture that the Spiricom messages can be ruled out?'

'The only criticism I can make is that maybe George released the news too soon. Maybe he could have waited for a back-up demonstration.'

'Are you sure, Walter,' I said, 'that you're not letting your enthusiasm run away with you?'

'The interesting thing,' Uphoff replied, 'is that I went through the whole background of psychic studies before I came to any conclusions at all. From agnosticism to skepticism to conviction. So I'm not too surprised when I learn that communication can be made with those on another plane. The whole universe is energy, and energy is never destroyed. So it's logical that it could be channeled for communication. It's not that far out.'

'Well,' I said, 'if all this is true, I guess we don't need to be so uptight about death.'

Uphoff laughed. 'I have a favorite phrase that Harold Sherman likes to quote. He's a former journalist, like yourself, who began to cover stories like this one. He's always saying, "You are part of creation. You cannot die out of it. We die from one dimension to the next. You can laugh at death when it comes. We dread it only because we don't know it."' It was an uplifting thought to end our conversation.

Uphoff's sober observations and reflections were a reinforcement of the potential of the O'Neil/Mueller tapes. Our chat did not remove all of my doubts, however, and I looked forward to finding out what the other qualified experts might have to say regarding the strange world of Spiricom.

* * *

My next visit was to one of Meek's associates, Hans Heckmann. Heckmann lived in a modest, tidy home in Lansdowne, a suburb of Philadelphia, not too far from Overbrook where I had grown up and gone to Friends' Central School. I had not been back there for many years, and as I passed by familiar landmarks on my way to Heckmann's house, I thought how strange this was to be returning to follow up on such an off-the-wall phenomenon as this. Anyone who mentioned the psychic in those school days would have been greeted with a fishy stare, and I would have been among the first to give it.

Heckmann had had his own heavy reservations when he tentatively began the explorations with Meek's Philadelphia group back in the early '70s. His work with computers and electronics demanded a methodical and analytic approach, and he kept applying that as he worked on the instruments that he hoped could break through to another dimension.

'I had to prove everything to myself, step by step,' he told me, as we sat in his Lansdowne living room over a cup of coffee. 'I always had doubts in my mind, and thoughts that there must be a rational explanation for all this. I was constantly vacillating between belief and disbelief. When we got the news about the Spiricom breakthrough, it hit like a bombshell. Here was hard evidence right on the tape that was to continue over a period of a year and a half. Everybody agreed that the process could be staged, but knowing Meek's unquestioned integrity, there would be no motivation for it. And for such a length of time? It didn't add up. If he and O'Neil wanted to fool someone, they could have carried it out for a handful of hours, and achieved the same results.'

His thoughts were echoing my own. The impossibly long hours of attrition would have been a useless redundancy in trying to convince the world they had accomplished the impossible.

'I've been thinking the same thing,' I told Heckmann. 'I don't think either Meek or O'Neil could be that deluded.'

'By no stretch of the imagination could I see anyone going through all these monotonous actions over such a protracted period of time,' Heckmann said. 'I've also considered a lot of other angles.'

'I have, too,' I said. 'What are some of yours?'

'Well, for instance, could Dr Mueller's voice simply be O'Neil's voice carrying on a conversation with himself?'

'What did you conclude on that?' I asked.

'Just about impossible,' Heckmann said. 'The voices of the two are entirely different, in tone and quality. In some cases, the voices overlap. The replies and questions are spontaneous and natural. George has some preliminary voice prints that show the difference, and in Japan the university there reported that Mueller's purported voice is neither Meek's nor O'Neil's.'

'How about a third party – a ham radio operator nearby coming in on the frequency to fake it?'

'That's an angle that has to be looked at,' Heckmann said. 'But keep this in mind. Most of the material was recorded between two and four in the morning, and again over that long period of a year and a half. He would have had to memorize and absorb Mueller's entire breadth of knowledge, his philosophy, his background, his unlisted but verified phone numbers, his Social Security number, his whole life span. What would there be in it for him? He would have less to gain than O'Neil – who had next to nothing to gain. I'm not saying it would be impossible, but it would be next to impossible.'

'It would take an incredible Stanislavsky method actor to keep this up,' I said. 'And anyone that talented wouldn't want to waste his time on this. To say nothing of the sheer boredom involved.'

Heckmann thought for a moment, then said, 'Another thing. I tried experimenting with an artificial larynx to see if I could duplicate the strange sound of both Doc Nick's and Mueller's voices. There was a vague similarity, but it wasn't even close. At one point, O'Neil says to wait until he adjusts the frequency – turns the voices higher. As O'Neil adjusts the audio tones up and down, the voice on the speaker follows the same tonal pattern. That wouldn't happen with O'Neil using an artificial larynx – which he couldn't do anyway with such a fast exchange of questions and answers.'

We continued talking for over an hour more. The upshot was that Heckmann had almost reluctantly – in the face of logic – come to the conclusion that the contact with Mueller had a more than 90 per cent chance of being real, and that it couldn't be chalked off by any means. Together we sat down and made a list of the plus and minus values of the probability that the phenomenon was genuine.

On the plus side were O'Neil's genuine desire for anonymity, which Meek finally persuaded him to give up; that Mary Alice O'Neil had observed some of the sessions, and believed in him; that several Mueller predictions had come true; the confirmed unlisted phone numbers; the change of pitch of the voices with frequency adjustments; the long months of sustained activity; the obscure facts of Mueller's life revealed; the voice prints and technical opinion regarding them.

On the minus side were the possibility of Bill's taking the part of both voices; possible availability of background data; a third person on the air; the fact that no one else had accomplished a two-way sustained conversation of this sort.

The plus column clearly outweighed the minus column; but a final conclusion still was begging. One thing was certain: an historic breakthrough could still not be ruled out, along with its implications for a confused and troubled world.

* * *

With my reservations still unabated, I tracked down Willard Cerney, President of Marine Electronics Services. He was sitting in his office at Fort Myers Beach, surrounded by a bewildering array of digital depth finders, radar equipment, radio direction finders, and other equipment designed to keep a ship on course. A patient and precise man, Cerney could tame the complexities of almost any marine electronic gear – and still have time to spend hours and months and years to join Meek's search to reach toward other dimensions. After several early experiences with precognitive dreams, Cerney often found himself pondering the question of life after death.

'What intrigued me was that there is a worldwide belief that we continue after this life. Also, historically, nearly all people from all races believe the same thing. I always apply the coldest possible logic to my work with circuitry, and I did the same with this question. I figured intelligence had to come from somewhere and if this energy in the spectrum exists after we die, it must exist today. My conclusion: it does exist, and there just might be a way to reach it.'

Cerney added that the real excitement of the Spiricom project came when Doc Nick's voice came through. When Mueller came through later, it was simply an improvement and refinement of the first breakthrough.

I asked him about the big question on my mind: could O'Neil have been carrying on a conversation with himself?

'Oddly enough,' Cerney replied, 'that's the first question I asked myself. But no matter how much a person tried to disguise his voice, the evidence would show up on the oscilloscope I used to analyze the tapes.'

He drew some sketches of the oscilloscope patterns, but they had little meaning to me. 'When you play the background tone alone, there is a smooth shape to the contours,' Cerney said. 'When O'Neil talks, there's a mixed pattern. You can see his words interweaving, but the tone is still there. When either Doc Nick or Mueller talks, there is a clear change in the amplitude. But beyond that, I checked other possible ways this could be faked. I tried to fake it exactly in a dozen different ways, but I couldn't. In fact I went up to Pennsylvania to check him out. He had neither the capability nor the equipment to accomplish such a long-term fakery – and he was far behind in the advanced electronics stuff in use today.'

'Do you think this is going to be replicated?' I asked Cerney.

'I'll tell you honestly,' Cerney answered, 'there is going to be so much stuff popping up in the next several years that it will make the Spiricom project look like a nursery school.'

'How do you figure that?' I asked.

'With the number of people working on EVP both here and in Europe,' Cerney replied, 'something is bound to happen. Of course, you never can be certain – that's part of the excitement.'

As a technical man, Cerney was a strong pillar of Meek's research, as Heckmann was. To get deeper into the puzzle, however, I turned my attention to probing the theory and philosophy of Meek's mission. Robert Jeffries, I was told, might have some of the answers for that.

* * *

Dr Robert Jeffries had been unable to attend the Washington press conference, but had been a close associate of Meek for 13 years, and admired him greatly. Jeffries interested me. Here was an outstanding executive, engineer, professor and university administrator who said in effect, to hell with everything else, the most important thing in the world is the basic nature of man and his relation to the cosmos. Yet he was living actively and dynamically in two worlds at the same time.

He remained on the board of trustees of the University of Bridgeport, of his mutual fund and advanced electronics corporation and other down-to-earth technical activities. But he went to live in Virginia Beach to help restructure the Edgar Cayce operation there known as the Association for Research and Enlightenment.

When I asked how he had developed his friendship with George Meek, he answered, 'We had a lot in common. We were both engineers. We were strangers in the paranormal field when we first met. But we began exploring it together. Meek enjoys going to the cutting edge of psychic research, and he has the courage to do it. He's single-minded, bull-headed, and sometimes treads heavily on other people's opinions. He doesn't take advice very graciously. I respect him and think he's on the right track. When you put things all together, what George has done is not that far removed from what we already know. The big problem is that all psi research is rather erratic. It doesn't lend itself to systematic study, and the psychic medium is often variable in his results.'

Like Meek, he thought the greatest contribution he could make to world peace was through the exploration of the ultimate destiny of the individual after this life. 'In scouting around this area,' Jeffries said, 'I came to the conclusion that if survival beyond physical death could be proved, this would have the greatest influence on attitudes and behavior on people and make them turn to a better life – individually and collectively.'

Jeffries, tall and commanding, was a persuasive speaker. I told him about my problem in trying to comprehend some of the hard-to-conceive physical elements in the paranormal field, such as materializations, poltergeist activity, possession and other phenomena. These were the things that were causing my deepest reservations about the Meek/O'Neil story.

'Many people feel that way,' he said. 'But the problem is that they haven't had the chance or taken the time to study the field in depth. Cayce, who to me is the most modern expression of a great psychic, said that thought has reality. It's as hard as concrete. The Yogis of India or Nepal take this sort of thing in their stride. They apparently have the ability to control the hormonal secretions in their body which can produce the unbelievable physical things they do, both inside and outside the body. Even the Menninger Clinic has done studies that show that if an individual develops the ability to control hormone secretions, he can manifest a variety of abilities that we would say are paranormal. I have observed a trance medium who produced a human hand, yet it dissolved when I grasped it. Apports – the carrying of material objects either across a room or simply reappearing in another location – have been clearly observed dozens of times. Cayce stated in his readings that some people are like geniuses as transmission links in a physical sense. The endocrine system, he says, makes it possible to take what are basically thoughts and convert them into physical expressions that can take the form of mere energy projections – like poltergeist action.' He paused a moment, then added, 'I guess you could sum up everything with the thought that what Meek is accomplishing doesn't really surprise me. In fact, I'd be surprised if someone didn't come up with what George has done.'

* * *

Uphoff, Heckmann, Cerney, and Jeffries: they were all credible people dealing in incredible worlds. They gave me fresh insights that reduced my reservations, but didn't fully eliminate them. I wanted to check with them first, however, before I talked to Meek's contacts abroad, many of whom had made strong progress in the EVP area, which could reinforce the concept of trans-plane communications if I could become convinced of its reality.

I planned my trip to Europe in the fall of 1982, but just before I left I arranged to visit Bill O'Neil. I wanted to see first hand the conditions under which he worked, and to see how he measured up to a skeptical eye. He had stubbornly refused to move from his fire-battered farmhouse, and continued to turn down all of Meek's offers to come to North Carolina. Mary Alice was still living several miles away, taking care of her ill and elderly father, but she and Bill were continuing to 'date' regularly.

O'Neil lived in a rugged area some 35 miles north of Pittsburgh, characterized by towns with such intriguing place names as Slate Lick, Girty, Gastown, Smitsburg and Punxsutawney. The house was hard to find. Elizabeth and I met Mary Alice in the town of Kittanning so that we could take advantage of her navigation through twisting roads along the Allegheny River. I was reminded of the time that Elizabeth and I had climbed to several high and remote monasteries in the Himalayas, where the Buddhists sought the isolation they felt brought them in closer contact with the mysteries of life and death. I wondered if Bill O'Neil didn't feel something of that urge, where he could reflect on the imponderable forces of the universe, as he found himself compelled to do. As a medium, he was a seer. As a non-theocratic believer in God, his course ran parallel to the Buddhist monks, in whose daily lives meditation and utter acceptance of occult miracles were commonplace. The continuous series of psychic adventures that Bill O'Neil had experienced over the recent years would be a burden under the most prosperous of circumstances. To undergo them in the chaotic atmosphere of a shell of a house and the lack of an adequate income added an extra burden.

And yet there was no question that Bill O'Neil chose to live this way, an ascetic life with the minimum of creature comforts, with a compulsive passion to turn his electronics into a spiritual reality, and to help the sick without regard for compensation. He was proud of his Seneca Indian ancestry, and perhaps this might have contributed to a way of life that O'Neil himself frankly admits is strange and inexplicable. The Senecas had a deep belief in the Great Spirit, in the strength and power of the Shaman, in the profoundness of the occult forces of nature everywhere. Many of these attributes must have come down through the genes to create the bizarre mixture of a Buddhist monk linked with the Radio Shack.

Throughout history, the isolated ascetic has been the most likely to reach out beyond the frenetic motions of the materialistic life. Maybe this was O'Neil, in latter day form. It was impossible summarily to dismiss his day-by-day activities that had taken place since the first moments of his mediumship. The sessions with Mueller, whether coming through the Spiricom instruments, or reported indirectly by O'Neil on tape, would have been senseless to conduct over a year and a half without his own deep commitment and conviction in their reality.

Just before Elizabeth and I left to visit O'Neil, Meek sent me a note to prepare us, more or less, for the encounter. 'Forget the condition and appearance of the house, and that sort of thing,' Meek wrote to me. 'You can have little concept of the talent locked up in this "eighth grade drop-out", as Bill refers to himself. In a strange way, he and Mueller have pioneered some developments which are almost beyond comprehension. In my recent visit, however, I found Bill on the first day to be remote, unco-operative, petty, withdrawn, morose and bitter. On the second day, while he was working with people at his little healing center, I found him to be charismatic, outgoing, exuberant, confident, and expansive. This will give you an idea of the range that Bill's personality covers.'

In spite of this preparation, I experienced something of a shock when we pulled into the rough and bumpy driveway at O'Neil's house. Mary Alice had warned us on the way out that it would hardly be a candidate for *Better Homes and Gardens*. It was a gaunt, two-storey clapboard shell, L-shaped, weatherbeaten and foreboding. Facing the driveway were two bleak open window frames, the scorched interior plainly visible beyond them. Straight ahead was a door frame, newly repaired with fresh clean lumber. Along one side was large plywood sheathing that had replaced the burnt-away clapboards.

O'Neil greeted us cordially, and led us through the doorway, through a partially gutted hallway to a small room on the first floor. If it had not been connected with the rest of the house, it would have been hard to believe that we were in the same building. Although it was far from elegant, the walls were paneled in random width knotty pine. The room was sparsely furnished with occasional chairs, a desk and a single bed along the wall, that served as a sofa. We chatted informally before going up the charred stairway to his laboratory. O'Neil brought up the lore and traditions of his Seneca lineage, especially what he called the 'live forever' plant, a plant for which he could find no botanical name. 'The Senecas knew about it, about how it can be broken off and re-planted and won't die. It comes up through the ice in the spring and the leaves have a healing action,' he said.

Up the shaky stairs leading to his laboratory, we found the room was still charred, with very little refurbishing. A maze of equipment was there, however, still in use for his continuing experiments, unsuccessful over the recent months.

At the top of the stairs, I had to put the question to O'Neil. 'Bill,' I said, 'this place is really in rough shape. You're freezing to death in winter, the walls are charred in all but two rooms, you have to haul wood and water – why do you stay here?'

O'Neil smiled. 'Remember what the Zen monk said when they asked how he got along when he wasn't meditating?'

'I can't remember,' I said, although I had read a lot of Zen material.

'He said, "I draw water, I carry wood."'

'Sure,' I answered. 'But George has offered you a nice place in North Carolina, and all the help you need to move there.'

'There's another reason, too, John,' O'Neil said.

'What's that?'

'Just stand here and listen,' he said. I started to say something, but he put his finger to his lips. So Elizabeth and I kept silent, for at least a full minute. We could hear absolutely nothing, except the sound of a few birds. Then O'Neil spoke.

'What do you hear?' he asked.

'Nothing, really,' I said. 'A few birds. A little wind in the trees.'

'There you have it,' O'Neil said. 'Peace and silence. Could there be a better reason?'

From O'Neil's point of view I could see what he meant even though I couldn't from my own. We moved on into the room that served as his lab.

'Over there,' O'Neil said, pointing to a darkened corner of the room, 'was where Dr Mueller first appeared, before his voice actually came through on the equipment. I looked up quickly, and there he was. I did some reality testing and asked him to do something to prove he was here. He knocked a book off the table, and that convinced me. His voice was clearly audible at the time, not as distorted as it was through the speaker and on the tapes.'

I made it plain to Bill that I had still to remain skeptical in the light of the fact that the Mueller communications had stopped, and were not repeatable.

He conceded that this was a great weakness. 'This blocks full credibility of what had happened over those many months of recorded communication,' he said. 'I *know* it is a fact, and am at the point of saying, to hell with what anyone else thinks. There is so much evidential material that Dr Mueller provided that I'm not the least concerned about anything but my own integrity. The material in his forecasts was right on the track of what actually happened. The unlisted phone numbers and personal information could have been known only by Mueller himself. Adding it all up, and no matter what happens, I will never give up my efforts to enlighten all of humanity as to the reality of life after death.'

Meek did have on record a number of forecasts by exact date that O'Neil had forwarded to him, all of them reasonably accurate. They involved events in Afghanistan, Rhodesia, Iran, Nicaragua, El Salvador and South America, the Middle East and Mexico, oil prices and crises, which, if the dates were correct, could not have been known at the time. In the healing area, there were over a dozen affidavits signed within a few weeks of our visit, reporting successful healings as the result of O'Neil's holistic treatments.

All added to the mystery, but still failed to provide the confirmed link with a different experimenter in another location who had been able to bring at least some kind of two-way conversation through a direct loudspeaker. In spite of my own research and travel, I was still having trouble conceiving of the idea that *any* kind of voice or message from a different dimension could be received, let alone such sequences as those recorded on the O'Neil/Mueller tapes.

Elizabeth and I were quiet for a long spell driving home from the visit. If ever there were an enigmatic puzzle, it was Bill O'Neil. Finally I asked Elizabeth what she thought.

'I think he's legit,' she said. 'Nobody could possibly fabricate such a wild sequence of affairs over such a long stretch of time. It just doesn't add up.'

'Don't forget,' I said. 'He calls himself Crazy Bill.'

'Yes,' said Elizabeth, 'but he's still got his wheels on the ground.'

'Forgetting everything else, like the healings and other phenomena,' I said, 'the one question I'm trying to answer is: did Dr Mueller actually speak from another world through electronic circuits? Everything else is on the periphery.'

'I think you have to go on the percentage of probability on that,' Elizabeth said.

'How would you figure that?'

'You start with the fact that this kind of communication is absolutely impossible. A lot of people don't even admit the possibility of life after death. A certain percentage do, however.'

'The Gallup Poll says nearly 70 per cent do believe in it. Also 20 per cent believe it will be scientifically proved someday.'

'Does the poll say how many believe we can communicate with those who have died?'

'I think about 70 per cent believe "no". That's a complete reverse of figures from those who believe in life after death.'

'In other words,' Elizabeth said, 'although you have a terrific number of people who don't question that we live on, there's an equally terrific number who think we could never reach them?'

'Apparently that's the way it is,' I said.

'So O'Neil and Meek are working against the odds.'

'They are. Yes. But the people in the survey haven't gone through the history of paranormal research. They haven't traced the whole history of the O'Neil/Mueller tapes. I don't see how anyone could even begin to believe this if they hadn't done so.'

'I think you're right there,' Elizabeth said.

'When you add it all up, what's your educated guess on the probability?'

Elizabeth thought a moment, then said, 'All right. I told you my gut instinct is that the tapes are legit. Making a wild guess, I'd say that the odds for that would be 75 to 25 that the tapes are real.'

'I feel the same way,' I said. 'Only I'd make the odds 80 to 20.'

'If you feel that close,' Elizabeth said, 'why don't you go the whole way and say you're completely convinced?'

'I'd have to see that duplicate experiment, if it ever happens. Entirely away from that farmhouse in Pennsylvania,' I said. 'Or at least an approximation. But let's see how I feel after I talk to Meek's experimenters in Europe.'

I was still determined to keep up the challenge, in spite of the fact that my skepticism seemed to be gradually weakening.

# CHAPTER 15

## *Other Voices – Other Worlds*

Meek had spent considerable time with EVP researchers in Europe. They all learned from each other, but Meek felt that EVP was basically the crystal set, rice-paper and match stick state of the art. He was hoping that their pioneer work in transcommunication could blend with the progress made in Spiricom, and reach that important step of replication. Long after his worldwide press announcement, no such breakthrough was in sight.

My knowledge of EVP was limited. I got hold of a few specimen tapes, and listened to them. The phrases were short and choppy. There was no direct response to questions. The operator still had to wait to play the tape back to get an answer. The noise level was extremely high. The percentage of clear, unambiguous statements was low. It was hard to get direct knowledge of the unseen persons responding, or to get long, meaningful phrases. Some did, however, and often asked for prayers. Many seemed to be from the lower levels, which Meek was not interested in contacting.

I studied a book called *Carry on Talking*, written by Peter Bander, the British writer and publisher who had interviewed several prominent clergymen about the voices. I was surprised to find the responses supportive. The Rev Fr Pistone, SSP, commented, 'I do not see anything against the teaching of the Catholic Church in the voices. They are something extraordinary but there is no reason to fear them, nor can I see any danger.' The Rev Prof Dr Gebhard Frei said, 'All that I have read and heard forces me to believe that the voices come from transcendental individual entities. Whether it suits me or not, I have no right to doubt the reality of the voices.'

I discovered that these opinions were more or less echoed by engineers and technicians who had studied the phenomenon. The consensus was that there was no question that the voices were real, that they were unidentified entities not from the living, and that they could not be explained in terms of the physical sciences.

Following in Meek's footsteps, I went first to Germany in the autumn of 1982 to talk to Professor Ernst Senkowski, the cheerful, whimsical gentleman I had met at the Washington press conference. He was an eminent EVP experimenter with a passionate desire to carry the Spiricom research along. As a lecturer in physics at the Technical College at Bingen, Germany, and a former UNESCO expert in physics, Senkowski was steeped in the subject and in electronics, which he also taught. 'We're at a critical point in the history of science,' he told me at dinner in the quiet dining room of the Nassauer Hof in Wiesbaden. 'Quarks are dead. The twistor theory is in. Twistors are massless fields that hit the exotic problem areas like bioenergy, interactions between hyperspace and mass-energy fields, even "twisted" photons. Any physicist who doesn't reach out into these new areas and beyond is going to be left behind. Including EVP and Meek's project.'

'What bothers me most,' I told him, 'is that none of the EVP communications have come anywhere near the hours of extended conversation on the O'Neil/Mueller tapes.'

'That is true,' Senkowski said. 'That's why I'm working hard to try to replicate them.'

'Have you had any luck?' I asked.

'So far I'm still in the EVP stage.'

'What chances do you think there are of a repeatable demonstration to confirm Spiricom?'

'I've been looking for the missing links between physics and metaphysics since my days at the University of Hamburg. It's impossible to predict in this field.'

'Do you consider EVP fully comfirmable?' I asked.

'Absolutely. It's not as articulate as Spiricom, but to me there's no question that it's valid. There are over 1,000 members of the German EVP organization. It was put together by a very interesting woman named Hanna Buschbeck. You must make it a point to see her.'

'How can you rule out the possibility that the voices are just wandering radio signals? That's another thing that bothers me,' I said.

'I'll show you when you come to my lab tomorrow,' he said.

At his home in Mainz the following morning, Senkowski demonstrated some of the results he had been getting on his EVP set up. Working from his log that indicated the numbers on the footage counter, Senkowski ran through one of his tapes. Unlike Spiricom however, he had to pose the question on the tape, then wait for several seconds, then play the tape back. However, the results were clear. At the 315 mark on the footage counter, Senkowski's voice could be clearly heard asking if someone could call him back with the code name 'Aurora.' Within seconds, a rather hollow voice came back: 'Aurora – yes!'

'Sounds spooky,' I told him.

'That's the way I felt when I first heard it. My wife and kids came in, and they almost ran out of the room. But you get used to it.'

Then he played another segment. At the 334 marker, Senkowski asked on the tape: 'Can you confirm this, please?'

Again the answer came back plainly: 'I can confirm.'

At the 364 marker, Senkowski asked a question with the background sound at rather high volume. It was hard to hear on the tape. But quickly, the unidentified voice came in: 'The tone is so loud.'

There was little question of the validity of Senkowski's work but, like Meek, he was striving for the confirmation of the sustained two-way conversation the Spiricom project had produced.

'What is being done over here in Europe about this specifically?' I asked.

'There's a researcher here in Germany named Hans Otto König. Lives near Düsseldorf. I'm keeping in close touch with him. I'm convinced that if anyone can do it, he can. He may just be the answer Meek is looking for.'

'Any idea when?' I asked.

'I wouldn't want to promise,' Senkowski said. 'But I've put Meek in touch with him – and you know George when he gets a lead on anything.'

* * *

The train from Mainz and Wiesbaden runs down the Neckar Valley, towards the Black Forest and the Swabian Jura, towards the village of Horb-am-Neckar where Hanna Buschbeck lived. It is ravishing country, with castles, moats, cuckoo clocks, and half-timbered rustic villages filled with charm. Horb was no exception. Hanna Buschbeck, a feisty gray-haired lady in her 60s, lived there and once each year lured EVP researchers to a conference at a lovely little inn in the village.

In her home on a winding thirteenth-century street, she told of how she had turned her general interest in electronics to EVP, after reading Jürgenson's book in the late '60s. She was skeptical at first. But she was startled when she played one tape back, and a voice clearly said: 'Hanna!' Her husband had died the year before, and in asking a question about him, the tape came back with a reply: 'Friedhof's Hotel.' This shocked her. *Friedhof* means graveyard. No hotel would be likely to carry that name.

In April, 1969, she was continuing her experiments, when the playback of the tape brought a voice that sounded exactly like that of her sister. 'At two o'clock the life was ended,' it said. Startled, she called her brother-in-law, fully expecting this to be a fantasy. It wasn't. Her sister had just died, and her husband had not even had time to call her.

But she wasn't satisfied with her own small personal communications. She helped the publishers of the German magazine *Esotera* to answer the flood of mail they were receiving about EVP, and went on to issue a newsletter. As many as 180 scientists and researchers came to the village of Horb for one conference. Collating group information convinced her of the reality and importance of the phenomenon, as she continued to probe it. The trend seemed to be away from the personal sort of messages to the impersonal, and to the attempt to find out what dimension the voices exist in. When a friend of hers said that she shouldn't try to talk to the dead, she replied: 'EVP shows us there's no such thing as being dead. We just go on living on some other level.'

She considered Spiricom as a logical extension of the EVP voices, but like the latter, she was sure it would be controversial. 'The Electronic Voice Phenomenon has got to be accepted by any open-minded person,' she said. 'It's there, on thousands and thousands of tapes, from Raudive to Jürgenson to all the others. Yet it is still challenged in spite of the concrete evidence. Specific names and situations are referred to, facts that couldn't possibly be attributed to stray radio signals. Evidence is constantly being recorded in the United States, Europe and elsewhere, by independent researchers. And though the quality is often bad, at least a quarter of the voices are clear and understandable. The only drawback is that the tape has to be replayed to listen to the voices which come only in short bursts. If Mr Meek's immediate two-way conversations can be duplicated here, I think the controversy may quieten down.'

But that wasn't forthcoming. Somewhere I hoped there would be a clue, in addition to Senkowski's mention of Hans Otto König, among Meek's other contacts in Europe. I could not help but be impressed by their qualifications and standing. Especially in Geneva, where I went to meet Alex Schneider, Prof. Diplom. Ing. ETH of the State College of St Gallen of Switzerland. As a Ph.D. and a professor of physics, as well as a specialist in high frequency electronics, he was highly respected in his country and was President of the Swiss Parapsychological Society. I talked with him the day after I had left Horb. We met in the lounge of the Dolder Grand Hotel in Zürich, where potted palms and chamber music were reminiscent of the elegant days of the turn of the century.

A distinguished, tall, gray-haired gentleman, Professor Schneider spoke in fluent English. Having worked for several years directly with Raudive, he felt that Meek's work was a substantial step forward.

'But we have to remember,' he said, 'that both EVP and Meek were not the first evidence of well-documented information. The experiments of thought-photography, where "spirit" forms clearly appear, are too many to be disregarded. Dematerialization, materialization and ectoplasm are also clearly established, except for those who refuse to look at the evidence. I see all these phenomena together as documentary information from the so-called dead. But the main problem as I see it is to eliminate the need for a human medium, and none of us has reached that point yet. This is what Meek was after.'

It was also what I was after, in the sense that technological proof – or even strong evidence of it – could eliminate those gnawing doubts about human interference or delusions that could convert fancy into assumed fact.

* * *

Throughout the rest of the trip in Europe, I was unable to pin down my own convictions or wipe out my lingering skepticism, in spite of some persuasive evidence from other credible sources Meek had referred me to.

At the tiny village of Aldbrough, on the edge of the North Sea just north of Kingston-upon-Hull, Raymond Cass, one of Britain's leading exponents in EVP research, lived in a pleasant cottage near the steep cliff that formed the eastern shore of England at that point. He was both an electronics and hearing aid specialist whose patient experiments with EVP had been fruitful in producing articulate and palpable results. He was also a penetrating scholar and analyst of the entire field with many interesting theories concerning it.

His conclusions were unambiguous: the EVP voices existed in fact, and could not be denied. They were clearly not stray radio transmissions or random noises on the tape recorder. The reception was enhanced, he thought, by the mediumistic capacity of the experimenter, although this was not absolutely necessary. Cass was also convinced that there is an unknown energy involved that possibly interacts with gravity fields, in the manner of poltergeist activity, where gravity is sometimes suspended.

'The interesting thing about the Meek and the Spiricom project,' Cass said, 'is that it carries the EVP material to an entirely new level. But the most intriguing thing is that you only have two choices with the O'Neil/Mueller tapes. Either you say they are a complete hoax – or – you admit that they are a direct telephonic communication with a surviving personality. There is no middle ground. There are no other choices.'

'How do you feel?' I asked him.

'I've gone over the tapes time and time again, as an audiophonic expert. There's one thing I'm certain of. There are two different voices. In other words, O'Neil is not holding a conversation with himself. Other voice tests are still being made by Meek, but I'm confident they'll show the same results. Those of us who know Meek and his track record are convinced that there is no fraud on his part.'

'What about a hoax set up from the outside?'

'You mean a conspiratorial group using "dirty tricks"?'

'Something like that,' I said.

'There would have to be carefully scripted and endlessly rehearsed material zeroed in to Meek's operating frequencies, sustained over a period of 18 months at the most outlandish hours of the night, and a high budget to finance an electronics expert who would be idiot enough to do this. And for what motive or reason? It doesn't add up.'

'How about replication?' I asked.

'That's critically important, and that's what Meek is zeroing in on right now. Actually, in a crude sense, he already *has* confirming evidence, with EVP. In other words, the O'Neil/Mueller voices are not an isolated occurrence, but simply a major improvement on previous results. This might not be the kind of replication Meek ultimately wants, but in a sense, it's here right now.'

'What about the political material and the forecasts Mueller apparently made to O'Neil? Some of them have been on the nose. In other words, does this bring in the question of Military Intelligence?'

'That raises a very interesting point,' Cass replied. 'I've been receiving a series of letters from an intelligent and perceptive gentleman named Philip Paul. He is extremely interested in EVP, and I've passed along to him what material I have on hand. His address was simply a Post Office Box in San Antonio, Texas. However, on one letterhead he sent was a more complete address – Kelly Air Force Base.'

'Do you think this was official interest on the part of Air Force Intelligence?' I asked.

'I'm not sure. It's a mystery,' Cass replied. 'He wrote me a letter when he learned about Meek and Spiricom, and said this development took him completely by surprise. When he heard the O'Neil/Mueller tapes, he wrote to me that he was prepared to give Meek the benefit of the doubt. Said it was possible that Spiricom was genuine. I thought from his previous attitude that he would dismiss it as preposterous.'

'He apparently had not?'

'I wrote back to him that in one or two places of the O'Neil/Mueller tapes, Mueller had yielded some high quality international information of a specific nature. I added that if the Soviet scientists studying the paranormal had made similar breakthroughs, a whole new source for scientific information might be tapped internationally. It's a big, very valid question.'

'What else did you learn about Mr Paul?' I asked.

'He had also been corresponding with Professor Senkowski,' Cass said. 'Senkowski was as mystified as I was – especially about the Kelly Air Force Base connection. The whole thing is still a mystery. Why did he have two different letterheads? One with just the box number, the other with the same box number, but the Air Force Base designation? And why didn't he ever mention directly his connection with the Air Force?'

From his letters, the enigmatic Mr Paul seemed to be as informed about the whole EVP phenomenon as those who had been researching it for years. Another factor was even more interesting: it was obvious from his letters that he never questioned the reality of the EVP voices as paranormal phenomena. He was interested in alternative explanations, however, other than communication with post-mortem sources. These were equally, if not more, exotic. One he called OD – standing for 'Other Dimensions'. Another was PU – standing for 'Parallel Universe'. The questions these designations posed was: was science fast catching up with science fiction? If so, this would go a long way in reducing my own reservations about the paranormal – including Spiricom.

There was one other strange item connected with the letters of Philip Paul. Each page bore a rubber stamp message that read: THIS CORRESPONDENCE/DATA IS OF A PRIVATE NATURE. DO NOT COPY, QUOTE OR SHARE THE INFORMATION CONTAINED WITH OTHER PARTIES. There was no designation that this firm statement came from any official source such as a Government or Military Intelligence agency, nor any official 'Top Secret' sort of designation. Why, then, did it appear?

When I returned to the United States after the brief European trip, I was as puzzled about this as I was about the entire mystery of EVP and Spiricom. I got in touch with George Meek to tell him about my visits to his associates abroad. I also told him about my curiosity involving Mr Paul.

'That's interesting,' Meek said. 'I've been aware of him for some time myself. In fact, I was in touch with him during the time you were in Europe. I'll send along some material about this to you.'

He did. Mr Paul had written to him on October 5, 1982, telling of his interest in Meek's work and Spiricom, and asking if he could visit Meek's lab in North Carolina in the near future. Before Meek had a chance to reply, another letter, of October 8, arrived. It read:

> Re my 5 Oct 82 ltr, I omitted some needed data concerning my professional status.
>
> I am assigned to the US Air Force Electronic Security Command, Electronic Warfare Directorate, Studies and Analysis Division, Systems Description Branch.
>
> Because of my affiliation with the DoD intelligence community, in accordance with AF Regulation 200-9, I am required to inform you of my status and also offer the disclaimer that my wishing to visit you is a personal venture and my visit represents no official interest or intelligence collection effort on the part of the US Government.
>
> Your understanding is appreciated and hopefully you can still extend an invitation to visit with you . . .

At least part of the mystery was solved. The unanswered question, as I saw it, was: did the 'personal' interest in EVP and Spiricom interlock with the obvious electronic activities of the US Air Force Electronic Security Command? When the *New York Times* reported, in February, 1984, on the Pentagon's interest in psychic research, there appeared to be a lot of straws in the wind. Representative Charles Rose of North Carolina, of the House Select Committee on Intelligence, stated in the article that the possibility of psychic warfare was all too real, and that it might call for a crash program for a development similar to the Manhattan Project in building the first atom bomb.

My interest in these practical applications of psychic research or EVP, however, was that they provided evidence of the reality of the phenomena. Also they were supportive in illustrating that research like Meek's commanded attention from anyone who was seriously interested in man's ultimate destiny.

To be convinced by rational evidence that physical death was merely a gateway into combined existence was more important than any limited practical use it might have, however sensational and dramatic. In Europe, the EVP research was providing increasing but incomplete reinforcement for Meek. Still lacking, however, was the replication of Spiricom, and without that, a solid confirmation was not possible.

* * *

I reflected a long time on the results of my visits in both Europe and the United States. I had absorbed so much information, ideas, and opinions that my review was kaleidoscopic. I had a hard time sorting everything out. Meek stood out as firm, astute and determined. O'Neil revealed an extremely sensitive nature beneath a rough exterior. There was no question of his sincerity or his dedication; they were genuine.

Uphoff was solid, analytical, dedicated to reaching beyond man's conscious limits. Heckmann was similar in outlook, his stolid Germanic approach weighing the evidence as much as I was. Jeffries was most impressive, bringing his distinguished technical and academic background to bear, and persuasive in helping me to begin to accept the far horizons of psychic experience. Cerney was a disciplined technician who looked at the electronic facts, and was persuaded by them.

Meek's associates abroad were men of stature and perception, skeptical enough to weigh and measure facts; open-minded enough to accept the unusual evidence they were amassing. None were proselytizers, fanatics, or gullible. All were willing to challenge Meek, and avoid any sort of blind acceptance. On balance, they accepted the strong probability that Spiricom had opened a new frontier. But all reserved that final acceptance for a repeatable experiment, as I was doing.

One important fact stood out: Meek was universally respected both here and abroad, and admired for his determination to keep driving towards the final goal. The fact that he was urging others to carry the project further, sharing everything he had learned to date and not attempting to keep his cards close to his chest, was laudable.

In spite of my reservations, I found that I was rooting for him to carry the project to that final goal. I also knew this was a priority for him, and that he would be off at the drop of an airline ticket to accomplish it.

# CHAPTER 16

## *Future Indicative*

After the Washington press conference, Meek had sent out the schematics of the Spiricom designs to several hundred technicians in the US and abroad. Over a year later, there were still no tangible results. At the same time, he was forming an organization he called the Life Beyond Death Research Foundation.* For the first time since his research began, he realized he would have to seek outside funding so that he could make research grants to those whose work seemed most promising.

One of these was Alex MacRae, the Scottish designer and electronics engineer who helped solve the helium speech problems for Skylab and the first Air Shuttle flight. Meek was impressed by his technical qualifications and his progress in exploring the EVP phenomenon. MacRae had come across the EVP voices indirectly. A heavy-set, balding gentleman, he had his own high tech lab in Portree on the island of Skye.

He was perfecting an electronic device for people who were afflicted with strokes and other forms of paralysis with equipment he called the Alpha system. On January 15, 1983, he decided almost whimsically to see if the system might possibly bring through any EVP voices. He had been studying the phenomenon off and on for three years, but had had little success in bringing any evidence through. He did, however, have a great deal of respect for those hard-science physicists like Harold Puthoff and Russel Targ at Stanford Research Institute, and Nobel Prize winner Brian Josephson who made no bones about the importance of paranormal research.

On this January day in 1983, he was surprised to find that his

* The Foundation furnishes excerpts and transcripts of the O'Neil/Mueller tapes and other Spiricom background at moderate cost. Write to Box 373, Franklin, North Carolina 28734, USA.

newly-designed Alpha equipment brought through a clear, distinguishable voice when he played back the experimental tape. He tried again, and got more voices. He continued the experiments over a period of weeks, and found that the definable utterances had increased from one in 20 minutes, to the rate of two utterances per minute.

In a letter to Meek, he described his procedure: 'I was taking a very gradual approach, after my initial surprise. I was quite happy to find that there was a phenomenon there at all. And there clearly was, without question. There were definite occurrences that could be described and defined and observed repeatedly. My research was based on measurement. First, the statements coming over the tape were short, but not random. The statements were complete, with a beginning, middle and end. They averaged only about one-and-three-quarter seconds. My job now was to try to explain them.'

MacRae's studies went on to answer the obvious questions asked by those who have not made a study of the EVP scene: were the voices stray signals from cab drivers, CB operators or local radio? MacRae found that the forms of speech he was receiving from whatever these entities were, consisted of a form of whistle speech, whispers, and the same sort of synthetic speech that characterized the O'Neil/Mueller tapes. None of these were characteristic of stray radio signals.

After more weeks of collecting the strange voices, he was convinced there was a phenomenon here that could not be explained by any known factor and that was not in any way like conventional radio patterns. He methodically catalogued the voices, and examined the context of the brief messages.

A clear pattern emerged. The strange whisper and whistling type of voices suggested hostility, similar to the lower levels of entities noted by other researchers. The more natural voices spoke consistently of heaven, life, death, and spirit. But more than that, a significant number of voices called MacRae by name, responded on replayed tape to questions, and mentioned relevant material. On top of that, the evidence was tangible and on tape for anyone to examine.

MacRae summed up his scientific opinion succinctly: (1) EVP is unquestionably para-physical, and available for frequent and predictable observation. (2) There is something there not yet recognized by science. (3) Communication rules exist that, when known, may alter appreciably our world view.

'Paranormal voices are real,' MacRae continued in his letter to Meek, 'and it is only the inability to absorb this admittedly incredible fact that has held up progress so long. EVP will bring the strongest evidence that all religions were right – but not entirely right with their theological squabbles. The tangible existence of this evidence will be a thorn in the side of Soviet Russia, where it has been reported that they have done their own experiments. They may have to re-write their philosophy to include EVP, and maybe we'll all see things in a better perspective.'

MacRae knew that Senkowski was conducting similar experiments in Germany, and compared notes. Both had found the same sort of experience, and both agreed that some intelligence was making speech patterns out of the 'white noise' transmitted by their own equipment.

Excited by MacRae's technical approach, Meek visited him in Scotland. He went over his work carefully, and found it to be of great importance. He was so delighted with MacRae's progress that when he returned home, he arranged to make a major grant from his new Foundation of $5,000 and gave MacRae a hearty endorsement. He felt that MacRae had found a promising clue to bringing evidence that would be acceptable to science, especially since MacRae himself was one of the top scientists in the field of voice analysis and synthesis.

But the problem still remained that the voices did not come directly through a speaker. They had to be heard in retrospect by replaying the tapes on which they were recorded. They still lacked the two-way direct conversation over a sustained period of time at a single sitting. Also missing was the detailed factual documentation, the biographical detail of the sort that Mueller had ostensibly brought through.

Eventually, Meek felt, that step would be bound to take place, with MacRae's expertise and sense of dedication. Meanwhile, he turned his attention to a letter he received from Professor Senkowski in January, 1983. It was about new developments by Hans Otto König, and they were startling. Although Meek was unable to be in Germany at the time, Senkowski spelled out the event in full detail.

* * *

At the very time when MacRae had conducted his first fully-successful attempt to bring through the voices – January 15, 1983 – the German electronics engineer Hans Otto König was invited by Radio Luxembourg to conduct a live, on-the-air experiment with his newly-developed, ultrasound technique that was showing great promise in bringing the two-way direct conversation with the operator.

As a private consultant to German industry in the electro-acoustical field, König had been experimenting with radio background noise, splashing water, and a variety of different acoustical sounds. He concluded that many background sounds seemed to have one thing in common: the upper frequencies pushed into the ultrasonic range. Most magnetic tape recorders don't go beyond the 15,000 or 20,000 Hertz range. When König began his EVP research 8 years before, he designed equipment to reach into the 30,000 Hertz range, using a complex mixture of frequencies and harmonics from four generators, beyond the audible hearing range for humans.

Radio Luxembourg is one of the most powerful broadcasting stations in Europe. When König arrived with his equipment, it was set up under the watchful eyes of the station's engineers and the presenter of the program, Rainer Holbe. No one, including König himself, was certain what would happen, because the attempt to reach the EVP voices would be made on the air directly, without pre-testing or rehearsal. Most important, of course, was the fact that the equipment was designed, like Spiricom, to achieve direct two-way contact without the intervention of the tape recorder.

Calling the device 'König's generator', Holbe announced that this would be a live experiment, and no one knew whether it would succeed or not. He assured the audience that the station engineers had thoroughly checked the assembling of the equipment, and that whatever results came over would come directly through the speakers, in two-way communication that would be conducted by the station staff, not by König.

The atmosphere was tense as the experiment began. One of the station's staff asked verbally if a voice could come through in direct response to his request. Within seconds, a clear voice came through saying, '*Otto König makes wireless with the dead.*'

Then another question was asked. Another pause followed. Then clearly a voice spoke through the speaker: '*We hear your voice.*'

Announcer Holbe's voice was shaking when he broke in to say: 'I tell you, dear listeners of Radio Luxembourg, and I swear by the life of my children, that nothing has been manipulated. There are no tricks. It is a voice, and we do not know from where it comes.'

What was interesting was that the EVP voices were as loud and clear as the questions asked by the technicians. The station issued an official statement afterwards: every step of the program was carefully supervised. The staff and engineers were convinced that the voices were paranormal.

More activity with König followed in the wake of the broadcast. At a meeting of the German EVP association in Fulda, near Frankfurt, König set up his apparatus before a large gathering. He invited the members to ask their own questions directly, for an immediate response. One woman asked if the deceased Raudive could identify himself. A voice came through immediately to announce, '*I am Raudive.*' Later, the voice was checked against Raudive's voice recorded when he was still alive. It was almost identical. König followed with another request to the equipment: 'Hello, friends, are you there?' An immediate response came over the speaker: '*Hello, we are here.*' A rapid duologue followed:

'Who are you?' König asked.

'*Achem*,' a voice replied.

'Tell me the name once more,' König responded. 'It is hard to understand.'

'*Achem*,' the voice replied, this time more clearly.

A few moments later, a voice on the speaker announced itself as that of Walter Steinneigel, a deceased friend of König who had worked with him on the project. Again the voice was later checked against a recording made when he was alive. Again, it was almost identical.

* * *

It took little persuasion from Senkowski for Meek to pack up and leave for Germany. If it were true that the phenomenon were reproducible, in front of witnesses and without the need of a taped replay, this was the sort of replication Meek needed and was looking for. But would it come through the speakers clearly? Would there be identifiable and relevant messages? And would König's ultrasonic carrier wave, as Senkowski had reported, make the voices clear and undistorted? If true, this would be a major advance.

Meek met Senkowski in Frankfurt. They were joined by Dr Ralf Determeyer, a distinguished scientist who had conducted successful EVP research in Germany and Switzerland. On the train to Düsseldorf, Determeyer and Senkowski filled Meek in on the observations they had already made of König's work. They were enthusiastic, pointing out that they were certain Meek would find the confirmation of his Spiricom experiments that he was looking for. Meek reserved his opinion, but their enthusiasm was contagious.

König met them at the station, a heavy-set man with a rather thick goatee, taffy-colored hair, twinkling eyes and a warm personality. They went to his apartment on the corner of a long modern apartment building. After a tasty and inevitable repast of German coffee and cake, they went down to König's basement laboratory.

He invited all his guests to inspect the equipment, an invitation which they accepted and a necessary step to prevent the ever-present possibility of a staged set-up. Determeyer and Senkowski, as experts, made minute inspections, while Meek satisfied himself with his own check of the equipment.

He was impressed with its sophistication compared to his own efforts with Spiricom which had not reached as high a level of technical development. As a leading acoustical engineer, König had spared no effort in assembling his equipment. Meek found himself impatient to get on with the demonstration. If the outcome were successful, he would be able to launch his new programs with renewed vigor and confidence.

With everyone satisfied, König flicked the switch to the 'on' position as the group waited. There was a faint sound of background noise, but nothing like the carrier wave that Mueller had had to speak over, the screechy sound of a Scottish bagpipe.

König spoke into his microphone. 'Good afternoon, my dear friends,' he said, as if he were addressing a business meeting. 'I have some visitors here who would like to speak with you over our equipment.'

There was silence for several moments. The faint background sound could barely be heard. Meek leaned forward in his chair, listening intently. He found it hard to believe that there could be so little distortion in the ultrasonic carrier wave, up to 40,000 cycles per second, and beyond the human hearing range.

There was more silence. Then suddenly a loud, clear voice came out of the speaker, almost as if it were in the room. '*Hello, George*,' it said. Meek was startled. He felt a chill run down his back. The others in the room, already familiar with König's project, smiled.

With Senkowski translating, one direct voice after another came through the speakers, with clearly identifiable and relevant messages.

Meek intervened. 'Where are you speaking from?'

There was a pause, then another clear voice answered, '*We are at König's.*' Not having to fight an audible carrier wave, the voice again sounded as if it were in the room.

Senkowski spoke up. 'Can you name the code word for my radio operation?' The name was Aurora. Senkowski waited, but not for long. Within moments, the voice on the speaker announced: '*The name is Aurora.*'

König addressed the equipment. 'Can my deceased partner speak with me?'

A voice answered immediately with the correct name. '*You have Walter Steinneigel.*'

'And where do you exist now, my friend?' König asked.

'*Merely on the other side*,' the answer came through.

'Can you tell me what you are working on?' König said.

'*Research*,' was the single word reply.

Meek was stunned. Not only was König's system a replication, but the voice quality was exceptional. Further, König was able to repeat his own experiments. The entities he was apparently contacting had not faded off as Mueller and Doc Nick had done. If this had been just a single demonstration, Meek would have had his doubts. But there was the Radio Luxembourg experiment under highly qualified engineering supervision, heard by hundreds and thousands of people in Europe, and repeated in other experiments later on the same station.

There were some limitations, but they were minor. The communications were still brief, not like the extended conversations that Mueller had carried out. No single entity identified himself with detailed biographical data at such length. But Meek was overjoyed. He found it hard to contain his enthusiasm. Senkowski and Determeyer were pleased and gratified that Meek could be a first-hand witness to what they had heard before.

Before his visitors left, König played them a tape of a previously recorded session, where two poignant colloquies occurred. One involved the parents of a deceased teenage boy whose parents spoke directly to him through König's equipment. He fully confirmed his identity in his own voice in a series of questions. The parents were so moved that they volunteered to go on Radio Luxembourg under the same controlled conditions to confirm it.

Meek listened as König played another sequence on one of his tapes. It was a conversation between a mother and her teenage daughter who had been killed in an automobile accident. After a series of questions that confirmed the girl's identity, the young girl's voice said on the tape, '*Mummy, I'm here*,' mentioning her name. '*I'm feeling well. I'll come back later*.'

* * *

Meek returned home with fresh optimism. With König's work as confirmation, he intensified his search for more researchers in Europe and the United States, who were themselves psychic as well as electronics engineers. By the beginning of 1984, Meek's bloodhound persistence began to bring in substantial grants for his new Life Beyond Death Foundation. One organization provided a grant of $30,000 with the comment, 'The spiritual implications of such discoveries are immense, and would contribute greatly to the cultivation of the recognition of individual responsibility in both health and spiritual matters.'

There were still questions to be answered, mountains to be climbed. If Mueller had moved on to a higher level of development, as Meek thought, could he be reached again by higher frequency electronic means? Could the group that had gathered around Professor Swann be brought into electronic focus, without the intervention of a medium? Could the world become truly aware of the importance of living forever and shape its destiny in more constructive terms? Could the knowledge of great inventors like Edison, Marconi, Tesla and others eventually be tapped to help solve current problems? And most important, could the modern, practical, technical mind realize that the spiritual world is a reality, that there is no death, whether we want it or not?

As a visionary, Meek was opening up new horizons for other researchers, snapping at their heels like a terrier and prodding them into action with an electronic cattle poke. Maybe he would never fully reach the impossible dream of perfection he had started out to capture 13 years before, at the age of 60. Still, he had reached part, if not all, of the replication he wanted.

Robert Browning wrote, 'A man's reach should exceed his grasp – or what's a heaven for?' Meek was just stubborn enough to try to prove Browning wrong.

# Afterword

One of the first items Meek sent me after the König demonstration, where EVP voices could be clinically confirmed in tangible form on a repeat basis, was a quotation by Leon Lederman, director of the Fermi accelerator, the most powerful atom smasher in the United States. Lederman stated, 'We have reached a crisis in physics where we are drowning in theoretical possibilities not based on a single solitary fact.'

The article containing the quotation was by Philip J. Hilts, of the *Washington Post*. It went on to say, 'New questions are being asked about what matter is, how it is formed and why it behaves as it does. Physicists do not understand why there are so many types of fundamental particles or why they vary so greatly. Some have virtually zero mass, while others are millions of times more massive.'

Meek scribbled on the bottom of the article, 'This is why the physicists have no basis for comprehending Spiricom or EVP.'

He might have added that paranormal research was at least in no worse a position than the physicists, who have as many questions as they do answers. And what is most interesting is the fact that there is a healthy stable of competent physicists, including Nobel laureates, who have no doubts whatever about the importance of psychic research, and who are willing to stake their reputations on it.

After carefully tracing the story of Spiricom and its EVP ally, the question that stood out most in my mind was why the hard sciences and psychical research seemed to be regarded as mutually exclusive. The dictionary definition of science is clear and simple: 'The observation, identification, description, experimental investigation and theoretical explanation of natural phenomena . . . or such activity applied to any class of phenomena.' Psychic research is certainly not excluded under that definition. But it most frequently is.

There are undoubtedly some good reasons for this. Paranormal events can be shifty, unpredictable, and elusive. They can at times be embraced by emotional and irrational investigators whose gullibility and stridency destroy any possibility of productive research. Because of the mercurial nature of the phenomena, the research is forced to become part art and part science. But then so is psychiatry and even medicine, in addition to psychic research. Just because psychiatry deals with disturbed and irrational personalities does not reduce its importance, or suggest that its researchers fall into that category.

The interesting thing about the Spiricom development and the whole field of EVP is that it is there, in tangible form, and can be repeated and examined objectively. Some of the results are weak. Some are sloppy. The sound is muddy. Some results are highly questionable because of their fragmentary nature. But the solid residue is clear and unambiguous. It is not hallucinatory. It cannot be brushed off or made to go away simply because conventional science has a tendency to say that it must not be considered, that it simply could not be. This is a most unscientific approach. Yet it is often the constant and only answer given, a form of pure prejudice instead of intelligent inquiry, even though those concerned with this viewpoint are intelligent.

I recall discussing the phenomenon of metal bending by mental concentration with an extremely intelligent friend of mine. This is now known as the Geller effect, and has been repeatedly demonstrated by qualified physicists in universities in many parts of the world. The only refutation to the reality of the phenomenon has been that certain magicians claim they can duplicate the feat by trickery. They further claim that scientists are right in every other aspect of their work. Just why the claim is made that physicists are dupes only in this one regard and not in others is not explained.

The logic that a phenomenon cannot exist simply because it can be done by trickery in some cases, is a most unscientific point of view. Nearly anything can be simulated by trickery or deception. It has been done in some of the most respectable laboratories in the country. A cancer researcher at Sloan-Kettering was caught falsifying his results. A cardiac researcher at Emory University was caught faking eight scientific papers and 43 research abstracts. These anomalies in no way negate the valid research that has been carried out and continues to be carried out.

When I invited my friend to study and observe the Geller effect in action, he said he had no interest in doing so. When I asked him why, he said, 'Even if I saw it with my own eyes, I wouldn't believe it.'

The point is that both EVP and metal bending are clinically observable and clearly demonstrable. There is certainly every reason to challenge them, but hardly any reason to keep them away from view. The rationalists who do this are most irrational in doing so.

A favorite expression of scientists in carrying out research is that a theory has to be 'kickable – and able to kick back'. Photons, for instance, were of doubtful validity until the Compton-Simon photographs showed that these elusive particles could be 'kicked and could kick back', proving that their existence was real. Now for the first time in psychical research, there are two phenomena that can be put to the same test.

Both metal bending and EVP have already been given the kick test, but the controversy still remains. Both have been observed palpably and both have been replicated. In the case of the Geller effect, literally thousands of others, including children, have shown the ability to bend metal by the mind. If they were all skilled magicians, as some claim, it would be a greater miracle than the event itself.

König's two-way EVP tests, MacRae's experiments, and Meek's Spiricom project appeared to have demonstrated the 'kickable' type of testability, with König's apparently furnishing the replication of Meek's experiments. Even if you believed only one of the experiments, there would still be 'kickable' evidence that we live after physical death. Actually, those who ignore this sort of evidence might do so at their own risk. For as H. H. Price once wrote, it might be more comforting for some to hope there was *not* this sort of life-continuation. In other words, there might be a prodigious amount of work to put in to gain further spiritual development, if the theory is right that the struggle and the educational process keeps right on going after physical death.

As far as the evidence goes, no one living today made any special request to be here. There is no evidence on record that any of us asked to be born. Very few have gone on record as wanting to die. But what the recent paranormal evidence shows is that we might have no choice about going on living after physical death. If so, the more we complete of our own development here, the less we might have to do later.

It seems to be not so much a question of morality, under these conditions, as of common sense. Morality is a stuffy word that often turns people away from it. Hemingway called morality 'something you feel good after'. If the theory is true that there is no such a thing as hell in the next life, that we create our own hell through self-judgment, then it makes sense to carry out actions in this life according to our best inner self-judgment.

Man's destiny seems to be a constant struggle. Now it appears possible that that struggle is going to continue whether we like it or not. But at least a struggle is something that isn't boredom, which would probably be the worst of hells, even if we were in heaven. The concept of work and self-development is probably the most satisfying thing in this life, regardless of the level on which the struggle starts. Again, the same may be true in what follows. There are enough palpable, 'kickable' hints that the journey might be tough, but interesting. Those who are lucky enough to have complete religious faith apparently know and accept this without question. Those who study the record for tangible evidence seem to be able to get close to this, and maybe even tip over to that comforting position. Meek's tireless efforts to help this point of view along might just bring this satisfaction to all who might be interested.

* * *

Elizabeth and I sat down to dinner on another cold November evening, two years after George and Jeannette Meek had come on their first visit to Connecticut to introduce us to the unlikely world of voices from an unknown domain. It wasn't quite an anniversary of the occasion, but it was close enough to be called one. I had almost finished the draft of the manuscript, and Elizabeth had gone over it with energetic interest and sanguine caution. Her reaction centered on the implications.

'The problem with the story,' she said, 'is that it deals with the most important question people have to face. And it's pretty heavy stuff. Most people don't walk around with a Spiricom in their handbag or pockets. How do you feel about it?'

'The basic elements of the story?'

'Yes.'

'I think I'm too close to them. Not only the months of research, but trying to put it all together.'

'If it's true,' Elizabeth said, 'the implications are enormous. I see the story hitting different people in different ways.'

'Which people, what ways?' I said.

'Well, I don't think it will make a dent in the hard-shell skeptic, but then that's not to be expected. For someone with an open mind, it might be a real eye-opener.'

'What did you find most important?' I asked.

'You can't really pick out any special part. It's like making a cake. You can't say the flour is any more important than the sugar or baking soda. It's the whole central theme that underlies everything – that there is strong evidence of life after death, and that we continue on with a full sense of personal awareness; that's what's important. Also, that there's evidence that we can communicate fairly clearly. And that there might be clear electronic proof of it. That's heady stuff also. And sort of a welcome thought with the mess the world's in today.'

'If this point were clear to a really hefty majority of people, do you think it could shift world conditions to a solid extent?' I asked.

'Definitely. I think we'd think twice before we began shooting bullets and rockets at people, especially when we know you can't kill thoughts and ideas with a piece of metal or radiation. But there's a long way to go. Conventional religion's been around for a long time, but it hasn't quite made a full impact on the world today. Maybe all this might give religion a technical push in a technical age. I guess that's an important point.'

We were quiet a few moments, then Elizabeth said, 'Look, you've been asking me all these questions. But you still haven't told me the bottom line about how you feel.'

I'd been afraid she was going to point that out, and in a way, I wished she hadn't. The deeper I had gone into the complexities of the story, the more confusing it had become.

And yet through all the convolutions, there seemed to be a steady ring of truth. What I could say, I could say with conviction: there is too much smoke here, both in this story and in the deep background of intelligent paranormal inquiry and unprejudiced scientific inquiry, not to say that something is *there* – and it should be pursued with all the modern tools that are available.